Rehab Right

How to Realize the Full Value of Your Old House

**by Helaine Kaplan Prentice
and Blair Prentice**

**City of Oakland
Planning Department**

Ten Speed Press

1☉
TEN SPEED PRESS
P.O. Box 7123
Berkeley, California 94707

Library of Congress Cataloging-in-Publication Data

Rehab right.

     Bibliography.
     Includes index.
     1. Dwellings—California—Oakland—Remodeling.
2. Dwellings—California—Oakland—Maintenance and repair. I. Oakland
(Calif.). City Planning Dept. TH4816.R429 1987   643'.7
86-5945 ISBN 0-89815-172-4

Printed in the United States of America

1 2 3 4 5 — 90 89 88 87

The preparation of this book was supported in part by funds from:

The National Endowment for the Arts, a federal agency, Washington D.C. The
findings herein do not necessarily represent the views of the Endowment.

The City of Oakland Office of Community Development, under the Community Development Block Grant Program, U.S. Department of Housing
and Urban Development.

The State of California, Office of Historic Preservation, under the National
Historic Preservation Act of 1966.

REHAB RIGHT is intended to assist the reader in making design decisions in
the course of rehabilitating an older house. REHAB RIGHT is neither a construction manual nor a safety handbook. Readers, therefore, are expected to
observe standard safety practices and exercise ordinary care while performing construction work. Since conditions in old houses vary considerably, the
reader may expect to seek such further advice as may be required before
undertaking any contractual commitment or building alteration.

The names and prices of products, suppliers and services are included for
illustrative purposes only. The authors do not suggest that these are the
exclusive or least expensive sources; comparative shopping is the buyer's
responsibility. No endorsement or warranty by the City of Oakland, or by
any of the supporting agencies, is expressed or implied.

TABLE OF CONTENTS

INTRODUCTION
   by Patricia Poore, Editor, THE OLD-HOUSE JOURNAL _____ ix

NOTES ON THE REVISED EDITION _____ x

PREFACE _____ 1

Chapter 1. THEY DON'T MAKE HOUSES LIKE THEY USED TO

Let Your House Be Itself _____ 3

The Difference Between Restoration, Rehabilitation, and Remodeling _____ 3

How to Use REHAB RIGHT _____ 5

Chapter 2. THE ARCHITECTURAL STYLE OF YOUR HOUSE

The Concept of Architectural Style
What's in a Name _____ 7
Architectural Portraits _____ 7

Architectural Portraits of House Styles Typically in Need of Rehab

Victorian _____ 8
   Italianate _____ 10
   San Francisco Stick _____ 12
   Queen Anne _____ 12

Colonial Revival _____ 15
   Classic Box _____ 17
   Neoclassic Rowhouse _____ 19
   Eastern Shingle Cottage _____ 20

First Bay Tradition _____ 21
   Brown Shingle _____ 21
   Craftsman Bungalow _____ 24
   Prairie School _____ 25
   California Bungalow _____ 27

Period Revival _____ 29
   Mediterranean Style _____ 29
   Provincial Style _____ 31

All-American Ranch Style _____ 32
   Wartime Tract _____ 33

Chapter 3. BEFORE YOU BEGIN

How Much Money Should You Spend On Rehab?
The Resale Value of Rehab Right _____ 35
Do the Basics First _____ 35
Recognize Over-improvement _____ 35
How To Finance a Rehab Project _____ 36

Before You Buy
Inspecting the Merchandise _____ 37
Disclosure Statements _____ 38
Termite Reports _____ 38

Codes and Permits
How To Determine Applicable Code _____ 39
Compliance Letter _____ 40
Building Permits _____ 41

Matters Of History
Federal Preservation Tax Incentives _____ 42
State Historical Building Code _____ 43
The National Register of Historic Places _____ 43

Chapter 4. EXTERIORS

Foundation _____ 45
Brick Foundation _____ 45
Concrete Foundation _____ 47
Posts and Piers _____ 47
Sill Plate _____ 48
Seismic Retrofit _____ 48

Crawl Space _____ 50
Clearance _____ 50
Vents _____ 50
Insulation _____ 51

Stairs _____ 52
Wood Stairs _____ 52
Brick Stairs _____ 52
Concrete Stairs _____ 53
Handrails _____ 55

Porch _____ 55
Wood Porch _____ 55
   Wood Damage _____ 55
   Posts and Piers _____ 56
   Joists and Decking _____ 56
   Columns _____ 56
   Railings _____ 57
   Roof _____ 57
Stucco Porch _____ 58

Cement Porch _____ 60

Front Door _____ 61
Wear _____ 61
    Panels _____ 61
    Veneer _____ 62
    Paint _____ 63
    Ornamentation _____ 63
    Threshold _____ 63
Hardware _____ 63
Security _____ 63
Garage Door _____ 66

Sheathing _____ 66
Wood Siding _____ 66
    Design _____ 66
    Damage and Repair _____ 67
Wood Shingles _____ 68
Stucco _____ 71
Mass-Produced Siding _____ 71

Ornamentation _____ 71
Wood Ornamentation _____
    Removal _____ 74
    Repair _____ 74
    Replacement _____ 74
    Re-installation _____ 75
Plaster Ornamentation _____ 75

Paint _____ 75
When to Paint _____ 76
The Painting Process _____ 76
Color Selection _____ 77

Windows _____ 79
Design _____ 79
Repair and Replacement _____ 82
Energy _____ 84
Security _____ 84

Roof _____ 84
Roofing _____ 84
Vents _____ 85
Flashing _____ 86
Gutters and Downspouts _____ 87
Eave, Fascia, and Soffit _____ 88
Chimney _____ 88

Chapter 5. INTERIORS

Floors _____ 89
Subfloor _____ 89
Finish Floor _____ 89
    Hardwood Floor _____ 89
    Softwood Floor _____ 94
    Ceramic Tile Floor _____ 94
    Resilient Flooring _____ 94

Walls _____ 95
Plaster _____ 95
Wood _____ 95
Lincrusta-Walton _____ 100
Paneling _____ 101
Paint _____ 101
Wallpaper _____ 103
Trim _____ 104
Removing Walls _____ 107

Ceiling _____ 109
Surface _____ 109
Space _____ 110
Special Features _____ 110
    Rosette _____ 110
    Trim _____ 111
    Beams _____ 111
    Coved Corners _____ 111

Doors _____ 111
Style _____ 111
Fit _____ 113
Damage _____ 113
Doorframe _____ 114
Hardware _____ 115

Fireplace _____ 116
Exterior Appearance _____
    Style _____ 116
    Repair _____ 117
Internal Workings _____ 117

Staircase _____ 119
Style _____ 119
Repair _____ 119

Utility Systems _____ 122
Electrical _____ 122
   Service _____ 122
   Wiring _____ 124
   Light Fixtures _____ 125
Plumbing _____ 127
Mechanical _____ 129

Chapter 6. FOR YOUR INFORMATION

When Should You Hire A Professional?
And When to Do-It-Yourself? _____ 131
Selecting a Contractor _____ 131
Drafting a Contract _____ 132

House History _____ 133

Access _____ 133
Ramps _____ 134
Other Design Considerations _____ 134
   Front Stairs _____ 135
   Front Door _____ 135
   Floors, Walls and Windows _____ 135
Doors _____ 135
Bathrooms and Kitchens _____ 135

Asbestos _____ 135

Earthquake Safety _____ 136

Chapter 7. SOURCES AND RESOURCES

City Offices _____ 138

Rehabilitation Assistance Programs _____ 140

Classes, Conferences and Workshops _____ 143

Books, Periodicals and a Film _____ 144
Architectural History _____ 144
Rehabilitation and Repair _____ 144
Buyer's Guides _____ 144
Periodicals _____ 144
Booklists _____ 145
Film _____ 145

Preservation Organizations _____ 146
National Preservation Organizations _____ 146
Statewide Preservation Organizations _____ 146
Some Special Interest Groups in Northern California ____ 148
Prominent Citywide Preservation Organizations in California _ 148
Oakland Groups with a Preservation, Design or Housing Focus _ 149

Preservation Administrations _____ 149
National Park Service Regional Offices _____ 149
State Historic Preservation Offices _____ 150
City of Oakland Landmarks Preservation Advisory Board _____ 153

How to Order RETROFIT RIGHT _____ opposite back cover

TABLE OF ILLUSTRATIONS

Index to House Styles Typically In
   Need of Rehabilitation _____ inside front cover

Chapter 1. THEY DON'T MAKE HOUSES LIKE THEY USED TO

Oakland, California, Residential Area Names _____ 6

Chapter 2. THE ARCHITECTURAL STYLE OF YOUR HOUSE

Victorian
   Italianate _____ 9
   Single-Story Italianate _____ 10
   San Francisco Stick _____ 11
   Queen Anne _____ 13
   Queen Anne Cottage _____ 14
Colonial Revival
   Classic Box _____ 16, 18
   Neoclassic Rowhouse _____ 19
   Eastern Shingle Cottage _____ 20

TABLE OF ILLUSTRATIONS, continued:

First Bay Tradition
    Brown Shingle _____ 22
    Craftsman Bungalow _____ 24
    Prairie School _____ 26
    California Bungalow _____ 27

Period Revival
    Mediterranean Style _____ 30
    Provincial Style _____ 32

All-American Ranch Style
    Wartime Tract _____ 33

Chapter 3. BEFORE YOU BEGIN

Categories of Applicable Code _____ 39

Chapter 4. EXTERIORS

Foundation
    How to Repoint _____ 45
    Typical Mortar Joints _____ 46
    Brick Patterns _____ 46
    Concrete Corner Repair _____ 47
    Post and Pier Elevation _____ 48
    Post and Pier Construction _____ 48
    Anchor Bolt for Existing Foundation _____ 49
    Seismic Anchor for New Foundation _____ 49

Crawl Space
    Vent Styles _____ 51
    Crawl Space Clearance _____ 51
    Crawl Space Insulation _____ 52

Stairs
    **Stair Dimensions for Brand New
      Construction Required by Modern Code** _____ 52
    Improving Drainage on Wood Steps _____ 53
    Steel Nosing on Concrete Steps _____ 53
    Stair Railing Reconstruction _____ 53
    Stair Railing Alternatives for the Neoclassic Rowhouse _____ 54

Porch
    Porch Balustrade Reconstruction _____ 56
    Porch Railings to Avoid _____ 57
    Stickwork Repair _____ 58
    Awning Substitute for Porch Overhang _____ 58

    Elephantine Column Repair _____ 59
    Elephantine Columns: Dos and Don'ts _____ 60
    Cement Porch Floor Repair with Flashing _____ 61

Front Door
    How to Replace Door Glass _____ 62
    How to Replace Door Threshold _____ 62
    Door Security: Reinforced Door Frame _____ 64
    Door Security: Braced Studs _____ 64
    Door Security: Non-removable Hinge Pin _____ 64
    Front Door: Dos and Don'ts _____ 65
    Door Security: Precaution for Exterior Hinge Pin _____ 65
    Door Security: One Architect's Solution _____ 65
    **Door Security: Original Door Knob
      as Handle with Auxiliary Lock** _____ 66

Sheathing
    Types of Wood Siding _____ 67
    Shingle Patterns _____ 68
    Shingle Installation Detail _____ 69
    Stucco Construction _____ 70

Ornamentation
    Ornamentation Vocabulary _____ 72
    Removing Wood Ornamentation _____ 74
    Proportional Reproduction: A Cornice _____ 75

Paint
    Color Wheel _____ 75
    Parts of a House to Paint _____ 76
    Value _____ 78

Windows
    Types of Woodframe Windows _____ 79
    Double-Hung Window: Dos and Don'ts _____ 80
    Parts of a Double-Hung Window _____ 81
    Double-Hung Window Frame Detail _____ 81
    Double-Hung Window Weatherstrip Placement _____ 83
    Window Security: Vulnerability of Aluminum Frames _____ 84
    Window Security: Key Lock for Double-Hung Windows _____ 84

Roof
    Soffit Vent _____ 85
    Porch Roof Flashing _____ 86
    Valley Flashing _____ 86
    Good and Bad Downspout Locations _____ 86
    Drip Strip _____ 87
    Maybeck Downspout _____ 87

Chapter 5. INTERIORS

Floors

Types of Strip Flooring _____ 89
Parts of a Floor _____ 90
Fixing Squeaky Floors _____ 91
Remedies for Loose Floorboards _____ 92
Sheet Vinyl: Dos and Don'ts _____ 94

Walls

Plaster Repair _____ 96
Extensive Plaster Repair _____ 97
Sheetrock: Dos and Don'ts _____ 97
Wainscot Styles and Vocabulary _____ 98
Re-creating a Wainscot _____ 99
Lincrusta-Walton _____ 100
Cross Section of a Plywood Panel _____ 101
Parts of a Room to Paint _____ 102
Basic Molding Shapes _____ 105
Molding to Avoid _____ 105
Reproducing Complex Moldings _____ 106
Adding a Window Cap _____ 107
The Difference Between a Structural Wall
and a Permanent Partition _____ 108

Ceiling

Ceiling: Dos and Don'ts _____ 109
Rosette Cross-Section _____ 110
Coved Ceiling Detail _____ 111

Doors

Types of Doors _____ 112
Victorian Doors _____ 112
Panel Door Construction _____ 113
Flush Door Construction _____ 114
Panel Door Repair _____ 114
Typical Problems on Interior Doors _____ 115

Fireplace

Installing an Add-on Mantel _____ 116
Parts of a Fireplace _____ 117
Rescuing a Remodeled Mantel _____ 118

Staircase

Newel Post _____ 119
Parts of a Staircase _____ 120
Staircase Carpeting: Dos and Don'ts _____ 122

Utility Systems

Identifying Your Electrical Service _____ 123
Adding a Wall Switch for an Overhead Light _____ 124
Socket and Switch: Dos and Don'ts _____ 125
How to "Fish" _____ 126
Light Fixtures: Dos and Don'ts _____ 127
A Clawfoot Tub with Added Shower _____ 128

Chapter 7. SOURCES AND RESOURCES

Oakland, California, Community Development
District Boundaries _____ 141

Ruler _____ inside back cover

TABLE OF "DO AND DON'T" ILLUSTRATIONS

Stair Railing Alternatives for the Neoclassic Rowhouse _____ 54
Porch Railings to Avoid _____ 57
Elephantine Columns: Dos and Don'ts _____ 60
Front Door: Dos and Don'ts _____ 65
Double-Hung Windows: Dos and Don'ts _____ 80
Good and Bad Downspout Locations _____ 86
Sheet Vinyl: Dos and Don'ts _____ 94
Sheetrock: Dos and Don'ts _____ 97
Molding to Avoid _____ 105
Ceiling: Dos and Don'ts _____ 109
Socket and Switch: Dos and Don'ts _____ 125
Light Fixture: Dos and Don'ts _____ 127

TABLE OF CHARTS

REHAB RIGHT Guidelines _____ 5
Permit Fees for Activities Typically
Associated with Residential Rehabilitation _____ 41
General Guidelines for Seismic Retrofit _____ 50
Window Prices _____ 82
Roofing Materials _____ 88

INTRODUCTION

The first edition of REHAB RIGHT was subtitled, "How To Rehabilitate Your Oakland House Without Sacrificing Architectural Assets." Oakland? The authors were too modest . . . the book was immediately a valuable addition to *The Old-House Journal* library. But we're a national magazine based in Brooklyn!

Actually, I've always felt that *The Old-House Journal* and REHAB RIGHT are kin, cousins on opposite shores. Our intentions are similar: present the case for sensitive rehabilitation using plain language and clear graphics. Don't proselytize, don't try to legislate good taste; just explain how to repair things and give lots of examples. In the first edition, the authors asked permission to use some material that had been published in the early days of *The Old-House Journal*. We've returned the compliment since, occasionally using a tip or a drawing of theirs. (And sometimes, when there's a basic concept that absolutely must be presented with clarity, I'll admit we sneak a peek at how REHAB RIGHT tackled the subject.)

REHAB RIGHT is, quite simply, the best regional preservation guidebook around. (We must have 50 or 60 of them.) And given the unexpected acclaim of the first edition beyond Oakland, the authors have made a conscious attempt to broaden the scope of the book in this edition. There is more useful restoration information here than in many of the fancier books from big national publishers.

After all, how-to information and the underlying "why-to" is the same for old houses everywhere, whatever their style or vintage. Oakland itself, with its stock of Victorian and post-Victorian houses, is typical of cities and suburbs all over the U.S. Therefore, even restoration hints on specific building parts are applicable outside the San Francisco Bay Area. And the information about residential architectural styles is superb! Style descriptions are uniquely intelligent: correct and astute, but sensible and accessible to those of us without a degree in architectural history. You won't find any of that murky "critic-ese" in this book.

What you will find is a crystal-clear introduction to your old house. And real good advice.

Patricia Poore
Editor & co-publisher
The Old-House Journal

NOTES ON THE REVISED EDITION

It has been eight years since REHAB RIGHT was first published, over ten years since the idea for it was conceived. The scene for old houses has certainly changed: there are many more suppliers of new and used houseparts, the preservation movement has taken hold and made inroads, and the renewed popularity of urban living has transformed tired neighborhoods into desirable real estate. Even the word "old" has become a badge of distinction.

As for the old house itself—it hasn't changed at all. It's just another ten years older. The problems of old age and disrepair persist, and the design-sensitive solutions remain the same.

Unfortunately, the common approach to rehabilitation—an approach which disregards architectural features—also persists under both public and private financing. This misguided method ultimately diminishes the value of older houses and their neighborhoods. Ten years have scarcely negated the need for a handbook on architecurally appropriate rehabilitation.

In the revised REHAB RIGHT, the basic philosophy, architectural profiles and, for the most part, construction guidelines stand unaltered from the first edition. They are just as applicable today. However, because new regulations, issues and data have surfaced, the text has been expanded to introduce recent topics and research. This is especially apparent in Chapters 3 and 6, and in the section on foundations in Chapter 4.

All prices have been updated to spring, 1986, and suppliers confirmed. Names of suppliers are provided to demonstrate that finding the right part is not impossible—but these are not necessarily the only, or least expensive, sources. Chapter 7 gives references to more comprehensive buyers' guides. The various other lists of resources in the same chapter have been revised and given a national scope.

Where reference was previously made in the text to *The Old-House Journal*, the citation has been updated to include recent articles. This is no substitute, however, for a cumulative index to the wealth of practical information about pre-1945 houses in that excellent periodical.

Since this book first appeared, similar manuals have been devised by planners in other locales to enlighten their constituencies and address regional styles. Many acknowledged REHAB RIGHT as source or inspiration. Fellow stewards of design integrity, we salute you!

We continue to receive enthusiastic reponses from new readers. It seems that time has not diminshed the impact of the drawings and ideas. To the many who shared their appreciation for the book, thank you. It was your support which brought REHAB RIGHT out of City Hall and into the bookstores. And to those who have tackled a rehab project and done it right, congratulations. You have enhanced the value of a single house, but more important, you have helped to preserve the fabric of your community.

Helaine Kaplan Prentice
Blair Prentice

PREFACE

In cities nationwide, popular interest in older houses has been directed toward historic restoration. Great sums have been invested in the re-creation of a landmark's original features for the sake of academic precision and frequently for snob appeal. But too often, when a more commonplace house deteriorates, most of the energy is directed toward just making the house liveable again. The goal is to eliminate hazardous conditions and to install basic amenities. Anything more is considered to be frosting.

While it is critical that shelters be made habitable, it is equally imperative that the architectural character of all buildings be respected in the process of structural improvement. Unfortunately, this is rarely the case. The intrinsic merit of a building is often sacrificed to the expediency of modern contracting technique.

This handbook was conceived as an *easy-to-use* guide to design decisions, in the hope that architectural integrity will no longer be unnecessarily lost. A *good* design decision for a repair problem requires satisfactory answers to three straightforward questions: How will it look? How will it work? And, how much will it cost? REHAB RIGHT addresses these questions for typical home improvement problems encountered in older residential building styles.

There are so many different people who influence the outcome of a residential rehabilitation project. REHAB RIGHT is written primarily for you, the **homeowner.** Use this manual to discover the built-in qualities you may not even realize your home boasts. These assets have resale value. Then, use this book to prepare for home improvement by recognizing which problems you have to solve and determining the best plan of attack. When you become acquainted with the technical jargon, you will be better equipped to communicate to a contractor or a hardware salesman that you want the job done the best way possible. Perhaps a previous owner made some so-called "improvements" and the changes are not to your liking. Use REHAB RIGHT to rectify past mistakes. On the larger scene, read this book to find out how the efforts of individual property owners can contribute to the upgrading of an entire neighborhood.

Maybe you are a **potential homeowner** looking for a place to buy. Lately many people are drawn to cities by the design quality and human scale of older neighborhoods. REHAB RIGHT will help you evaluate houses that are for sale and make an intelligent selection among them. It should also give you some idea of any additional investment necessary beyond the sale price to bring the house up to legal standards or to the standards of your personal taste.

Real estate agents, eager to discover which features make a house marketable, will find REHAB RIGHT a useful tool in appraising the value of residential architecture and passing this knowledge on to the consumer. The characteristics which help sell the house this time should be retained by the new owner to help sell the house the next time around.

Some people turn to **professional contractors** for advice on home improvement. While most contractors know how to get the job done, many could profit by more design sensitivity. REHAB RIGHT will stir the imagination of any skilled craftsperson. Esthetics notwithstanding, this book provides the contractor with a handy checklist of rehab problems.

Some **public employees** are in a position to design rehabilitation projects. Others review applications for special low interest rehabilitation loans. Still others must make daily decisions regarding code compliance, land use regulations, permit issuance and the like. REHAB RIGHT is directed at honing public employees' appreciation of distinctive residential styles, so that a professional understanding of local architecture will be intrinsic to any related recommendations made.

Actually, **any property owner** can benefit from REHAB RIGHT. Many of the design concepts apply equally well to commercial structures or apartment buildings. And finally, **anyone** can broaden his or her environmental perception by learning to recognize different house styles by name. An awareness of our architectural heritage fosters common sense decisions about residential rehabilitation, and an enthusiasm for doing the job the right way.

Chapter 1

THEY DON'T MAKE HOUSES LIKE THEY USED TO

LET YOUR HOUSE BE ITSELF

One of the best things about cities is the vital mix of cultures among the people who live there. The social diversity is stimulating, the way life in a city is supposed to be. Likewise, the fabric of the city, having been gradually developed over time, presents a pleasing diversity of building styles. In Oakland, California, houses of strikingly different appearance —from 1875, 1905, 1935, 1965—stand side by side, creating a physical setting as varied as the social environment.

These days, individuals of many different ethnic backgrounds are intent upon tracing their cultural history. They value the role that the past has played in determining their personal identity; they treasure the unique qualities of a distinctive heritage. It is disheartening to realize that the integrity of many a culture has been diluted in the great American melting pot, the valuable distinctions homogenized. So it is with architecture too. A house reflects history —the attitudes, the technology, the spirit of the era in which it was built. Most houses built before World War II also reflect great care and quality in their craftsmanship and materials. Every house has its own story to tell. What a shame that the integrity of many an older house has been needlessly dishonored by modernization techniques which, like the melting pot, tend to make everything look the same.

Of course, most older houses are in need of some improvements to make them safe and convenient. But **you can make your living environment feel new without eliminating what is old and valuable.** The architectural style of a house imbues it with a distinct personality, and it is this architectural character that REHAB RIGHT aims to preserve— not the inconveniences or unsafe conditions which may accompany it and which do merit change. An old house respectfully renewed feels fresher, even younger, than a modern house which, after a few years' occupancy, shows disrepair and rapid aging due to the lesser quality and durability of many of today's building materials. Let your house be itself, and it will survive the strains of time and fashion for yet another 50 to 100 years.

There's a big difference between structural improvements and interior decoration. Structural improvements are home repairs related to the skeleton of the house—the floor you stand on, the roof over your head—the "nuts and bolts" that have a permanent importance for you and any subsequent owners of the house. REHAB RIGHT will help you to make and implement those important design decisions. Interior decoration, on the other hand, is more superficial and shorter lived. It's the selection of a wallpaper pattern—not the installation of wall studs; it's the selection of curtain fabric—not the replacement of a dryrotted window sill. This book is not about decorating; rather, it is a guide to creating the sound framework upon which any truly effective decorating scheme depends.

While it is appropriate to use your individual taste in decorating your home, resist the temptation to impose your personality on the structure of the house. If, for example, you like vivid colors, consider hanging bright posters in the living room instead of painting the outside of the house a garish hue. If you have a collection of souvenirs from Mexico, you need not stucco your house, roof it with red tile, and surround it with white gravel to achieve an interesting display.

Think of your house as a whole, a single unit with no removable parts. Every change you make chips away at the integrity of the whole, every feature removed is drastic surgery. Before

you know it, efforts to personalize and update a house will leave you with an assortment of miscellaneous parts that bear no relation to each other, let alone to the original design. Wrought iron columns, asbestos shingles and aluminum frame windows have only one thing in common: the local hardware store. A house is not like a car which has available options to obscure the mass production. It's just the opposite: older houses were built one at a time, and such added options obscure their individuality.

An article in the *Wall Street Journal* points out that because people invest such a large portion of their earnings in the purchase of a house they focus their leisure activities on the home too. Home improvement has become a form of recreation. Whether tools and lumber, brushes and buckets are your idea of fun, or a matter of sheer necessity, be sure that the "improvements" you make respect the form and the materials of the original house. The spaces and details were deliberately arranged and selected for proportion and consistency when the house was first built. The design as a whole has a visual purpose and an economic value that are yours to appreciate, yours to safeguard, yours to benefit from when it's time to resell.

THE DIFFERENCE BETWEEN RESTORATION, REHABILITATION, AND REMODELING

There is so much activity these days in the improvement of older housing that a new set of verbs has been introduced into common parlance. Most of the words start with the prefix *re*—which means to begin anew—and it is not hard to become confused among the definitions. The variations in meaning between *restore, rehabilitate,* and *remodel,* may seem subtle, but the words represent powerful attitudes which make all the difference in the way a job turns out.

To restore a house is to return a building to its original condition, as if it were a precious museum piece. This technique is typically used for structures of significant merit, like historic landmarks, where accuracy will serve an educational purpose as well as a visual one. Restoration is the most painstaking improvement process, and often the most expensive because it requires technical skill and academic precision for successful results. It can involve the removal of extraneous, anachronistic elements, as well as the re-creation of original features which have deteriorated or been destroyed. For example, on a Victorian house, the wood portico may have succumbed to dry rot. In restoring the house, the best replacement for the defective overhang would be an honest reproduction of the original—the same dimensions, the same joinery, even the same materials as its predecessor. An enormous challenge lies in accurately discovering the past and sensitively restoring that heritage in the present.

A fine example of a restoration project in Oakland is the Camron-Stanford House. This Italianate mansion built in 1876 on the shores of Lake Merritt, at Lakeside Drive, went through several incarnations: as the lavish residence of newlyweds Alice Marsh and Will Camron, as the lively hub of Josiah Stanford's social circle, as the headquarters for the Oakland Museum and, in what many feared would be its dying days, as an abandoned and desolate mansion dubbed "Lady of the Lake."

In 1971, through the efforts of the Camron-Stanford Preservation Association, the restoration project began. The needed repairs were substantial. The rear annex had to be demolished and the interior walls reconstructed. Three years later, after a fresh—and accurate—paint job, the Camron-Stanford House was reinstated as a public architectural gem. The house is now the headquarters for special programs on Oakland history, with an emphasis on residential architecture.

Remodeling a house is normally at the opposite end of the improvement spectrum from restoration. Unless it is done with unusual sensitivity, **remodelling a house means redesigning it so that the generic features are lost and the basic character destroyed in the name of modernization.** A remodeling job is too often considered a "success" if the original structure is unrecognizable at the outcome. This technique is appropriately

used for buildings which were constructed of inferior materials or for buildings which have fallen into a state of irreversible disrepair due to vacancy or vandalism. Remodeling can also be a proper course of action when a structure undergoes a dramatic change in use, say from a single-family residence to commercial office space.

Unfortunately, it is quite common for a house to be remodeled and totally divested of its valuable characteristics when conditions do not require such radical treatment. Hence, the expression "remodel" has acquired a bad connotation. To many people, it suggests a shameful waste of valuable resources, even it is possible to remodel with sensitivity, especially with the help of a talented architect.

Examples of remodeling jobs can be found in Oak Center in West Oakland where many houses were so devastated by abandonment, theft and a complete lack of maintenance that the only feasible solution was to "gut" the interior—that is, to remove all remnants of original style. Doors, molding, rosettes, coved ceilings, wainscotting, everything down to the studs in the walls were dismantled and construction started all over again from the eviscerated frame. The new version is typically distinguished by sheetrock walls with a hint of baseboard, aluminum windows, and snazzy light fixtures. Other examples of remodeling can be found in homes where the owners were convinced, sometimes with the help of a contractor or salesman, that, without qualification, "old" is bad and "new" simply wonderful.

In the vast space that separates restoration from remodeling we find rehabilitation. **To rehabilitate a house is to take corrective measures which will make the structure liveable again.** The British use the word "recondition," and lately we've adopted the abbreviation "rehab." **Some aspects of rehab work entail renovation—the introduction of brand new elements.** For example, the electrical circuits may have to be rewired to provide adequate service for today's appliances.

The other face of rehabilitation is preservation, the retention of valuable existing elements. For example, it was a matter of course in 1905 to construct oak floors, inlaid with geometric borders, in the living and dining rooms of Colonial

Revival houses. Preserving these floors is intrinsic to proper rehabilitation and is accomplished in two stages. First, during construction, the hardwood is covered by a protective dropcloth to avert any additional damage while other carpentry is underway. Later, when the floors are ready for attention, the oak is sanded and varnished, returning the irreplaceable hardwood to its original richness. In contrast, a remodeling job would treat the valuable oak as if it were ordinary fir, leaving paint cans and lumber on the floor during repairs, and then covering the fascinating, textured grain with homogeneous shag carpeting when the job is done.

When rehabilitating a house, **it is essential to protect the structural and decorative characteristics which belong to the architectural style. These are the very features which constitute the visual integrity and economic value of the building. Modern elements should only be introduced when absolutely necessary for legal or utilitarian purposes. Modern elements should only be introduced in a manner that is sympathetic to the original design spirit, and never at the expense of irreplaceable assets.** That is what is meant by REHAB RIGHT.

Good examples of REHAB RIGHT can be found in homes where family members have done the repairs themselves, lovingly, and where a limited budget prevented the family from purchasing all new hardware. Forced financially to appreciate what they have, these households actually end up with a finished product more valuable for its integrity than any assemblage of replacement parts could ever be.

The rewards of sensitive home improvement are manyfold. First, there is the satisfaction of knowing you've done the job right. Second, there is the gratification of compliments from other people who appreciate the care you've taken. Third, there is the limitless pleasure of living in an attractive and comfortable home. While these benefits are difficult to measure, a fourth reason to REHAB RIGHT can be quantified in dollars and cents. A perceptive combination of restoration and renovation will actually contribute to the resale value of your home. Finally, a good rehab project can be surprisingly influential

REHAB RIGHT GUIDELINES

• **Retain original houseparts and materials wherever possible. As a rule, if damage is present, repair is visually and economically preferable to replacement.**

• **If replacement is necessary, replace parts and materials in-kind.**

• **If replacement in-kind is impossible due to unavailability or cost, the replacement should at least reproduce the salient visual characteristics of the original, such as material, composition, proportion and color.**

• **If used, modern house parts should be incorporated with sensitivity to the architectural style.**

• **Wherever possible, replace missing house parts and remove inappropriate modernization.**

on an entire block. Improvements in neighborhood quality can also be calculated in monetary terms when it comes to real estate.

HOW TO USE REHAB RIGHT

This handbook is written to tune-up architectural awareness and to convince you that good design makes good economic sense. If you study the book from first paragraph to last you'll know more than enough to make wise rehab decisions. But most readers will have acquired a copy of REHAB RIGHT with a specific residence in mind and they will be anxious to get to the solution of their repair problems without delay. In fact, even in formal discussions about home improvements with architects and contractors, the conversation invariably turns to the professional's own home. Recognizing that each reader will focus on the portion of the manual which affects him or her personally, REHAB RIGHT is organized so that the information you and your house need can be quickly selected.

First, **discover your house.** Step outside and take a good look at the building. Walk around it. Touch

it. Explore the materials. Do you find clapboard siding or stucco? Wood shingles or asbestos? Single out the details. Are there columns on the porch, pediments on the windows, finials on the roof? Cross the street and look at it from a distance. Appreciate its mass, its overall shape. Is the structure tall, narrow and rectangular or low, spreading and irregular in form? Try to sum up its personality. Is your house noble and ornate? Natural and handcrafted? Traditional and trim?

With a refreshed image of your house in mind, come back inside, find a comfortable seat near a reading lamp and turn to **Chapter 2, "The Architectural Style of Your House."** There you'll find drawings and descriptions of 13 Oakland residential styles typically in need of rehabilitation. By leafing through the illustrations and reviewing the definitions, you'll likely experience a burst of recognition when you find just the right name for the architectural style of your own home.

The name provides useful clues about the structural and decorative features which merit respect and deserve retention. The name also alerts you to potential repairs, because within each of the architectural descriptions, you'll find that specific rehab problems are predicted for the different styles.

How much should you spend on a rehab project? Are you entitled to tax incentives? If you are looking for an old house to buy, what are some shopper's considerations? House inspection, rehab budget and resale value are among the topics addressed in **Chapter 3, "Before You Begin."** Also described are the codes and permits which govern rehab construction. Become acquainted with terms like "applicable code" and "historical building code" in order to protect important features of the house which are perfectly legal, albeit not perfectly modern.

Now you're at the heart of REHAB RIGHT. **Chapter 4, "Exteriors," and Chapter 5, "Interiors,"** present over 100 repair problems commonly encountered in the improvement of old homes. (Don't worry, you won't have to face *all* 100 in your house.) For each problem, one or more solutions are described and illustrated, with an indication of cost. The cause of existing damage is explained. Code restrictions are mentioned where appropriate to remind the reader that, in addition to physical

and financial constraints, there are legal limitations on home improvement. Consult the **Table of Contents** for the page number of the precise topic that interests you.

Chapter 6, "For Your Information," discusses an assortment of subjects of interest to the rehabber. These include guidelines for hiring contractors, measures to abate earthquake and asbestos hazards and a method for researching the history of your house. Should you desire to make an old house accessible for disabled users, there are suggestions for improvements which respect the building's architectural character.

Chapter 7 lists **"Sources and Resources."** If REHAB RIGHT has left you with questions unresolved, this chapter will direct you to people and places that can help.

On the back cover you'll find a built-in ruler, in both centimeters and inches, for taking quick measurements when you are so motivated that you can't take the time to look for a yardstick, and so engrossed in REHAB RIGHT that you just can't put the book down. ⌐⌐

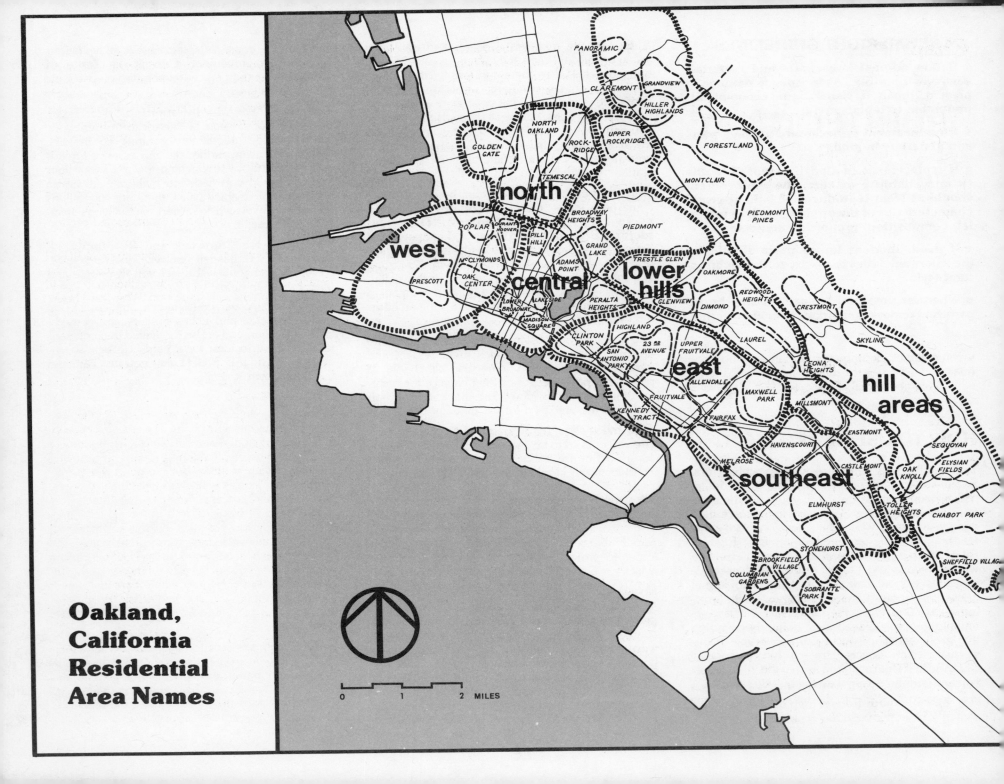

Oakland, California Residential Area Names

Chapter 2

THE ARCHITECTURAL STYLE OF YOUR HOUSE

THE CONCEPT OF ARCHITECTURAL STYLE

What's in a Name?

There are so many ways to remember a house. The smell of it, the feel of it, the sound, the cost, the look of it. In addition, every house has a name which communicates the picture in just a few words. The architectural style is a convenient handle which sums up the **form** of the building: the size, shape, room arrangement, interior spaces—and the **details** within that form: the ornamentation, hardware, doors, floors and fireplace. When a building is a style its appearance is not just a random collection of parts. All the features of the building work together to produce a single image. The dimensions of the windows are proportioned to the height and width of the entire house, and the materials selected for siding complement the structural shape. Every choice is a deliberate choice for a consistent overall impression. An individual component may stand out for its craftsmanship or flair, but its most important role is its contribution to the visual integrity of the building as a whole.

The forces which bring about architectural style are many: technology, materials at hand, fashion trends, cultural baggage, family needs, budget, topography, climate, transportation, public utilities and a host of others. So the name of a style tells us more than what a house looks like. The name can tell us where the house came from, how it was constructed, when it was built, even who lived there.

Architectural styles are classified at two levels. The more general category indicates a resemblance due to common origin, like a person's last name does. The more specific category sorts out the distinctive characteristics that define a unique personality, like a person's first name. For example, "Victorian" is the name of an architectural family in which all the kin were built in the late 19th century, with wood siding and flashy decoration. Within the family, each relative has its own expressive appearance. The Italianate is tall and thin; the Queen Anne, broader with gables; the San Francisco Stick, flat and boxy. If you know enough to call a house "Victorian" that's good, but calling it an "Italianate Victorian" is that much better. The more precise the name of the style, the more explicit the picture, and the more likely you are to REHAB RIGHT.

Architectural Portraits

The architectural portraits in this chapter are in both words and drawings. The verbal descriptions supplement the sketches, so what you can't find in the illustration you might discover in the text. The portraits are prototypes of 13 common pre-war house styles as they are found in Northern California. Elsewhere you will find houses of similar character, or regional variations which reflect the building materials, conditions and attitudes of a particular place and time. Some variants are close cousins to the Northern California version. Our broad-gabled bungalow, for example, is easily recognized in colder climes although clad in brick and with porch enclosed. Other relationships are a little less apparent. The Period Revival style in your region may have a Dutch motif instead of the Mediterranean flavor predominant in warmer states which were once under Spanish rule.

A handbook on regional architecture, available from

a local preservation group, library or bookstore, can apprise you of the name and identifying features of residential styles in your area which correspond to those portrayed here. Look for similarities in form or massing, layout and characteristic details. The handbook may also include styles which do not appear in these pages because they are unrepresented in the West. Some preceded the development of Oakland and its environs, such as the colonial and gothic styles of the 18th to mid-19th centuries. Other styles, developed later and are rather common in other parts of the country, but were simply not fashionable here, like the mansard-roofed second-empire style.

In theory, identification should be fairly simple if you compare your house with the one pictured. If the details, or the form, or both, jibe, then you are in luck. In reality, however, even your West Coast house may possess characteristics that are not shown, or may lack some that are shown. Do not despair. There is great variety within architectural families, and crossbreeding among the separate styles often produces one-of-a-kind hybrids. You might say, for example, "I have a Brown Shingle with classical porch columns."

Years of remodeling efforts also make it difficult to identify an architectural style. The obvious clues to a building's rightful name may have been hidden or destroyed by well-intentioned repairs. If you find yourself in that position, look around the neighborhood for houses with similar patterns to yours, but with more original features still intact. The arrangement of windows and doors, for example, and especially the presence of bays and porticos, are useful clues when the columns have rotted, the brackets have been removed, or the clapboard siding has been covered with asbestos shingles. If you can give a name to the house nearby that's an "older" version of your own, like Neoclassic Rowhouse, then you can call yours a "denatured" Neoclassic Rowhouse.

Some houses are hard to categorize because their plainness borders on the nondescript. Again, look for clues, no matter how subtle, in the volume, the proportion, the construction, the ornament, the age. If you come up with a name, like Prairie School, you can call your house "simplified" Prairie School.

Other houses are camouflaged by the addition of a commercial structure built up to the sidewalk at the front of the first floor. This may keep overhead down, but it doesn't do much for the appearance. Commercial conversions are often found on Queen Anne cottages and Neoclassic Rowhouses.

Most architectural styles occur in a large and small version. Both sizes may share the same name, like the mansion-sized Queen Anne and the cottage-sized Queen Anne, or they may assume different names, like the large Brown Shingle, and its smaller counterpart, the Craftsman Bungalow. Design trends were cleverly adapted to variations in family size and budget, without sacrificing quality or aesthetics. There is no reason why the same can't hold true today in the process of rehabilitation. The illustrations show the styles as they should look (not necessarily the way they do), so you can use the sketch as a guide for preservation or replacement.

This chapter does not include every house style in Northern California and intentionally so. The gallery illustrates only those styles in need of rehab. Several styles were omitted because they are too rare, too new, or are consistently well-maintained. Even if your house is not pictured, the general design principles and repair techniques offered in this book still apply.

The design and technical recommendations are as applicable to multi-family residences as they are to single family units. Unlike modern apartment buildings in California which could be mistaken for motels, many older apartment buildings have the appearance of a "house" and warrant sensitive improvement. The REHAB RIGHT design approach is also useful for commercial structures in older neighborhood centers. Too often these attractive blocks have been awkwardly modernized.

Students of architectural history may take issue with unqualified praise bestowed on each architectural style. This primer is not meant to be an academic critique. REHAB RIGHT is a tool to improve appreciation of an architectural heritage, even if some styles are not outstanding in the realm of international building design. In fact, architect-designed houses are only incidental to the discussion. This is a book about vernacular architecture, the old houses in which most people live.

In Chapter 1, under the heading "How To Use REHAB RIGHT," you were encouraged to step outside, take a walk around your house, and become reacquainted with its appearance. If you have not yet done so, try it now. A fresh look at the architectural style you inhabit will make this chapter a lot easier for you to use.

ARCHITECTURAL PORTRAITS OF HOUSE STYLES TYPICALLY IN NEED OF REHAB

Victorian

Say "Victorian" and colorful scenes of pomp and sentiment come to mind, like a richly embellished greeting card of the times. Women in bustles and bows twirl their parasols, strolling down the rose-covered walk in celebration of May Day at Oakland's Arbor Villa. Mustachioed men, their black bowler hats hung on polished brass hooks, mingle at the Forum Bar on Broadway. Slamming their mugs of Wieland Lager on the solid oak counter for emphasis, they extol the exploits of Sheriff Harry Morse who nabbed the notorious Narrato Ponce with the help of his ivory-handled six-guns.

The word "Victorian" literally describes an era of 64 years, the exuberant period from 1837 to 1901, when Victoria was Queen of Great Britain and Ireland and Empress of India. Domestic arts and inventions thrived in her domain, but architecture flourished nowhere better during this period than in California. Here, the contagious optimism of gold rush and silver strike, wheat harvest and cattle round-up, was translated into physical expressions of prosperity. By the 1880s, the life of these aggressive pioneers assumed an aura of grace as the middle-class built themselves homes as spacious and spectacular as purse or parcel would allow. The building facade was embroidered with elaborately carved brackets and spindles, luminescent stained glass and plaster-cast garlands. Inside, the parlor was filled, even cluttered, with fringed lampshades, draped flags, potted palms, patterned throw rugs,

marble busts and appliqued pillows proclaiming the virtues of religion, motherhood and "Home Sweet Home." Life was spirited in late 19th century California, and the unrestrained taste in ornamentation proclaimed the excitement of the times.

Advances in technology went arm-in-arm with pronouncements of prosperity in prompting such individually expressive residential styles. The introduction of standardized lumber and machine-made nails in 1839 made possible a spectacular new construction technique known as the balloon frame. Previously, house construction had required that hefty posts be positioned in the ground, with great difficulty, and that the cross-beams be joined to the posts with great care, by the painstaking mortise-and-tenon technique. This framework was so sturdy that the building would stand by itself without the help of supporting walls.

In sharp contrast, the revolutionary *balloon frame* utilized lightweight, pre-cut lumber instead of cumbersome timbers, and wire nails in lieu of hand-crafted joinery. Studs, the upright members, extend in one piece from the foundation to the roof, and joists, the horizontal members, are nailed to the studs. The frame gets its rigidity from the siding or diagonal sheathing instead of from reinforced joints. Construction with the balloon frame, typically used for two-story houses, requires only a facility with hammer, saw and tape measure, so the responsibility for house building was taken from the master carpenter and placed in the hands of ordinary, ambitious handymen. In fact, with the development of a variation on the balloon frame known as the *platform frame*—built one story at a time, with each floor serving as a platform for the next level of construction—it was quite possible for an entire structure to be erected by only two people. Platform frame construction is still used today.

The job was further simplified by the proliferation of house plan books which offered the novice or the merchant builder explicit architectural direction. Periodicals such as the *California Architect* and *Building News* motivated subscribers with the latest ideas for "tasty" residences, and provided them with floor plans and specifications.

When new machines were invented to mass produce elaborate building ornaments previously hand-hewn, house parts catalogs were distributed by the milling firms to promote and sell their products. By studying the illustrations the way farmers pore over seed catalogs, any builder could express his personal Victorian spirit by designing a unique composition of colonette and comice, balustrade and bracket, festoon and frieze. (Refer to the illustration of ornamentation vocabulary in Chapter 4.)

While the description of Victorian architecture sounds quite lavish, the fact was that between the balloon frame, the plan books and the parts catalog, handsome, well-constructed and fashionably adorned homes were efficiently erected on a wide scale for families of practically all income levels.

In Oakland, the flat and ample acreage afforded opportunities for building that the steep, narrow lots in San Francisco could not rival. The climate in the East Bay was far better suited to the Victorians' interest in horticulture, and the abundance of inexpensive land here offered generous lots for the practice of gardening. A wealth of native trees shaded the avenues, while experiments with exotic plant material lent a distinctive tropical aspect to the growing Victorian neighborhoods. Visitors to the West would ferry across the Bay and hire carriages to view the "elegant mansions and tasteful cottages" they had heard so much about as far away as New York. Even San Franciscans themselves would travel to Oakland to enjoy a sumptuous eleven-course meal at the Grand Central Hotel or a bucolic Sunday picnic underneath the coast live oaks.

Oakland not only lured new arrivals with a striking physical setting: it offered its inhabitants cultural pursuits as well. In the 1870s, for example, the public library opened under the direction of Ina Coolbrith, California's first poet laureate; the State's first women's club, the scholarly Ebell Society, was formed; the Chickering Club convened for amateur poetry readings; Snell's Seminary, one of the city's more select finishing schools, relocated from Benicia; and seven-hundred voices harmonized in a local choral group. How appropriate that Oakland Victorians inhabited house styles befitting their life and times: the expressive architecture of Italianate, Stick and Queen Anne.

ITALIANATE

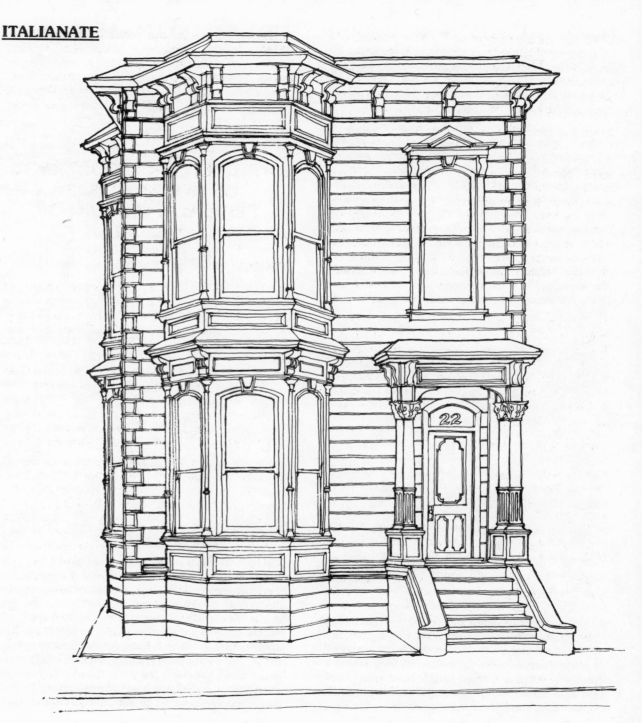

Italianate (mid-1860s–1880s)

Tall and stately, the Italianate house is a dignified neighborhood member in Prescott, Oak Center and Clinton Park, easily identified by its pronounced vertical lines. A two-story, slanted bay takes up about two-thirds of the front, and a raised porch with handsome portico fills the remaining third and visually balances the prominent bay. At the roofline, a projecting cornice is supported by concave, curved brackets, although the roof itself may be actually lower than this "false front" suggests. In the past, cresting was the crowning touch, but most of this iron lace was lost to metal salvage in post-Victorian war efforts.

Because the Italianate style is a California adaptation of stone structures built in 17th century Italy, certain architectural elements have been translated from stone into native redwood and douglas fir. The square quoins at the corners of an Italianate house are decorative versions of the original masonry reinforcements, and the Corinthian columns on the porch are carved from wood, not chipped from marble. Other imitation elements, such as brackets, panels and keystones, communicate substance and stature critical to the successful appearance of the facade.

The windows on an Italianate house have a three-dimensional quality that makes them resemble sculpture more than conventional panes of glass. Long and narrow, the measurements of the window and its many accessories are carefully proportioned to the size of the whole house. The shape, as well as the size, of the window frame, for example, is as graceful as it is distinctive: arched, notched or indented, it is rarely just rectangular. Slender colonettes to either side of the window, a protruding sill beneath, a decorative shield above and a squeezed pediment, segmented hood or bay cornice to top it all off, turn the window into a spectacular event, not just something to look through.

The front door also reaches out to the street. Beginning with sculpted newel posts at the bottom of the front steps, the extended entrance continues right up the staircase with turned railing balusters to the partially fluted columns on the front porch. Overhead, a portico, which may in turn support another balustrade, shades the front door, itself much more

SINGLE-STORY ITALIANATE

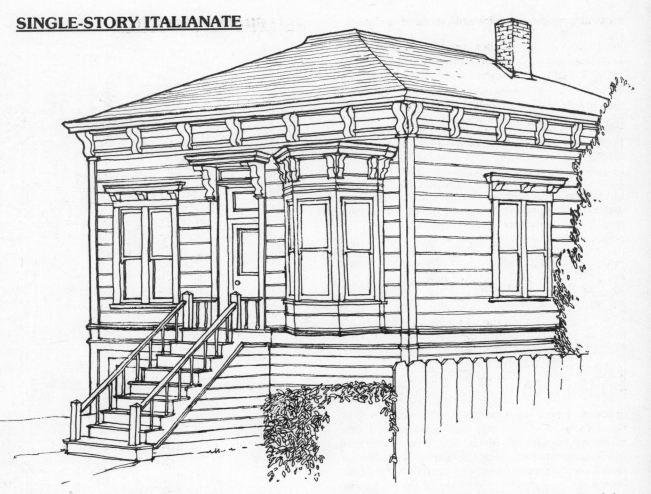

than a flat, plain surface. The solid wood is divided into recessed rectangular panels, and the glass is cut for sparkling highlights.

Inside there is a long hall with a series of doors. The first leads to the gentlemen's parlor, the second to the ladies' parlor with an additional bay window of its own, the third to the dining room and the last, at the back of the house, to the kitchen. Within the rooms, arched passageways, reminiscent of the window shapes, provide a more formal transition from one space to the next. Sliding wood panels, solid and incised like the front door, close off the rooms for privacy as well as more efficient heating. Even the white fireplace picks up its decorative theme

from the facade, with its mantel supported by curved brackets and its round, arched opening, just like the cornice outside.

The ceilings are high, often twelve feet or more. To break up the expanse of wall, wood wainscotting or lincrusta-Walton covers the four feet from the floor. A strip of molding circumscribes the room a foot or so below the seam where wall and ceiling meet. Wallpaper, typically floral and sometimes garish, extends from wainscot to molding. These techniques make the tall rooms more in scale with the size of people. Some builders installed a coved ceiling instead of a cornice because it was a less costly design feature. The rounded corners give these airy spaces a comfortable sense of enclosure.

When you look up to see just how high that high ceiling is, you discover an elaborate plaster rosette, some three feet in diameter, from which to suspend chandeliers. Originally, the ceiling was wallpapered and the rosette was painted a rainbow of colors— the grapes purple, the leaves green, the roses rose. When your neck gets stiff and you look down, you find yourself standing on wall-to-wall carpeting with an Oriental rug on top. The Italianate room envelopes you with things to see.

In Oakland, a smaller version of the Italianate house was also developed. A one-story building with front bay, bracketed cornice, pedimented window, simplified portico and raised first floor, the details are the same as the two-story type, but the overall proportions are different. In San Francisco, the heavy demand for real estate from the gold rush onward forced construction of tall, thin buildings which sometime appear almost unnaturally elongated, but in Oakland the wider lots permitted such luxuries as side yards, side bays, and a local variant: the relatively short and broad Italianate house. Other variations found locally include a two-story Italianate with a one-story bay window and a flat-front Italianate with no bay window at all.

Since the Italianate buildings date from as early as the 1860s, they have succumbed to many repair problems associated with old age. Prime victims of modernization, these once elegant Italianates are demeaningly concealed under pastel stucco or asbestos siding, mercilessly stripped of their brackets, colonettes and keystones, and thoroughly divested of their original character.

A striking example is found at the corner of 18th Street and Castro, where each in a row of five Italianate houses has a radically different appearance. The first and fourth have been left substantially intact, testimonials to their successive owners. The second has been modernized or, as some people say, "barbarized." Not only have the double-hung windows been ousted by sliding aluminum frames, but the window openings which were too tall for the conventional metal module have been reduced to suitable size by inserting a plywood flap. A once-bold front door has been

replaced by a meek hollow core, and the handsome drop siding has been sheathed in salmon-colored asbestos shingles.

The third house has been mysteriously transformed from an Italianate row house into a Spanish villa. With the whimsy of Walt Disney, some carefree remodeler troweled the house with white stucco, roofed it with red tile and planted thorny triton cactus right in front. The fifth Victorian house is, alas, just a memory. It was demolished in favor of the drab concrete box built in its place.

San Francisco Stick (late 1870s-1890s)

The San Francisco Stick Style, as its title suggests, originated across the Bay and emphasizes straight lines and right angles. Flat, narrow boards are nailed to the outside of the building to boldly repeat, and blithely reinforce the structural skeleton beneath the clapboard skin. Diagonal braces, installed parallel to the façade instead of projecting from it, frame the porch. The roof projects over the front of the house so that the gable end forms a separate plane. Its composition of right triangles, incised with sunrays and starbursts, casts a shadow on the façade behind.

The structure of the San Francisco Stick house communicates lines and right angles in a more subtle way than does its ornamentation. A rectangular bay window, which does also happen to be easier to construct, replaces the slanted bay window of the Italianate. The straight roofline of the earlier style was bent into a gable that creates the illusion that the sides are perpendicular. The horizontal siding is reoriented to vertical and diagonal positions, especially around the bay window where the structure is exaggerated by the board and batten technique. Furthermore, the square tower appears for the first time.

By the late 1870s, builders were finally treating wood as wood. For a decade before they had used wood as a medium to imitate stone in the adornment of Italianate houses. The two-dimensional design of the Stick decoration was a product of scrollsaw and jigsaw—the same tools which introduced those intricately carved puzzles for Victorians' entertainment. Local redwood and Douglas fir offered seem- ingly inexhaustible supplies of high-quality timber with clear open grain that did not split or splinter when nailed. Surprisingly, the price of redwood remained relatively constant through the turn-of-the-century, despite the increase in demand, a brief period of inflation and a duty on foreign trade which could have easily encouraged a competitive rise in domestic lumber rates.

A decorative variation to the San Francisco Stick style, known as "Eastlake," carried the exploration of the properties of wood one step further—to the three-dimensional. Knobs and newels, turned out by chisel, lathe and gouge, and most closely resembling table legs, typify this architectural mode mistakenly named for British designer, Charles Eastlake.

Seven years after the publication of Eastlake's book *Hints on Household Taste,* a treatise eschewing excessive decors in favor of more "chaste and sober designs," the Londoner's work was displayed at the 1876 Centennial Exposition in Philadelphia. His furniture was straight and square, its flat surfaces impeccably pierced with abstract floral or geometric patterns. Builders and architects, quick to catch on to the latest fashion, applied Eastlake's cutouts directly to Stick houses. But soon the ornamentation assumed a life of its own, and the simple, chaste designs evolved into sculptured, almost voluptuous, decorations. Flowers and foliage, columns and spindles as shapely as the contemporary hourglass corset, came to be known as the "Eastlake Style." Needless to say, the somber Briton was appalled at the application of his name to such chicanery. "The specimens I have seen illustrated," he wrote regarding the architectural version of his once simplified standards, "burlesque such doctrines of art as I have ventured to maintain."

When explosive Eastlake motifs are found combined with the straightforward San Francisco Stick style, the result is often referred to as Stick-Eastlake. However, extensive research by Judith Waldhorn and Gary Kray reveal that there is very little to differentiate the actual building design of houses with Stick and/or Eastlake adornment. Even though some of the exterior ornamentation may be repeated inside—diagonal braces or spindles on archways, for example—the plan itself is usually reminiscent of its Italianate precursor, and provides inconclusive evidence for a separate Eastlake or Stick-Eastlake category.

President Herbert Hoover lived in a modest, two-story Stick house with fancy shingles and a spindled arch on 12th Street, near Chestnut, when he was an office boy in Oakland in 1896. That house probably cost $2500 to construct. Julia Morgan, the prolific architect whose own work will be mentioned in later sections on the Craftsman Tradition and Period Revival, grew up in a more lavish Stick home at the corner of Brush and 14th Street, a residence which showed elements of Queen Anne architecture as well. Perhaps the best Oakland example of the San Francisco Stick style is the Alfred Cohen house on the east side of 29th Avenue just above East 14th Street. It is presently being restored under the sponsorship of the Oakland Heritage Alliance. Stick houses are also found in West Oakland where 9th Street and Chester intersect, on 15th Street, east of a Grove Street warehouse, nestled between modern apartment buildings on the ridge above Grand Avenue, and quite by coincidence, east-of-the-lake.

As the 1880s approached, the urge to combine architectural styles was encouraged. Stick and Eastlake features were enthusiastically incorporated in the Queen Anne style.

Queen Anne (1883-1890s)

When an 1883 issue of *California Architect and Building News* introduced what came to be known as the Queen Anne style to the Bay Area, it marked a dramatic departure from the rigorously vertical Italianate and San Francisco Stick-style houses. The Queen Anne house is certainly more horizontal in appearance, but more important it is an absolute concoction of volumes and textures. Round corner towers with peaked witch's caps intersect steeply pitched gables with appliqued sunbursts. Recessed upstairs balconies with turned balustrades overlook prominent front porches trimmed with arched lattice-work. The arrangement of forms appear haphazard, and the assortment of surfaces is totally unrestrained. Horizontal bands of masonry, scalloped shingles, colorful tiles—or stucco made to look like tiles—carved woodwork, plaster garlands and "artist's

QUEEN ANNE COTTAGE

glass" mark an irregular progression of stories from foundation to oriel to attic. There is no single roofline, but a picturesque composition of merging shapes. Nor is there a single window pane: the upper portion of each double-hung window is surrounded by small squares of flashed glass. And sometimes, to add still more color, two pieces of glass are installed together to create the hue of a third.

If the Italianate house is like a svelte, prim dandy standing at attention, his frilled cravat spilling over velvet lapels, then the Queen Anne house is like a buxom gypsy, her ruffled skirts, billowing blouse and patterned kerchiefs infinitely artful, but always in disarray and never quite matching. Despite the discrepancy between the two images, both styles are expressive, even extroverted, in true Victorian spirit.

The striking change in image was eased by central heating, admittedly more important in the East. There, by the late 1870s, it was no longer necessary for rooms to be shut off to keep the heat in and the cold out, so the circulation pattern was not constrained to long corridors with an endless series of doors. The influence spread westward, and thus the Queen Anne has a grand hall at the heart of the house—a symbol of gracious living—and the rooms radiate out from the central core. Rejecting the strict lines of the Italianate and San Francisco Stick floor plans, the interior spaces in the Queen Anne house flow from one to another, with dimensions as irregular as the exterior silhouette suggests. Sometimes a freestanding staircase rises like an island in a two-story-high living room; sometimes an inglenook provides a cozy recess next to the fireplace with a comfortable bench for reading and rest.

Derived from the rambling manor houses of British Norman Shaw, the Queen Anne style was popularized under the banner of "picturesque." Style books like *Palliser's,* magazines like *Harper's,* and essays like those of Andrew Jackson Downing promoted the picturesque mode as the pinnacle of good taste. It was most desirable, even democratic, to design a building whose informal arrangement of forms and textures communicated a "wild ruggedness." Asymmetric patterns, emphasizing shape, light and color, were the calling cards of domestic design.

In the San Antonio District of Oakland, a rhythmic progression of tower houses marches up 23rd and 24th Avenues, from East 21st to East 27th Streets. Some of the towers are enormous cylinders, almost like silos. Some are prism-shaped turrets perched high on the corner, making the house resemble a mid-eastern spicebox. Other towers are simply rectangular in shape. A neighborhood collection of tower houses like this is exceptional, an architectural resource that few cities other than Oakland can point to.

In the 1880s, a rowhouse version of the Queen Anne style popped up in cities from Boston to San Francisco, adapting the popularity of the picturesque to a broader range of budgets. In Oakland, it had been over ten years since the completion of the transcontinental railroad married the East Bay to the rest of the country in 1869. The demands of a growing population for new housing were accommodated by a proliferation of Queen Anne cottages. You'll find their giant gingerbread gables city wide: in North Oakland, west of Telegraph Avenue, in West Oakland near McClymond's High, in San Antonio near Foothill Boulevard, and in Chinatown around Madison Square.

The Queen Anne Cottage is a one-story building practically consumed by an oversized gable. A veritable billboard for textural effect, the ornate gable may be clothed in decorative shingles, framed with intricate bargeboard, pierced by flashed glass windows, stamped with a sunburst and topped with a proud finial. A less elaborate gable might only have scalloped shingles, a perimeter of dentils, and a modest topknot. The Queen Anne Cottage is very common in Oakland, and can be seen in a row on Harrison at 29th Street, as an antique store on College near Clifton, sprinkled along 97th and 98th Avenues between Bancroft and East 14th Street and scattered throughout San Antonio and Clinton Park.

The gable overwhelms the front bay window, and this arrangement of volumes creates cut-away corners and a recessed porch. For each of these new architectonic features, special ornamentation evolved. At the corner, spindled brackets support the overhang, and a pendant—a turned, wooden tear drop, the opposite of a finial—punctuates the projection.

The porch has a circular arch (Queen Annes show a fondness for circular forms) which reaches from the bay window to rest on a single column. The column represents no single motif but, like the Queen Anne itself, is a mixture of styles, as its beaded base, truncated shaft and ad-hoc capital indicate. In fact, the Queen Anne style is such an unabashed composite of borrowed elements that it behooves the owner to read the other sections in this manual on Victorian types as well.

The floor plan of the Queen Anne Cottage is not as palatial as the countrified Queen Anne style. The limitations of rectangular urban lots and working-people's budgets combined to condense the sprawl of gables and turrets into a more succinct package. The grand central living hall is reduced to a modest vestibule, but there is still no corridor. The rooms are arranged in succession like Italianate or Stick, but the spaces merge together through spindled archways.

In some cases, Queen Anne Cottages were built by speculators who advertised them as a wise investment because the one-story structure had a built-in option for expansion: the attic under the gable. In other, more select situations, architects designed Queen Annes. Examples of the collaborative work of the brothers Newsom, prominent California architects of the time, still stand in Brooklyn, that section of Oakland incorporated in 1872 and also known as Clinton Park. Look for one on the southeast corner of East 18th Street and 10th Avenue, and another on the southeast corner of East 23rd Street and 9th Avenue. In 1890, the same year that his plan book was published with instructions for a "suburban style suitable to Oakland," Samuel Newsom cheerfully announced: "Nowadays, beauty . . . is becoming happily less and less of a luxury."

Colonial Revival

As the 19th century drew to a close, and the gaiety of the nineties subsided, the nation's homebuilders, almost penitent for their Victorian excesses, looked toward an architectural style more refined than the bombastic Italianate and more orderly than the quaint Queen Anne. Things European lost their snobbish allure as the new world filled with working-class immigrants, and Americans turned to their own country's history in search of an architectural image.

The New England exhibit at the 1876 Philadelphia Centennial Exposition sparked the nostalgia. Then, with improved train service, people began to travel for pleasure. In Massachusetts and Rhode Island they discovered the charm of colonial houses "mellowed in place as nothing else in America seemed to be," in the words of one architectural historian. The colonists' homes were rich in elements derived from the Greek and Roman humanistic tradition: symmetrical façades and floor plans, and sensitive proportion. Known as "Georgian," "Federal" or "Adam," and "Jeffersonian," the various styles built between the Revolution and 1820 were typified by their classic columns, prominent porticoes, molded geometric patterns in low relief, rectangular windows with small panes of glass and a semi-elliptical fanlight over the front door. These features were easy enough to imitate with the materials and technology available a century later. The Colonial Revival was on.

The 1893 Columbian Exposition in Chicago clinched the Neoclassic trend. Beaux-Arts architecture, named for the Parisian design school which professed Greek and Roman precedents, was the theme of the world's fair. For years thereafter, everything from public monuments to office buildings to single-family residences picked up the classic features—capitals, pediments, colonnades, etc.—that bespoke a civilized culture.

Meanwhile, back in Oakland, major streets were suddenly striped with parallel metal tracks, and the air literally buzzed. The electric trolley had arrived. Along Grove Street in 1889, along Piedmont and East 14th Street in 1892, along Telegraph, San Pablo, Broadway, Foothill, and numerous other streets in subsequent years, the electric trolley brought the blessing of efficient transportation to the city, and with it, a halo of development. Business enterprises lined the trolley routes, genesis of the commercial strips which cling to those thoroughfares to this day.

On the side streets, in a grid pattern perpendicular to the electric cable, Colonial Revival houses sprung up like mushrooms which feed on a tree's roots, boldly tracing the roots' clandestine pattern above ground. In return, the mushrooms provide nutrients

CLASSIC BOX

to the host tree and similarly, the trolleys' existence depended on ample patronage from the very development it created.

The wealthy built Colonial homes of grandiose proportions. In the East Oakland foothills, the Dunsmuir House stands as an impressive example of Neoclassic architecture. Its white Doric columns, majestic pediment and grand interior spaces create a splendid setting for a lavish, annual Christmas fête enjoyed by the general public.

Another large Colonial Revival building can be found at 7th Avenue and East 18th Street. It has a substantial pediment supported by two-story-high Ionic columns, sidelights flanking the front door, and a protective brick wall with cannonball topknot defining the yard. But its modern use is in contrast with that of the Dunsmuir mansion: this is a boarding house.

For the average family, the separation of work place and residence was at last a convenient reality, so several simplified versions of the Colonial Revival were designed to suit its needs. The subdivision of residential land near the trolley lines was noted for its narrow street frontage which, coincidentally, minimized the distance from front stoop to car stop. What the lot lost in width it made up for in depth, and a long shoe-box shaped building was the architectural response. Architectural historian Sally Woodbridge has dubbed this style the Classic Box. For lack of a more formal designation, we call the other working-class styles the Neoclassic Rowhouse and Eastern Shingle Cottage. These houses exhibit Neoclassic details, although their form maintains obvious hold-overs from the Queen Anne Cottage, like the raised basement, recessed porch and bay window.

The Colonial Revival style was more popular in the East Bay than in San Francisco, and was generally short-lived in California. It just didn't fit in. Charles Keeler, in his 1904 book *The Simple Home,* harangued "the meaningless white-painted, fluted columns of hollow wood" as "wholly incongruous in the glare, newness and rush of western life." In response, Californians directed their attention to the State's heritage in search of a style more attuned to the local light and landscape. The California counterpart to Colonial Revival became the Mission

Revival, although few, if any, residential examples exist in Oakland.

Despite its brevity, the few years of popularity enjoyed by the Colonial Revival style coincided with a large demand for housing. The Oakland population tripled from 48,682 in 1890 to 150,174 in 1910. Urbanization reached out along the fingers of the electric trolley lines, reorganized and greatly expanded in 1902 as the Key System under the strong hand of F.M. "Borax" Smith. And the City boasted the lowest death rate in the entire world! Less than thirteen mortalities per thousand inhabitants for the twelve-year period between 1886 and 1898. Thus, the large number of Classic Boxes and Cottages found in Oakland belies the limited period Colonial Revival was fashionable in California.

Neoclassic Rowhouses are quite common in North Oakland. The trolley, after all, spread its influence up Grove Street, Telegraph, Claremont and Shattuck. You'll recognize examples of this style along Temescal Creek, near Bushrod Recreation Center and by Mosswood Park. The rowhouses are sited close to the sidewalk on fairly narrow sidestreets, like Locksley and 58th Street. There is but a patch of front yard wedged between the prominent front steps, the sideyard driveway and the paved-in planter strip. Obviously the very urban Colonial Revival was not known for its integration with nature. In fact, this was the last hurrah for formality because the earthy First Bay Tradition followed soon thereafter. The Eastern Shingle Cottage provided the transition.

Classic Box (1890-1910)

It's not a very appealing name, Classic Box, but it certainly is descriptive. A two-story structure, resembling a Kinney shoebox in shape and a Roman temple in detail, this style is typical to West Coast cities which experienced a burst of population growth at the turn-of-the-century—Seattle, Portland and Oakland. Don't think of the "box" as an unimaginative geometric shape. Consider it, instead, a creative response to site constraints and fashionable trends. The Classic Box pulled in its wings in contrast to the spread-eagle posture of the Queen Anne. The parts of the house were retracted into an orderly package, with flush planes, flattened ornamentation

and few protruding parts. Even bay windows, when they exist on the side or front, are compressed, a broad angle minimizing the distance of the projection.

At the same time, the rectangular layout recalled the floor plan of the colonists' homes they had set out to imitate. The earliest settlers in the 17th century had designed the first American dwellings no more than one room deep under the main roof. The more sophisticated Colonial style which soon followed, and persisted as the most common style in the 18th century, was just as wide, but twice as deep. Called "double-pile," this floor plan consisted of two rows of rooms, broadside facing front. Reinterpreted a hundred years later in Oakland, the long, narrow lots demanded that the double-pile plan be reoriented, with the short end addressing the street instead.

Typically the front door is on one side, leading to a foyer devoted to a "U" or "L" shaped staircase sporting two knobbed railing balusters per step. The stairway landing, bathed in pastel light from the stained glass overhead, boasts a built-in bench whose hinged top reveals a hidden storage bin. Behind the foyer there's a closet, then a bathroom, and at the back, the kitchen. On the flip side of the double-pile plan, the living room, dining room and wash porch are lined up.

Colonial Revival details include hefty ceiling beams, waist-high wainscotting, and classic columns in the archways—all in a dark finish. This was the period when hardwood floors came into their own, and the regularity of the floor plan was emphasized by the parquet border inlaid around the perimeter of square rooms. A plan book published by the Pacific States Savings, Loan and Building Company around 1900 offered an elegant but economical ten-room house that we would call a Classic Box. Its construction cost? Only $10,000.

The Classic Box is capped by a broad peak. A dormer window sticks its head out from the middle —a hipped roof within a hipped roof. At the cornice, the eaves are usually enclosed, either a shallow relief of plaster patera or swag garlands on the frieze. Patera are abstracted petals in concentric circles. Swag garlands are carved compositions of fruit and flowers, draped like a piece of cloth over two supports, and "tied" with plaster ribbons. Also known as festoons, the garlands sometimes appear

CLASSIC BOX

in a band between the first and second story. While this decoration recalls Victorian ornamentation, other variants of the Classic Box anticipate the Craftsman era. On these later versions, the eaves are no longer enclosed, and the exposed rafters constitute decoration derived directly from structure.

There is great variety among window shapes on a single Classic Box. The dormer window is short and broad, like a winking eye. The double-hung windows on the façade have a squarish appearance, and on some, the upper portion is partitioned into eight smaller panes, akin to its colonial ancestors. The window arrangement is fairly symmetrical in front, but on the side, windows of assorted size are scattered chaotically across a large page lined by slender, clapboard siding. Some of these windows are as small as twelve inches by eighteen inches; some are stained glass; some have diamond-shaped leaded partitions and do not even pretend to open. Despite the discrepancies, every window in a Neo-classic Box is invariably framed by a wide strip of flat, wood trim.

Colonial Revival houses are known for Palladian windows, and these appear on selected Classic Boxes in Oakland. A Palladian window has three parts, a high arched central section, and, on either side, a lower section underneath an entablature. This distinguished feature is named after its designer, Andrea Palladio, a Venetian architect of the Italian Renaissance. In the 17th century he revived the use of classical forms and proportion, and his work has been imitated ever since. Look for a Palladian window on the Claremont Avenue apartment building next to Hardy Park and the professional offices that overlook Lake Merritt near Perkins Street.

Other classic details of this residential style may have Palladian origins too. Hugging the corners of the house are fluted pilasters. Pilasters are like columns, having a base, shaft and capital, but pilasters are flat instead of round or square. The front door is enshrined beneath a portico complete with Ionic or Corinthian capitals. When the portico is flat, it is topped by a turned balustrade, and sometimes the portico extends across the house, creating a spacious front porch. In other homes, the portico is peaked and hipped, repeating the theme established by the roof and dormer. Even the front steps are in keeping. The tread and risers are flanked by a terraced stoop, each level covered by a flat, overhanging cap.

Originally, Colonial Revival houses were painted white or subdued tones of gray, with white trim and black window sash. Some modern owners, jumping on the Victorian paint wagon, have chosen to highlight details with bright, contrasting colors. As successful as this technique is for extroverted Italianate and San Francisco Stick houses, it is of questionable value for the more sedate Neoclassic style. Another dilemma faced by contemporary occupants is the lack of off-street parking. Classic boxes were designed to fill their narrow lots, and besides, they were built for riders of mass transit.

Neoclassic Rowhouse (1895-1915)

Not every family needed a ten-room home. A smaller East Bay residential style which grew out of the Colonial Revival genre is the Neoclassic Rowhouse. A one-story house on a raised foundation, with a hipped roof and dormer window, the Rowhouse shares many classic details with its brother the Box. Its form, however, is more reminiscent of its forebear, the Queen Anne Cottage. Although "rowhouse" suggests attached units, it is used here to mean detached houses built side-by-side, in a line.

The front portico that is so pronounced on the Neoclassic Box is absorbed within the rectangular perimeter of the Rowhouse. The front door is recessed to one side. On the same corner, the large peaked roof reaches out over the door, and rests on one, two or three classical columns. The columns are abbreviated, resting as they do on a three-foot-high wall which encloses the porch and accentuates the squared-off plan. The character of the columns varies from house to house. They can be square and chunky with Doric features, or turned and slender with simplified Ionic capitals. On remodeled Neoclassic Rowhouses, the columns are often camouflaged in asbestos siding, or replaced by curlicued wrought-iron supports. In some cases, the porch and its columns have been eliminated altogether, walled-in and weatherized to create more interior living space.

Alley-like sideyards are the result of narrow lots.

Designers of the Neoclassic Rowhouse were forced to capitalize on the front and back of the house for natural light. On the street front the living room has a slanted or square bay with double-hung windows; in the rear, there is an airy sleeping-porch. Where space allowed, a modest bay projects into the side yard, the way an elbow sticks out when your hand is in your pocket, no matter how close you hold your arm to your body. Notice the difference in proportion between the broad and austere bay window on the Neoclassic Rowhouse, and the elaborate and elongated bay window on the Italianate.

The dormer window plays an important part in visually breaking up the roof and ventilating the

NEOCLASSIC ROWHOUSE

structure, but it does nothing to supplement the supply of light. Behind the dormer is an attic space rarely converted to living quarters. It is not surprising then, that when the glass in the dormer breaks it is replaced with plywood or odd-lot lumber.

Like the Box, narrow white clapboard covers the Rowhouse, wide, flat trim frames its assorted windows and a terraced stoop flanks the front steps. Since the main floor is raised as much as ten feet from the ground, it can present a long climb to the front door. For safety purposes, most steps have supplemental railings that were not a part of the original building. A railing design sensitive to the colonial motif is graduated like the steps themselves.

The more common, hardware store solution is a straight wrought-iron rail installed on the diagonal, but its appearance is jarring.

The raised main floor creates opportunities for in-law apartments, rental units and garages underneath. Tempting as this extra space is, efforts to utilize it are often accompanied by violations of building or planning codes. Similarly, the handyman, beckoned by the dormer window to expand into the attic, faces legal constraints pertinent to family safety. Before invading the attic or basement of your Neoclassic Rowhouse with an army of tools and good ideas, check with the zoning, Inspectional Services and Housing Conservation Departments. (Their services are described in more detail in Chapter 7.)

Eastern Shingle Cottage (1895-1910)

The Eastern Shingle Cottage is so named because its A-frame shape and shingle surface are holdovers from a larger, East Coast style. Its details, however, are strictly classic, and firmly in the Colonial Revival tradition. In fact, close examination shows that the ground floor of the Eastern Shingle Cottage is almost identical to the Neoclassic Rowhouse: a raised first story, a recessed front porch with classic columns, and a bay window to one side. But the second level is astonishingly different. A gigantic gable twice as tall at its apex as the height of the first floor, and as wide as the house itself, dominates the scene.

The front and sides of the gigantic gable meet at a perfect seam. If this were more of a Craftsman house, the eaves would extend beyond the face of the gable, and the supporting beams would be exposed. The concealed structure and flush edges are among the reasons the Cottage belongs in the Colonial Revival category, despite its frequently brown-shingled surface.

The gable is pierced by one or two windows, which are surrounded by broad, flat trim. This is similar in spirit to the attic window which interrupts the hipped roof of the Neoclassic Box, because emphasis on the window compensates for the ungainly expanse of the roof plane. Several design techniques are used to accomplish this. On many examples, the double-hung window is underlined by a wood railing with closely spaced balusters and the window and

EASTERN SHINGLE COTTAGE

railing composition complements the proportion of the enormous isosceles triangle in which it sits. Unfortunately, this railing is often removed when new siding is installed. The window has no visual anchor without it, and the gable looks miserably empty.

On other examples, the window sill is exaggerated and supported by protruding brackets, something like a pouting lower lip. On still others, the window panel is recessed within the gable, and the shingles curve inward to meet the sash.

On the side of the house, which is to say on the side of the gigantic gable roof, there is a large

dormer-like projection with several double-hung windows. A dormer is a window placed vertically in a sloping roof, with another sloping roof of its own. The name derives from the French word *dormer* (they pronounce it door-may) which means "to sleep" because the space the dormer window affords usually serves as sleeping quarters. Sure enough, in the Eastern Shingle Cottage this feature is the upstairs bedroom.

Architect Ernest Coxhead, an English expatriate, practiced in the Bay Area during the Colonial Revival period. His rather eccentric designs for churches and residences are characterized by an over-sized

20

gable for the roof, sheathed with shingles and punctuated by carefully placed windows. His influence on the merchant builders who distributed the Eastern Shingle Cottage throughout Oakland and Berkeley is obvious.

First Bay Tradition

There's a saying that "history repeats itself," and when it comes to architecture this conventional wisdom really applies. In "germinal" or original styles, a new building esthetic is established; in "revival" styles, the homebuilders of a particular era look to these historic forms for inspiration and imitation.

The First Bay Tradition, as the name suggests, was the beginning of a regional style which was destined to reappear. It emerged in the 1890s, developed for the next 25 years or so, and peaked in the mid-1920s when over 14,000 bungalows were erected in East Oakland. The Second Bay Tradition began in the thirties, and for its duration urban residences in California resembled rural farmhouses. As development moved upward into the hills, post and beam construction was reinterpreted to accommodate the steep slopes and incorporate the panoramic views. By the Third Bay Tradition in the sixties, the redwood sheathed vertical box was in vogue with vocabulary borrowed from the tract builder's language.

First Bay Tradition houses are characterized by a communion with nature, sensitivity to basic materials and appreciation of structural form and craftsmanship. The unfinished redwood and fir, the expressed beams, the built-in bookcases and the informal floor plan, have tremendous appeal to a new generation of homebuyers seeking natural quality for their living environment and financial investment.

Four architectural styles constitute the First Bay Tradition, and they fit in two subcategories: Craftsman and Prairie. As we found with other Oakland styles, there seems to be a small and large version of each. The Craftsman Bungalow is a more modest expression of the Brown Shingle home. The California Bungalow is like a compact counterpart of the winged Prairie School.

While house trends in the Victorian era were established by merchant builders, the First Bay Tradition derived from the work of professional architects. Although only a rare reader will own a house designed by one of the great masters, their influence is seen in so much of Oakland's architecture that they deserve mention here.

In 1869 Joseph Worcester, Swedenborgian minister, left Boston for San Francisco, and brought to the Bay Area the transcendental teachings of Ruskin, Emerson and Thoreau. "The most beautiful styles of art and architecture," they believed, "are those that closely imitate the forms of nature." As a physical statement of this design philosophy in 1876, Worcester built himself a house in what was then an unfashionable section of Piedmont, a rough-hewn cottage constructed entirely of unfinished redwood, inside and out. Imagine what a striking departure this reserved and rustic bungalow was from the highly ornamented and ostentatious Victorian homes of the same period!

By the 1890s, the Bay Area had the benefit of a population of well-educated architects. Each picked up the thread of Worcester's plea for the unaffected and wove it into a new architectural fabric. A. Page Brown, A.C. Schweinfurt, Willis Polk, Bruce Porter and Bernard Maybeck collaborated on the design of Worcester's house of worship. The Church of New Jerusalem (2107 Lyon Street, San Francisco) is a masterpiece of serenity, and a milestone in the First Bay Tradition for its consistent use of handcrafted natural materials.

The influence of Worcester on the work of Ernest Coxhead, John Galen Howard, Louis Mullgardt and Julia Morgan was less direct, but the outcome was similar: an architecture of shingles, stained wood, exposed rafters and picturesque spatial arrangement.

Despite similarities, there was no formula. Each architect pursued a personal building style. Polk's work was flamboyant, Schweinfurt's was primitive, Coxhead's was wry. Of them all, Maybeck best embodied the Arts and Crafts attitude because, when the blueprints left the drawing board, he participated in the construction. Woodworker, stonecarver, postpainter, Maybeck has become something of a folk hero in the Bay Area for his unrelenting commitment

to fine craftsmanship. The many examples of his residential work, which can still be discovered in the neighborhoods of Berkeley and Oakland, offer a rallying point for architectural enthusiasts.

The famous architect Frank Lloyd Wright was a contemporary of the First Bay Tradition design circle, and despite the two-thousand mile distance from Wright's home base in the midwest, his influence was felt here in three ways. First and foremost, Wright "invented" the Prairie School house. According to *A Guide to Architecture in San Francisco and Northern California,* "With the exception of Chicago, there is no urban community which contains as many examples of the Prairie Style [as the Oakland-San Francisco metropolis]."

Secondly, Wright trained several architects, among them A.C. Schweinfurt, Frederick Langhorst and Aaron Green, who later came to California to achieve prominence and contribute to the evolution of the local genre. Third, Wright was imitated by Bay Area practitioners in all three phases of the regional tradition. The gently sloping roofs, low proportions, sheltering overhangs and indigenous materials which typify Wright's style were incorporated in the work of architects John Hudson Thomas in the teens, William Wurster in the thirties, Lois Langhorst in the forties, Charles Callister and Jack Hillmer in the fifties, developer Joseph Eichler in the sixties and countless other Bay Area building designers throughout the 20th century.

The preceding paragraphs may read like a telephone book, there are so many names mentioned. But the point is a simple one. The architecture of the First Bay Tradition in Oakland displays an unusual design awareness—unusual for homes built by contractors, and this can be attributed to the Tradition's origins in the work of talented, professional architects.

Brown Shingle (late 1890s-1915)

The spacious, two-story Craftsman house is called either Brown Shingle or Western Stick Style. These interchangeable names are as straightforward as the style itself. They are no-frill descriptions of the building's trademarks: the redwood shingles, weathered

BROWN SHINGLE

to a raisin-brown, and the projecting structural members, which look like elongated and exaggerated sticks. This frankness was hardly the case in the Victorian era when houses were so decked-out that they earned pretentious names derived from European dignitaries.

A Craftsman house was once cleverly described as "looking more natural than nature itself." The characteristics of the Brown Shingle style justify this quip. The shingles cover the entire house like bark on the trunk of a tree. They bend where the building bends and bulge where the building bulges. On a beautiful example in Oakland's Pill Hill (384–34th Street), the shingles form a hood over the window, circling it the way that cambium encases the bole when the bough of a tree is removed.

The shingles are typically 2' long and 8" wide, paper thin at the leading edge and nearly half an inch thick at the base. Because they overlap to keep out the rain, the shingles look more like horizontal rectangles than vertical ones, once installed. Many Brown Shingle houses are shingled in a manner which looks as if each slat is a double image. In reality, the broad and narrow bands are all the same size shingle, but the spacing varies to create the pattern.

Shingles change color with age and acquire a rich patina that is desirable, even sought after—but in some cases they do look shabby. To freshen up shingles use stain, never paint. Paint harms natural shingles because it clogs the pores. Water collects with no way to evaporate, and accelerates decay.

The word "stick" was used in the 1880s to describe the flat boards applied to the facade of Victorian houses to echo the structure underneath. Here too, the stick work is a structural expression. While the Victorian stick style capitalized on the ornamental opportunity the stick work afforded, the Craftsman stick style emphasizes the structure itself. The tie beams, for example, are not concealed within the roof, but extend beyond the eaves into plain view. The protruding end of the beam is finished with a simple diagonal cut, a set of notches, or a Swiss or Japanese motif. Braces are attached to the gabled end of the house to support the heavy rafters. Constructed like a right-triangle, each brace is finished with a slash, a notch, an Alpine cut-out or an

Oriental twist, to match the beam itself. Between the braces and the broadly pitched roofline a barge-board is added, a sturdy two-by-twelve, from the days when lumber dimensions were literal and "two inches" did not mean "one-and-five-eighths."

Living and sleeping porches are an essential feature of the Brown Shingle style not only because they obscure the threshold between indoors and out, as the Craftsman credo commanded, but also because they provide another opportunity for stickwork. Porch posts often stand in pairs—two sticks are better than one—and the horizontal framing members project a foot or more beyond the posts. Many a veranda is covered by a trellis, and what is a trellis but the barest skeleton of structural form? Even the choice of wisteria as the vine which is typically trained over the trellis cooperates with the overall image. In warm seasons, wisteria may camouflage the trellis with its profuse foliage or upstage the stickwork with pendants of lavender blossoms but as winter approaches, the vines lose their leaves and the structure prevails.

The incorporation of plants into the architectural form is but one way Craftsman style houses use natural materials exclusively. Shingles and shake, rough stone and redwood were acceptable, trimmings were unnecessary, and oil paint generally frowned upon. According to the Hillside Club, early East Bay conservationists and arbiters of taste, "No colors are so soft, varied and harmonious as those of wood." Despite this, or perhaps rising to the challenge, Bernard Maybeck developed his own palette of Pompeii red, blue-green, salmon and beige which were, in fact, soft, varied and harmonious with wood.

The chimney is made of clinker brick, a brick more coarsely textured than the conventional type because it has been overfired in the kiln. Originally discarded seconds, clinker bricks became so popular that correct overfiring became a craft in itself. Outside, the dark red clinker brick blends well with the grooved shingles and redwood grain; inside, the clinker brick fireplace is the visual focus of the living room and the symbolic focus of the home. Gustav Stickley, editor of *The Craftsman Magazine,* a periodical which monitored craftsman-like lifestyles with a religious fervor from 1901-1916, wrote that the fireplace should "sound the keynote of comfort

and hospitality." The Craftsman movement had social as well as architectural standards to maintain.

The windows of the Brown Shingle house are typically casement or double-hung with pronounced wood frames. The upper segment may be cut into six, eight or even twenty-four smaller panes by wood partitions. The Hillside Club preferred hinged windows which swing outward for an unobstructed view, and French doors, the logical extension. However, Gustav Stickley's recommendation of 1912 is a more fitting description for most Brown Shingle houses in Oakland: "Wherever possible, the windows should be grouped in twos or threes, thus emphasizing a necessary and attractive feature of the construction, avoiding useless cutting up of wall spaces, linking the interior more closely with the surrounding garden, and providing pleasant views and vistas beyond."

The only curtains deemed suitable for the Craftsman window were denim, burlap or cotton crepe, natural fabrics in an age which predated synthetics. Even now, polyester just wouldn't look right with the wood grain which abounds on the interior. Boxed beams criss-cross the ceiling, wainscotting covers the walls, oak boards cover the floor and redwood moulding surrounds the doors. The built-in china cabinet with leaded-glass doors, the built-in closet "for wraps" under the stairway, the built-in bookcases and desk are handcrafted of redwood, or more commonly, fir. If there are built-in columns to boot, they are likely to have a plain Doric capital.

Consistent with the use of natural materials, the form of the Brown Shingle house is "organic." That is, it appears to have grown of its own accord, rather than adhering to a formal floor plan. In one typical arrangement, two gables intersect at right angles to form a cross whose longer arm runs the length of the rectangular lot. From this cruciform, rooms project on an as-needed basis: an upstairs porch to capture a view, for example, or a five-sided bay for a breakfast nook, or an entire wing for the master bedroom.

Because of their size and asymmetry, Brown Shingle houses in Oakland are found on relatively large parcels. The yards are filled with big evergreens (deodor cedar, lawson cypress, redwood, even sequoia), trees which are in scale with the building and consistent with a philosophy revering nature. Many of these houses have been reorganized inside as apartment units or business offices, with the fortunate outcome that more people have the opportunity to enjoy the craftsmanship and quiet comfort of the Brown Shingle style.

CRAFTSMAN BUNGALOW

Craftsman Bungalow (1905-1925)

Having just discussed the meaning of "Craftsman," the word "bungalow" remains to be defined. The bungalow is typically a single-story house with one or more broadly pitched, overhanging gables. On most, a small gable caps the entry porch, echoed by a larger gable behind and to one side. The roofline recalls a child's drawing of mountains: a series of overlapping, inverted triangles. Another bungalow style found in Oakland shows the broadside of the roof to the street instead of the gable peak. In this style the space beneath the roof is adapted for use by the installation of a dormer window.

To describe houses which do their best to look like bungalows, the awkward word "bungaloid" was coined. While this word is typically used to categorize larger homes designed by architects for wealthy clients, it also applies to a vernacular building style that may be unique to Oakland. Many families find that the bungalow is too limited in size, that the two or three bedrooms do not provide enough living space. Because the lots are small, the only direction that remains is up. The more spacious, but rather ungainly, two-story result is rightly called bungaloid. Examples can be found on Carrington Street in the Fruitvale District.

The etymology of the word "bungalow" is a curious one, and we must travel to the country of India to discover it. In the early 1800s, the Indian Government built resthouses along the main road to aid travelers en route. These thatch-roofed shelters were temporary dwellings, low in profile and surrounded by verandas. The British administrators anglicized the Hindustani adjective *bangla,* which means "belonging to Bengal," and called these way stations "bungalows."

The Craftsman Bungalow is recognized by the deliberate use of natural materials, an emphasis on structural form and a casual relationship with the outdoors—traits reminiscent of its Indian namesake. The Craftsman Bungalow has exposed beams beneath overhanging eaves, projecting brackets and a propensity toward Swiss or Japanese motifs. Brown shingles persist, though sometimes wood siding is used instead.

Two large pillars, broad at the base, slightly tapered at the top and somewhat foreshortened, support the front porch gable. Made of wood or stone, the columns rest on pedestals which rise up out of the foundation and serve as endposts for the porch railings as well.

Ideally, the foundation of a Craftsman Bungalow is constructed of local stone so that the house seems to emerge from the earth. In the Oakland flatlands, where building stone is not indigenous, most bungalows have a raised cement foundation sheathed with sculptured cement, brick or quarried stone for a more textured appearance.

The front window on a Craftsman Bungalow is as individual as a signature. Although they are all divided into three parts, no two look exactly alike. One house has a trio of double-hung windows with sixteen small panes on top. Another house has fixed windows filled with leaded diamond shapes. A third has a dramatic stained glass inset, another has mullions in an irregular geometric pattern, and so forth. The design can prove a helpful clue to the precise construction date.

The central window is always the largest of the three panels. Often, for consistency, the front door arrangement is handled in the same way as the front window. Two sidelights, narrow panels of glass (leaded, paned, stained or otherwise), flank either side of the entry. The windows on the Craftsman Bungalow are decisively outlined with wood molding and grouped in horizontal bands to complement the dwelling's broad stature. Even the dormer window, with its broad overhang, is designed in careful proportion to the rest of the house.

The interior finish of the Craftsman Bungalow is a showcase of wood. The wall, floors, beams, built-in cabinets and benches are a treasure trove of grain. The owner has a choice of clear stain, to keep the redwood a light russet; medium, to enrich the surface to cherry; or dark, to deepen the grain to somber walnut. Above the plate-rail, a wood mantle which caps the dining room wainscotting, there is a strip of wall about a yard high. This is commonly used as a neutral backdrop for decorative plates, bottles and bric-a-brac propped up around the ledge. The *Craftsman Magazine* of that period recommended a more creative idea; abstract floral designs which could be hand-stencilled like a frieze around the perimeter.

If informality is a corollary to naturalness, then the floor plan of the bungalow is another expression of the Craftsman ethic. The formal entry hall of earlier styles is discarded completely in favor of the front porch. The front door opens directly into the living room, which itself spills directly into the dining room. The space is so free-flowing that the dining room is used more for "living" than "dining" and the bedrooms are within earshot of the living areas. Privacy can be hard to come by.

The old-fashioned, subdivided kitchen of Victorian times is here incorporated into a single room. The pantry, the work counters, the cooking surface and the sink are reorganized into a "work triangle" for the modern housewife. As Gustav Stickley wrote in a 1912 issue of the *Craftsman Magazine,* "The most sensible plan is to have the kitchen large enough to allow some of the meals to be taken there. For there is no reason why this part of the house should not be cheerful and attractive as any other, and certainly where the mother has to do all

her own work both she and the family would get more real comfort by simplifying the serving of meals as much as possible."

This new attitude toward comfort and convenience meant much more than the demise of the formal dining room. It marked the introduction of the 20th century California way of life. At last, the Golden State had a residential style all its own, an architecture suited to its landscape, derived from native materials and adapted to West Coast culture.

Seventy years ago, Craftsman represented a lifestyle as well as an architectural style. Today, the wares of that lifestyle are easy to come by at the many popular crafts fairs in the Bay Area. The pottery mugs, hand-woven rugs and hanging candles fit in perfectly, as do the efforts of indoor gardeners. A Craftsman Bungalow on Hudson Street in the Rockridge section of Oakland is a good example. The small size of the lot precludes extensive landscaping otherwise suitable for the Craftsman house. Instead the owner has designed a magic forest of potted plants which cascade down the steps, fill in the porch, hang from the rafters, obscure the foundation and generally sequester the house—as if it were nestled in a wooded hillside.

Prairie School (1910-1925)

It's confusing, isn't it, that a style with a Midwestern accent is mixed up in this discussion of the Bay Area's own regional architecture. While Frank Lloyd Wright, the renowned Chicago architect, is credited with the invention of the Prairie style, his product was brought to California by those who worked directly under him, and those who emulated descriptions of his buildings in the architectural journals. The expression "Prairie School" refers to the followers, the imitators and the reinterpreters of the design concept initiated by Wright.

Although the Prairie School style was created to meld with the Midwestern landscape, its attributes are remarkably analogous to the features of the Craftsman tradition in Northern California. Both emphasize natural materials, horizontal proportions and a kinship with the earth. Wright's design philosophy that "form follows function" blended with

the attitudes, material and landscape of the East Bay as easily as it did with Illinois prairie land.

The Prairie School house in Oakland is noticeable right off because of its size. Two or 2½ stories high, it is taller than neighboring bungalows or cottages. Room wings project to either side, making it wider than the typical Oakland house, as well. The long, low walls are plastered in pastel colors; hence its nickname, "Stucco Villa."

The Prairie School house is a juxtaposition of broad boxes which allow the building to adapt to differing site conditions. If the lot is flat, the boxes are at equal elevation; if the lot is steep—as many are in the Grand Lake District where the Prairie School style abounds—then the boxes step up the hill. Likewise, the roof plane is broken and steps up the hill. The side expansion of room wings is seen more often on corner property whose size and frontage is more conducive to the expanded arrangement.

Each box is capped by a very low-pitched tar and gravel roof. The eaves overhang to the point of real or suggested cantilever. The shadows cast by the overhangs modulate the stark stucco walls. On some, the rafters are exposed beneath the eaves in a Craftsmanlike manner. On others, a perfectly horizontal board, whose broad side is parallel to the facade, describes the perimeter of the flat roof and enunciates the eave. This is called the fascia.

When one of the wings is a porch, or on rare occasions a portecochere (a covered driveway at the front door), then the flat roof is supported by heavy piers. Remember these. Their influence is felt in the California Bungalow as well as in other features of the Prairie house itself. The weight and proportion of the porch piers are reiterated in the massive, terraced stoop which flanks the front stair progression from sidewalk to front door. The posts' chunky quality is also repeated in the heavyset chimney.

Horizontality is also a design element of the casement windows. They are grouped in bands, with shared projecting sills, and appear to wrap around the building. In some examples there are geometric mullions, but more often the pane of glass is left entire, a plain rectangular surface just like the building's walls. In fact, the Prairie School house is

a careful composition of planes and voids, like a Mondrian painting.

On the inside, the bands of glass flood the rooms with natural light. While this is desirable, even Craftsmanlike, in concept, it can pose a disadvantage with western exposures. The Prairie School house in Illinois did not have to contend with the strong, late afternoon sun of California. Also, in a dense urban situation like Oakland, the picture window can make privacy a problem, a dilemma not encountered in the more sprawling Chicago suburbs. Because of this, passers-by typically see the soft folds of opaque drapes drawn behind the windows of the Stucco Villa.

Life in a Prairie School house can be sumptuous. The broad proportions evident on the exterior make for spacious rooms on the interior. Even the staircase is wide and the landings ample to match the opulent, airy spaces. The scale of a Prairie house lends itself to the display of large oil paintings, hand-woven wall hangings and other oversized pieces of art which demand a gracious wall and enough room to step back and view them from a distance.

The cool pastel exterior of the Stucco Villa belies the warm interior, where earth tones predominate and the extensive woodwork is stained a golden oak. The hardwood floor, the hallway paneling and the bookshelves made of gumwood are all subtly ornamented by strips of darker, mahogany-colored wood inlaid in geometric patterns. The fireplace is built of rough fieldstone and placed at a focal point in the living area. Light colors and fine craftsmanship are the attributes which typify the Prairie School house and sustain its image of elegant simplicity.

In 1916, California architect Irving Gill summarized the new architecture of the West in an article entitled "The Home of the Future." The language is inflated, but the description is fitting for the Prairie School house in the Craftsman Tradition: "If we omit everything useless from the structural point of view, we will come to see the great beauty of straight lines, to see the charm that lies in perspective, the force in light and shade, the power in balanced masses, the fascination of color that plays upon a smooth wall left free to report the passing of a cloud or nearness of a flower, the furious rush of storms and burning stillness of summer suns. We

will also see the glaring defects of our own work if left in this bold, un-ornamented fashion, and therefore, swiftly correct it."

California Bungalow (1910-1925)

The last style in this discussion of the First Bay Tradition has a little bit of everything that came before. The California Bungalow shares small size and low-pitched roof with the Craftsman Bungalow, stucco and horizontality with the Prairie School house, and front porch and exposed rafters with the Brown Shingle. The California Bungalow in Oakland is the builders' distillation of the more sophisticated features of its architect-designed predecessors. Although extremely plain, especially compared to the

bungalows designed by Greene and Greene in Pasadena, the California Bungalow offered comfortable living at popular prices.

In 1920, 216,261 people lived in Oakland, more than three times the number residing here in 1900. Obviously, there was a need for a house style that could be quickly constructed at reasonable cost and yet perpetuate the California image that had enticed the newcomers in the first place. The California Bungalow filled the bill.

Almost fifty years had passed since the introduction of straightforward woodframe construction in Victorian times. Time and experience perfected the stud-and-joist technique, and simplified it even further. The studs, for example, were placed in a

CALIFORNIA BUNGALOW

standard 16″ pattern, in contrast to the Victorian merchant builders who placed studs more arbitrarily and at wider intervals. The shorter distance from floor to ceiling in the bungalow, combined with the reduced spacing between the studs, resulted in shorter, lighter lumber which was easier to handle. Next, diagonal sheathing was abandoned as the means of crossbracing. Instead, rigidity was achieved by placing 16″ long 2 × 4s horizontally between the studs.

Concrete greatly simplified the foundation. Although Portland cement had been discovered in 1824, its versatility was not fully realized until the 20th century. It took experimentation with the new product by Wright and other respected architects to bring concrete into the builder's arsenal. Formerly, the foundation consisted of bricks or stones, placed and mortared individually. With concrete, a trench is dug to define the building's perimeter, board forms lined up, reinforcing bars inserted, and the concrete poured in one fell swoop.

Similarly, the siding operation was greatly simplified by the introduction of stucco. Made of Portland Cement, sand and a small percentage of lime, stucco is applied in a plastic state (hence the word "plaster") over a wire mesh curtain that is wrapped around the building. How much easier this was than using a level to keep each strip of clapboard horizontal, or nailing several thousand shingles on, one at a time!

If anything persisted from the Victorian Era it was the availability of plan books. Printed first in Southern California and later in Seattle, Chicago and Minneapolis, these publications offered the prospective homebuilder an incredible assortment of bungalow designs. Working blueprints could be ordered for $5 to $25, usually less than one percent of the estimated production cost, which started at under $1,000 for a four-room bungalow, and ranged upwards to $7,000 for larger, very elaborate models.

The plan books provided more than design details, however; they also influenced taste and values. The introduction to the promotional brochure "Little Bungalows," distributed by the Los Angeles firm E.W. Stillwell and Company in the 1920s, presents a convincing argument in favor of the "genuine California Bungalow" whose plans they had for

sale. "It is better to build a small house than to overburden the budget with debt for a larger one. A beautiful small house is just as expressive of character, aims and aspirations as the large house. Mere size is a waste of money and human endeavor."

As new materials, construction techniques and mass-produced blueprints simplified house building, so the floor plan of the California Bungalow simplified housekeeping. One room merged with the next, and this meant fewer steps for the footworn homemaker. There were no hallways to collect household tumbleweed, no formal parlors to keep "company-clean," no knick-knacks to accumulate dust. The plan books boasted the efficiency their drawings offered. "The economic use of space" was a positive way to say "small," and "cozy" an optimistic word for "crowded." Besides, built-in conveniences more than made up for the lack of room because "movable furnishings," as the brochure argued, "so complicate the labor of the cleaning day."

According to the 1925 *Oakland Tribune Yearbook,* 12,312 one-story houses were built in Oakland between 1907 and 1920. Between 1921 and 1924, in one-fourth the time, an astounding 12,822 more sprung up. Most of these were California Bungalows, concentrated in the new East Oakland subdivisions. The rest were scattered throughout the City, making it the most widely distributed house style in town.

The feature unique to the California Bungalow is the pair of elephantine columns which support the small gable over the front porch. On their own, these heavy-looking posts with broad base and tapered top seem too short and awkward, but in place they are clearly in proportion to the overall bungalow design. Covered in stucco, the columns have a wood framework underneath which is subject to both termite damage and dry rot. Replacing the columns with anything less substantial in appearance than the elephantine originals—like wrought iron posts or 4 × 4s—looks skimpy and regretfully out of place.

The origin of the bizarre bungalow columns is a matter of speculation. They were obviously influenced by the hefty piers on the Prairie School house, a style sometimes considered to be the California Bungalow's larger counterpart, and by the arroyo

stone columns on the Greene and Greene bungalows in Southern California. Or, they may be descended from an ingenious Craftsman detail used by architect A.C. Schweinfurt. In 1897, he designed the First Unitarian Church on Bancroft Way in Berkeley for a congregation whose membership included Bernard Maybeck, Charles Keeler (author of *The Simple Home,* a Craftsman manifesto) and representatives of the sylvan Hillside Club. Schweinfurt used massive redwood tree trunks, peeling bark and all, for the front porch columns on the church. Short, slightly tapered and mammoth in dimension, the tree trunks may well have been the unwitting precedent-setters for the oversized porch columns which became the bungalow trademark.

The interior of the California Bungalow resembles that of the Craftsman Bungalow, but it is generally plainer. The ornamental use of wood is limited to the moldings, baseboards and hardwood floors. Sliding or French doors between living room and dining area may persist, but the leaded glass has been eliminated.

The California Bungalow in Oakland stands on a small lot (typically 40′ × 100′) with an abbreviated front yard and narrow side yard. This lack of land may frustrate the enthusiastic gardener, but the unified appearance is terrific. Look down a block of closely spaced bungalows and you will appreciate the up-and-down rhythm of the rooflines, the in-and-out rhythm of the projecting porches. Critics call the parade of pastel bungalows monotonous but in fact, a closer look reveals interesting variations within each house. There is enough repetition to establish a unified framework, yet enough variety for individual identification. This is the essence of good neighborhood design.

Unlike many Victorian neighborhoods whose visual unity has been destroyed by ad hoc demolition or thoughtless remodeling, Oakland's bungalow blocks are still intact. The pleasant, human scale of these neighborhoods, combined with the convenient size and reasonable price of the bungalows, has begun to attract young couples and single people in the market for their first home.

Period Revival

The 1920s in California were a prosperity decade not unlike the exuberant period which had launched the Victorian Era seventy years before. This time oil, rather than gold, was the cause. Three enormous oil strikes in the Los Angeles Basin in the early twenties surpassed all previous development in oil production nationwide. Until this time, gasoline had been a troublesome by-product, useless and dangerous to dispose of. But the Los Angeles strikes were coincident with the arrival of the automobile age, and the refineries were immediately redesigned to extract as much petrol as possible from every barrel of oil. Quite literally, oil stoked the fire of California's headlong expansion. Valued at 2½ billion dollars, the crude oil produced in California in the twenties alone was worth more than all the gold ever mined in the Golden State.

By 1925 in Alameda County, more than 100,000 automobiles were registered, and the popularization of the car precipitated three major changes in the Oakland land use pattern. First, the hill areas, once off-limits from development because the trolley cars could not negotiate the steep slopes, were now available for residential buildings. Second, the moguls of the auto industry—General Motors, Fisher Body, and Durant—located their factories in Oakland, spurring employment, population growth and housing starts. Third, the local street network had to be reorganized to accommodate automobile traffic.

In 1927, the Major Highway and Traffic Committee of One Hundred was convened to devise "a comprehensive plan for the reconstruction of the ill-arranged collection of streets of Oakland into a well-ordered system of traffic arteries." They commissioned the notable firm Harland Bartholomew and Associates of St. Louis to conduct the study and prepare recommendations. One illustration in their report shows that although practically all the flat land was already urbanized (that is, served by sewer and water), there was only a limited number of streets with permanent pavement outside of the central business district. Other than Broadway, Telegraph Avenue, East 14th Street, and a half-dozen more, the thoroughfares were worn macadams "in such condition that the traffic avoids them whenever

possible." The report then enumerated major street improvement projects which were the key to fulfilling Oakland's "prospects and promises for the future."

Progress was the priority, and the twenties were downtown Oakland's finest hour. The commercial buildings which now form the backbone of the central business district were erected in a single decade. Included in the roster are Capwell's, the Hotel Leamington, the Tribune Tower, the Fox Theater, the Central Building and the Bank of America tower.

At the tail end of the downtown building boom in 1931, an enclave of Art-Deco commercial structures appeared in the vicinity of 20th and Broadway. A façade of terra-cotta, turquoise tile and incised angular patterns typify this style, which is also known as Zig-Zag Moderne. The Breuner's Building, the Oakland Floral Depot, the Singer Shop, I. Magnin and the Paramount Theater are fine examples. They are known throughout the Bay Area, not only for their individual merit as fine architecture, but also for their proximity which creates a theme for the uptown commercial district.

Meanwhile, back in Los Angeles, the young cinema industry had begun to infiltrate the mass culture with the glitter of its own prospects and promises. Gilded movie palaces, bearing the names of major production companies like Fox, Paramount and RKO, brought Hollywood to the rest of the State, where the silver screen convinced the public that fantasy is reality. This attitude, combined with the flamboyant spirit which accompanied the oil strikes, the automobile age, and a period of prosperity, produced an outrageous architecture. The Californians chose a building style better suited to a film set than the local landscape.

In the twenties and early thirties, theaters, shopping centers and middle-class houses alike were designed to conjure up romantic times and faraway places. The frankness of the Bay Region style had given way to the pretense of Period Revival. No longer did the houses appear to emerge naturally from native soil; instead they looked as if they had been plucked from the 13th century English countryside and deposited in 20th century urban America.

The longing for a foreign atmosphere was so great that entire tracts would be developed in a Provincial

or Mediterranean mode, as if they were miniature European settlements. In Oakland, there was one called "Court of All Nations." Another, "Normandy Village," is still intact on Holly Street, east of 73rd Avenue. Local builder Walter W. Dixon went one step better than just developing the eclectic houses. He published a magazine from Oakland called *Home Designer* to nurture an appreciation of Norman arches, Tudor half-timbering and Spanish pergolas, and to promote his product.

Another valuable, and somewhat less biased, guide to housing fashion in the twenties was the professional journal *Western Architect and Engineer*. Their report of the California Complete Homes Exposition conducted in Oakland in 1922, for example, shows Spanish residences with "cheerful" interiors, and two-story stucco houses with window shutters and arched doorways, designed by the architectural firms Miller and Warnecke, and Reed and Corlett. Equally informative are the advertisements, which confirm the popularity of oak floors, fold-up wallbeds and pastel paint, and provide the historical sleuth with meaningful clues to a building's original materials. Both periodicals are available at the Fine Arts Desk of the Oakland Public Library. The library building itself was designed by Warnecke in 1949.

As with earlier house styles, there is a large and small version of the Period Revival prototype in Oakland. The larger examples resemble the Stucco Villa and the smaller ones the Bungalow, primarily because they had to respond to the same subdivided lot sizes and utilize the same available building materials. No matter what the size or sub-category, all Period Revival houses have one outstanding feature in common: incredibly tidy owners. The lawns of Provincial cottages in Oakland are always mowed to crewcut precision, the prominent picture windows are always streaklessly clean, and the welcome mats are placed perfectly parallel to the front door.

Mediterranean Style (1915-1935)

The Mediterranean Style house is easily identified by red roof tile. This is not to say that it has a red tile roof. Rather, most smaller houses are covered by flat or low-pitched tar and gravel roofs concealed behind a parapet or the front porch gable. Typically, it is only the porch or parapet which is covered in red tile, but the suggestion is enough to set the Mediterranean mood for the entire house.

Originally, when the semi-cylindrical tiles were handmade by peasants in the Spanish countryside, wet clay from the native soil was shaped over the workman's strong thigh. Today, the tiles are made in molds and held together with wire, but the installation process is basically the same and the textural effect almost identical. The tiles are placed in interlocking rows, alternately facing up and down. The water that runs off the rounded back of the top tiles is collected in the swale created by the u-shaped bottom tiles. There is a pleasing unevenness to the rows of overlapping pottery that even machine modules cannot regulate.

The Mediterranean Style house is invariably sheathed in stark white stucco, a dramatic counterpoint to the undulating tiles. There is little color on the house, save the terra cotta of the tile and the wood frames of the six-part casement windows which are painted burnt sienna, or occasionally turquoise blue. The earthy red, clean white and bright aqua are a lively and attractive palette.

The ornamentation on the Mediterranean house is restrained compared to the explosive Victorian styles, but a bit pompous compared to the ascetic Prairie School. Wood or wrought iron is used for second-story balcony railings on larger homes, or for window grills on cottages. On some houses, distinctive twisted columns support the front porch roof in post and lintel fashion, or frame the living room picture window. These twisted posts and similar baroque features characterize the "Churrigueresque" style (pronounced chi-ree-ga-resk), named after the Barcelona architect who first designed them in the 17th century, Jose de Churriguera. His decorative style, which dominated Spanish and Mexican architecture in his own time, was revived at the San Diego Panama Pacific Exposition in 1915 and incorporated in the vogue for Mediterranean architecture which followed.

The Hearst Castle at San Simeon has the most exaggerated examples of Churrigueresque towers and spires. Its architect, Oakland native Julia Morgan, was mentioned as a practitioner of the Craftsman

MEDITERRANEAN STYLE

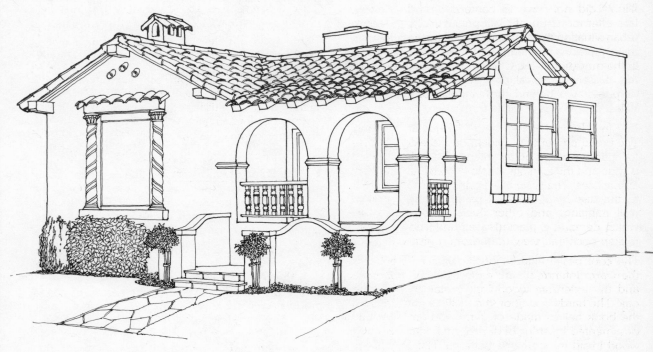

Tradition, but she was so prolific, with over 1000 commissions to her credit, that she was proficient in the Mediterranean style as well. The Berkeley City Club on Durant Avenue, which she designed, has a Hearst Castle flavor, but her residential work in Oakland and Piedmont shows the flair and expression possible on a smaller scale in the Mediterranean vein.

We use the inclusive name "Mediterranean" for this style because the architectural elements are assembled from the lands which border the Mediterranean Sea—Spain, Italy and the Islamic world of North Africa. The coastal climate of California is classified as Mediterranean, one of only five such areas found in the world. (The other three are the coast of Chile, southwest Australia, and southwest Africa.) Because climate determines the plants and animals that survive in a given environment, the natural setting of California is very much like that of the countries on the Mediterranean shore. As a result, the house style that derives from Spain, Italy and Northern Africa can look extremely convincing in California.

If there's red roof tile, you can be sure there are arches on the house too. Either the porch, the front window, the front door, or all three, have an arched opening. The arch may be pointed, rounded, flattened, or a circle with a peak in the Islamic manner. Even the weep holes which stick out through the façade to allow the tar and gravel roof to drain, or the attic to air, are arranged in an inverted curve. Extending from the side of many Mediterranean houses is a stucco wing wall with another arched opening. This provides a gracious entrance to the backyard, when the arch is the size of a door, or a ceremonial entrance to the garage, when the arch is as wide as the driveway.

The front walk and the driveway are an abstract composition of paving stones cut at acute angles and installed in a random manner. They are usually painted a brownish red to match the roof and trim, a startling contrast to the patch of kelly green grass to either side. Originally, it was fashionable to paint the different stones assorted hues, and East Oakland homeowners who enjoy striking color combinations have perpetuated the trend.

Inside the Mediterranean house the walls are covered with a rough, almost lumpy plaster that is either white or an integral earth tone which simulates adobe. Dark wood beams are exposed across the ceiling. The Churrigueresque motif is picked up in staircase bannisters, and the arch—in whatever form it took outside—is used for a passageway between rooms. The fireplace is sheathed in white, integrated into the wall adobe-style, and surrounded by ceramic tiles. There is an arched recess to either side for display of candlesticks, keepsakes or religious icons.

In Oakland, large Mediterranean Style houses are found in the Lakeshore Highlands, Oakmore and Trestle Glen and scattered in Piedmont Pines. Architect/builder Fred L. Confer was responsible for some of the most handsome examples in Rock-

ridge, above Broadway. In North Oakland, San Antonio and East Oakland, smaller Mediterranean houses are more common, filling the space left between California Bungalows, Neoclassic Boxes and Queen Anne Cottages.

There are three Oakland tracts composed entirely of Mediterranean homes which are so well integrated with one another that a visit there is a cross between a trip to Spain and a tour of Universal Studios. One is found on the loop road comprised by Castello and Cordova Streets, just off Fruitvale Avenue. A second is located on 77th and 78th Avenues between Holly and East 14th Streets. The third, largest, and most varied, fills a six-block area around the intersection of Monterey Boulevard and 35th Avenue. The residents of these three "villages" take exemplary care of their homes and maintain a quality neighborhood image. They make it clear that this is a good place to live.

Provincial Style (1919-1935)

When William the Conqueror invaded England in the year 1066, he brought from France the Norman style of architecture. Peaked roofs and gothic arches proliferated and became the trademark of the English country home. Nine hundred years later, when the doughboys returned to the United States from the Continental battles of World War I, they brought home a taste for the quaint cottages and picturesque settlements they had seen abroad. Yet somehow, when the medieval imagery was transposed to California soil, the result resembled a dollhouse.

Provincial Style houses in Oakland are small in scale and fussy in texture. They can be identified by a gambrel or steeply pitched roof that is covered with slate or a composition shingle which was especially designed to look like thatching. Gladding, McBean and Company, the largest West Coast tile manufacturers of the period, advertised that the coloring of its roofing product "reproduces the stains of lichens and storms" and they bragged "that it smacks of storied antiquity."

The walls of the single-story Provincial house are built of rough stucco on a frame of 2×4s, but stone, brick and wood are incorporated for decorative effect. The wood is used in the manner of half-

timbering, a technique associated with English Tudor style houses of Shakespeare's time. In real half-timbering, the spaces between the hefty structural members are filled with plaster or brickwork; the resulting triangles and rectangles form the façade. In the 20th century version, however, the exposed wood is only ornamental. The geometric pattern of dark timbers and white spaces is applied over the structure, not as part of it.

Originally, stone was used for foundations and front steps; a convenient way to recycle the boulders strewn across Britain's fields. But when the Norman and Tudor style houses were reinterpreted in the 1920s, technological advances made it more convenient to built a concrete foundation, and to cover it with a rock veneer. Stone is also used as a decorative trim around windows and doors, appealing to the person who believes a "man's home is his castle," and should look like one.

A castle is impenetrable, and indeed the Provincial house has very few openings. The simple board or paneled door has only a small lookout window, if any. The living room has a large, arch-shaped picture window, but this is typically partitioned into very small panes by heavy lead mullions. The casement windows are small, sometimes hooded, and occasionally reduced to narrow slits suited at best to an archer's bow.

As expected, the interior is cool and dark, private and secluded, with limited access to the yard and little connection to the foreign, urban landscape outside. A floor plan as irregular as possible adds to the mystery, as do hidden stairways, passages between rooms and real or suggested changes in the floor level. The roughly plastered rooms are small in size and unconventional in shape—romantic perhaps, but not always comfortable. As we have noticed with every house style since the 1870 Italianate, the fireplace picks up the architectural theme. In the Provincial house, a large hearth of coarse brick or unmatched stones is indispensable to the image.

While this style was promulgated by architects such as W.R. Yelland, Carr Jones, Walter Ratcliff and Henry Gutterson, a simple builder's variant of the Provincial house is common in both North and East Oakland. Its plain stucco walls, single story and front porch are also suggestive of the California Bungalow, but the steep roof and Tudor arch picture window distinguish the imported Provincial Style from its regional neighbor.

An outstanding example of Period Revival architecture in Oakland is the Idora Park tract between Telegraph and Shattuck, 56th and 58th Streets. Until 1927, this was the site of the most spectacular amusement park ever built in the East Bay. At the turn-of-the-century, F.M. "Borax" Smith and the Realty Syndicate developed this extravagant attraction to lure potential investors to nearby real estate. Extensively landscaped, Idora Park was an ideal picnic

PROVINCIAL STYLE

ground. When the beer and sandwiches were consumed, there was so much more to do for "fun, frolic and jollification": the Laughing Gallery, the Scenic Railway, the Great Coal Mine, a Tea Garden, a Merry-Go-Round, a full-fledged theater, a Friday Night Amateur Contest and countless other entertainments —all for the price of a single dime. According to the 1909 Oakland Chamber of Commerce, Idora Park was as exceptional for its "cleanliness and wholesome atmosphere" as it was for the facilities it offered.

When Idora Park changed from an amusement park to a housing tract, every trace of the original

landscape was razed, the native oaks included. The Period Revival house, after all, was not mean to fit in, but rather to stand out. Each Provincial Style house in the enclave has a large living room window on the right and a recessed front door atop three or four red front steps on the left. The picture window is treated in a variety of ways: one is surrounded by flat, irregular stone; another is barely shaded by a projecting, shingled hood; a third is partitioned by mullions; and a fourth is concealed by a striped metal awning. The steep peaks, cylindrical towers and gambrel roofs calmly alternate with the low-pitched tile roofs of their Mediterranean neighbors. What a wonderful fantasyland! The unusual glass-globe streetlamps are not even 15 feet tall and there are no overhead utility lines.

All-American Ranch Style

The make-believe world of Period Revival was jolted back to harsh reality by World War II. In the thirties, housing starts slowed down for lack of funds; in the forties, for lack of materials. No longer could architecture afford pretense. The few dwellings that were constructed had to be erected quickly and efficiently in order to house the workers who migrated to war-related industries, the meccas of employment.

California became a center of manufacturing for the defense effort and received more than a proportionate share of federal spending. During the war years, Washington pumped some 3½ billion dollars into the California economy, fueling employment and consequently boosting housing demand. The airplane industry was centered around Los Angeles, but thanks to Henry J. Kaiser, shipbuilding was concentrated in the Bay Area—Richmond, Oakland, Sausalito and Vallejo. The shipyards were in operation 24 hours a day, and at peak capacity in 1943 a new freighter was launched every ten hours.

It took a work force with three shifts and no racial or sexual barriers to operate these enormous factories. So many people had never before been employed in Oakland. To provide them housing, and to anticipate the wave of soldiers who would need a place to live when the war ended, a major re-zoning effort was necessary between 1942 and 1944, and three new subdivisions were developed in Southeast

Oakland. The 460 acres near the area where the Nimitz Freeway and 98th Avenue now intersect, which had been zoned for industrial use, were re-zoned for residential use.

The Wartime Tract houses which were subsequently built there are an early species of the All-American Ranch Style, a style that would dominate the national housing market from the late 1940s on. What better way to package democracy for a returning soldier and modern consumer both, than a plot of land, a detached home and a private parking space for every family. Later examples of the All-American Ranch Style found in Oakland, but not discussed here, are in the Crestmont, Sequoyah Hills and Park Ridge Estates subdivisions.

Once the demand for housing clearly outweighed the supply, it was necessary to impose municipal regulations to protect a public no longer able to pick and choose. Well over 600 subdivisions had been platted in Oakland before 1939, but for the most part, improvements were at the behest of the developer who recognized amenities as an aspect of promotion.

In 1939, the City of Oakland adopted its first set of subdivision regulations, and the three Southeast Oakland tracts mentioned above were early examples of its implementation. The subdivision ordinance, which has since been expanded, determined the width and turning radii of streets, designated the size of the blocks, and required that the developer provide paved streets, curbs, sidewalks, storm drains and sanitary sewers. The evolution of the All-American Ranch Style went hand-in-hand with the gradual sophistrication of subdivision regulations which governed the development of site plans for what has likely become the most widely distributed architectural style in the United States.

Wartime Tract (1942-1945)

The Wartime Tract house is a small, one-story building on a concrete perimeter foundation with five rooms and a pitched roof. The roof is shingled and the exterior walls are finished with either stucco or rustic siding. In Oakland, the Wartime Tract houses are concentrated in Columbian Gardens, Brookfield Village and Sobrante Park. They are also scattered among the California Bungalows between 80th and 90th Avenues, below East 14th Street.

The three subdivisions mentioned were the work of three different contractors—Phillip Heraty, The Brookfield Corporation and Shultz Construction Company, respectively—so each has modifications of its own. However, the Wartime Tract house is basically rectangular in shape with the broad side facing the street. The roof overhang is supported on 2×4s to create a recessed front porch. The parking area is usually a detached pad or carport, although in Brookfield Village, where the houseplan is U-shaped, the garage is incorporated into the body of the house.

Mysteriously, in Sobrante Park, many houses have two front doors. This is attributed to the wartime custom of inviting defense workers to board in the family home. The extra door leads to a room which could be closed off from the rest of the house on the inside, securing privacy for both the boarder and family members.

The interior of the Wartime Tract houses consists of a living room, a dining room, a kitchen, two bedrooms and a bath. The limited dimensions of the rooms and the constraints the small size imposes on a growing family are the same drawbacks of the California Bungalow. To overcome this, some families have expanded the house to the back with the addition of a family room, an extra bedroom, or just a sliding glass door leading onto a patio. Other property owners have converted the garage to living quarters, and still others have added a second story above the garage.

WARTIME TRACT

What little decoration there is on the Wartime Tract house is typically an imitation of some earlier, more established style. Window shutters are meant to suggest colonial architecture, the diagonal brackets on the porch posts are a souvenir of Victorian times. The porch railing may have some Craftsman-like stickwork, or the living room window may be subdivided by wooden strips in imitation of Period Revival leaded glass. On many examples, a veneer of brick is mortared over the lower portion of the façade to simulate a masonry foundation and lend an air of permanence. Ironically, the chimney brick, which is truly structural and not decorative, is often camouflaged with paint, the same pastel color as the rest of the house.

The Wartime Tract house is sited further back on the lot than the typical Oakland bungalow or row-house. This gives the impression of more land, as befits the All-American style. However, the lots are only 75 feet deep to begin with, so the effect of more land in front is achieved by sacrificing precious backyard space—a hard bargain. The sidewalk is next to the curb, with no planting strip in-between, and this too makes the lawn seem more spacious than it really is.

Thanks to the site planning, Sobrante Park has one of the most successful examples of street planting in Oakland. There is a London plane tree, or two, in the front yard of every house, instead of in the planting strip as elsewhere in urban locations. Placing this tree on the house side of the sidewalk gives the roots ample space for nourishment, promoting vigorous growth while precluding the risk of sidewalk damage. The canopy of leaves is especially graceful because the trees are mature and the streets are curved. The landscape seems to predominate the house, an impression entirely befitting the style which heralded the revolutionary era of American tract development and the preoccupation with landscaping which characterized the new suburban way of living.

Chapter 3
BEFORE YOU BEGIN

HOW MUCH SHOULD YOU SPEND ON REHAB?

The Resale Value of Rehab Right

Establish your goals, understand your motives. Rehabilitating as an investment is quite different from rehabbing to improve your living quarters. Improvements to your own living space will probably cost more than a neutral design suitable for resale. However, if you plan to live in the house for many years (say over five), the resale value of improvements is less important because the costs can be amortized over several years, and the changes can be enjoyed for that much longer.

REHAB RIGHT advocates that, whatever your goal, you **do not impose your personality on the house. Let the house express its own character.** This is the economical approach right from the outset, since you are spared the expense of excessive or unwarranted alteration. But additionally, it has been shown that **rehabbing right pays off later in increased property value.**

In a 1986 study, Susan A. Wiesner, at the Graduate School of Business Administration, the University of California, Berkeley, measured the impact of architectural integrity on resale value. Her sample was taken from a target area in North Oakland, and the houses correspond directly to the styles portrayed in this book. If any of seven cardinal changes had been made to a building in the sample—

windows, porches and columns, doors, steps, awkward additions, siding or ornamentation—then the historic integrity was considered lost. (The research of necessity was limited to exterior features.)

The results of Wiesner's multiple regression model demonstrated that among the factors affecting sale price, architectural integrity was more important to buyers than the total square footage of living area, the number of bedrooms and the presence of a fireplace. Condition of the house was found to be the most significant factor, and second, just slightly ahead of integrity, the number of bathrooms. Weisner's analysis concluded that "historic architectural integrity does have a positive effect on the value of older real estate."

For resale, therefore, it is advisable to stick to the fundamentals, improving the condition of the property and leaving architectural features intact. Rehabbing for immediate resale is not disreputable if, as a result, the building's basic problems are solved rather than concealed behind cosmetic changes.

Your goal may be limited to correcting code violations. When bringing a building up to the applicable code, try to understand exactly what needs to be done, and do your best to accomplish this without destroying the very architecture you set out to preserve.

Whatever your goal...

Do The Basics First

1. **Life and Safety Hazards:** Electric and heating systems should be up to code. A fire can cause injury or death, and destroy all of your investment.

2. **Weatherproofing:** Roof, gutters, flashing, sheathing, paint, windows and drainage should be in good condition. Water leakage means costly repairs and ruined rehab efforts.

3. **Plumbing:** Pipes and fixtures must be in good enough condition to preclude water damage. Never conceal faulty pipes behind new or improved walls.

4. **Dry Rot and foundation problems.** Structural damage must be corrected before walls and ornamentation can be restored. Attend to seismic protection.

After these basic repairs have been accomplished, funds remaining in the rehab budget can be used to improve the comfort or value of the home by rejuvenating exceptional architectural features, updating the kitchen or bath and other more visible and compliment-fetching projects.

Recognize Over-improvement

A house is considered to be over-improved if the money expended on rehab or alteration cannot be recovered when the house is sold. It is important to note, however, that the concept of over-improvement does not take into account the owner's enjoyment of changes to the house during his or her term of occupancy.

Two key factors which govern the over-improvement threshold are the sales value of particular improvements and the location of the house.

It is a common misconception that the cost of a particular home improvement will increase the value of the house by an equal or greater amount. In fact, among popular home improvements, most only add 40%–75% of their cost to a home's market value, according to *New Shelter* magazine.

While fundamental rehab differs from the secondary home improvements cited in the *New Shelter* survey, the way to recapture costs for either is to manage construction expense so that the outlay is in line with the market value of the end product. The Enterprise Foundation Rehab Work Group of Columbia, Maryland, recommends this approach: **component rehab + sweat equity + discounted materials**. As explained in their newsletter *Cost Cuts* (August/September 1986), component rehab means replacing only those houseparts which are broken beyond repair, severely out-of-date or major energy-losers. It is the opposite of substantial rehab, or what is sometimes called "gutting." Substantial rehab, they argue, can decrease the potential resale value of the alterations. Because several different improvements are undertaken at once, and not one of them can recoup its own cost, the losses are compounded.

Sweat equity means do-it-yourself whenever practical because labor costs usually far exceed the bill for materials and supplies. To keep materials costs down, use standard consumer savvy, and ask for contractor's discounts. You are, after all, in the business of rehabbing houses, albeit one at a time.

As for location, the value of a house is heavily influenced by the value of surrounding property and the quality of the neighborhood. Some areas are experiencing dramatic increases in property values; others are stable; and yet others are deteriorating. Improvements to one home that are in concert with improvements to other homes nearby can push property values up. In other cases, however, **improvements beyond a critical threshold will not add to resale value,** or even have a spin-off effect on the rest of the block.

Whether moving into a new house, or fixing up the place you live now, determine the direction in which the neighborhood is heading. Call the appropriate City offices (listed in Chapter 7) to learn if parks, sidewalks, street trees, loan programs, or any other publicly sponsored projects are slated for the area. Ask about the schedule and the precise boundaries. Check out the neighbors' contribution to environmental quality by driving around the neighborhood. From the street you can judge the interest and energy owners and tenants put into their property. Yard upkeep, fresh paint, general maintenance and overall cleanliness, are good indicators. Look for signs of work in progress: debris boxes, trade trucks, scaffolding.

Investigate the market value of houses comparable to your own. Ask a realtor active in your neighborhood for sales—not listing—prices of similar homes. Or play detective at the county recorder's office. (In Oakland, the County Recorder's Office is located at 1225 Fallon Street, Room 100; open 8:30–4:30 pm.)

Ask that same realtor about listing your property. Request a price tag for your house "as is" and with selected improvements. In Oakland, members of the Board of Realtors have access to a computer print-out which lists asking and selling prices of all reported real estate transfers in the City. Your agent will undoubtedly refer to this source to derive a price for your home.

Calculate the difference between the approximate market value of your house with the desired improvements and the amount of investment you now have in it. This is the leeway you have for rehab expenditures if profit or breaking even are your only concerns. However, if you plan to live in the house yourself for several years, then your enjoyment of the neighborhood has a meaning and a value of its own, irrespective of real estate trends.

How to Finance a Rehab Project

Establish a rehab allowance before you spend any money or sign any contracts. Determine how much you can afford either outright from pocket, or monthly in loan repayments.

If you already own the house, there are three common ways to generate rehab funds from a bank: a home improvement loan, a home equity loan and a refinancing of the original deed of trust. Basically, the bank evaluates the applicant's ability to repay the loan, and charges the customer in the form of interest rate, points and assorted fees for the privilege of borrowing. The interest rate is usually higher for principal under $15,000. Compare charges among lending institutions to find the most favorable terms.

A home improvement loan can be used for any home improvement purpose. The applicant's qualifications are judged on income, not on the property itself. The bank requires a contractor's or architect's drawings, specifications and cost breakdown for the proposed work. If you are planning to do much of it yourself, be prepared to demonstrate your qualifications in construction, or to work with a licensed contractor who will take responsibility and supervise. The bank is concerned about the quality of the end product, as the house is their collateral on the loan.

At today's rate, a $5,000 home improvement loan would cost $62/month for 15 years. The maximum home improvement loan is limited only by the customer's income and other outstanding debts.

With the upsurge in real estate values in California over the last decade, and the recent lowering of interest rates nationally, two prominent sources of funds for those who have owned their house for several years or more are the refinancing of original deeds of trust, and home equity loans, which are second deeds of trust. These loans are not restricted to house purposes, but are frequently used for rehabilitation or additions.

With a refinanced first, or a new second loan, you are borrowing against the amount the house has increased in value since you purchased it. This differential value is determined by a bank appraisal for which you will be charged about $200, and have to wait four to eight weeks. At today's rate, a $30,000 loan would cost $350/month for 15 years.

Factors which affect the bank appraisal are the conservative values of real estate: comparables, location and upkeep. The appraiser will use three sales of like property in the immediate neighborhood or, for lack of three, the adjacent neighborhood. By law, no neighborhood can be excluded or "redlined" by a lender, but clearly neighborhood has an indirect bearing on the appraised value. It is, after all, the source for comparables, and the essence of location.

The house is evaluated as is, with no consideration as to its future value when the improvements are complete. The appraisal is based on evidence, not vision.

A low appraisal may mean that the difference between the outstanding loan on the house and the present market value is not enough to borrow against. To get some idea before you go to the bank—or while you're waiting your turn for bank appraisal—ask a realtor active in your area for a rough estimate of the market value of the house, or at least some comparable sale prices. Take 70–75% of this approximate market value, then subtract the amount outstanding on your first mortgage. The result is an educated guess at the amount the bank will lend in a home equity package. For a refinanced first mortgage, the principal will be 80% of the new appraised market value.

If you are of modest income and unable to qualify for a bank loan, you may be eligible for one of the City of Oakland's subsidized rehab loans. These emphasize correction of code violations, but can also pay for other work. Consult Chapter 7, "Rehab Assistance Programs," for descriptions and contacts. Outside Oakland, contact your City or State Department of Community Development. Nationwide, some 40% of Community Development Block

Grant disbursements are used for residential rehab programs. (Metropolitan areas larger than 50,000 population receive federal block grant funds directly; in smaller locales, they are handled by the state.)

If you do not yet own a house and are looking to buy a building in need of work, be certain to consider the amount of money needed for improvements and where it will come from prior to buying the property. **Failure to account for needed rehab funds is a common mistake in the passion of house-hunting.**

A recent buyer with a large mortgage has little recourse for bank loans, having yet to build up equity and having already assumed a major bank debt. The primary solution is to buy a house whose purchase *and* phase-one rehab you can afford without undertaking complicated and expensive loans which, in the long run, are depleting. Try to retain as much cash as possible to use for improvements when drawing up the purchase and loan agreements. Approach the bank directly or through your influential broker, to combine an improvement loan with the first mortgage at the more favorable mortgage rate. The interest rate for a first mortgage is more favorable than that for second or home improvement loans, and the monthly outlay will be much lower than for two notes. However, when demand for loans is high, don't expect the bank to respond favorably. Another approach is to whittle the down payment below 10%, if the bank's stipulations for doing so are not prohibitive, then use the retained down payment money for rehab.

Another way to generate cash for rehab before you buy is to have the broker negotiate a second deed of trust from the seller as part of the transaction. Instead of taking a down payment completely in cash, the seller takes back a second for a short term loan, with a balloon payment at the end of the term, say five years. At that time, and with the improvements, the house may qualify for an equity loan from the bank. But remember, **the cost of the improvements will probably be more than the value added to the property as a result of those improvments.**

Talk to the real estate broker about other options. There is a sizeable private market for second deeds of trust or, the broker may be able to arrange a joint venture or shared equity situation and attract an investor in the project. **While trying to resolve your problem of rehab funds, don't forget the long term financial costs of the solutions.**

If your employer has a credit union, inquire there about home equity loans. Its rates may be lower than the bank's. Also, credit unions offer a personal note of credit, a type of loan not available at most banks. As with a short term, private second, the credit union note can be used for construction and pave the way for refinancing or an equity loan at a better rate in a few years' time.

If you are looking for a loan to buy your first house and you are within the income and purchase price ceilings set by a single-family house bond program, you may be eligible for a low cost mortgage and rehab loan. The Oakland program is described in Chapter 7. Elsewhere, contact your presiding Community Development Department.

In brief, the bond is used by a tax-exempt agency to support single-family house purchase. The limits on income and purchase price are sufficiently high to offer working and middle-class families a large selection of houses. In the present City of Oakland Issue C, a portion of the bond funds have been set aside to finance rehab along with purchase. The maximum amount of the combined purchase and rehab loan would be 95% of the value of the house when the rehabilitation work is complete.

If you are rehabilitating a house for trade or business use—say a bed-and-breakfast establishment, or consultant's offices—or for rental housing, you may be eligible for federal preservation tax incentives. That topic is described under the heading "Matters of History" later in Chapter 3.

BEFORE YOU BUY

Inspecting the Merchandise

Either you love it or you don't. That much you'll know. But is it in sound condition? And is it as good —or bad—as it looks?

A thorough home inspection can give you the objective data to quell or buoy up your emotional response to an old house. Problems undetected at purchase time can quickly sour your honeymoon with the lovable old wreck when you must live and cope with them, especially all at once.

Professional house inspectors offer their services in the Yellow Pages under Building Inspection Services. Some are members of the American Society of Home Inspectors, Inc. (ASHI), which accords membership status on the basis of education, experience and examination. Professional inspection, according to ASHI literature, requires a comprehensive knowledge of building practices, house systems and maintenance. This broad expertise is beyond the realm of any single building profession. As Jane Spangler, an ASHI member in Oakland, puts it, "A good inspector understands how a house ages."

Choose an inspector who will conduct a thorough investigation and provide a written report, including the checklist of the systems, structural components, built-ins, etc. which were reviewed or excluded. Ask to see a sample report in advance to assess the actual scope of work (what does "thorough" mean?), the amount of information provided for your fee, and whether the observations are interpreted for your use.

Ask for references from other old-house clients, particularly those who own buildings of the same era as your own. An inspector who concentrates on 1950s tract homes may not recognize problems unique to the pre-war styles. An inspection report costs between $250 and $300, depending on the size of the building.

To inspect a house yourself, begin with the "Inspection Checklist for Vintage Houses" available from *The Old-House Journal*. A seminar in house inspection is offered through the Owner-Builder Center by Ms. Spangler, and she has annotated the OHJ checklist to reflect local conditions. Another broad-based source is the book *What's It Worth—A Home Inspection and Appraisal Manual*, by Joseph V. Scaduto, available from TAB Books, Inc., Blue Ridge Summit, PA 17214.

In your own locale, check with local preservation groups or restoration architects. They may have devised an inspection checklist sensitive to regional styles.

After performing an inspection yourself, you might choose to call in a professional inspector, architect or engineer, builder or tradesperson to evaluate specific areas of doubt or problems.

Use the revelations of the inspection for more than a yes-or-no decision on whether to buy. You now have the basis for determining initial and secondary rehab costs. Apply this valuable information in the form of a rehab budget, and determine the source of the funds needed *prior to purchase*, as discussed in the preceding section. If you cannot afford the basic structural, safety and weatherproofing repairs, you probably cannot afford the house.

Disclosure Statements

Buyer beware? Now it's "seller beware" too. Effective January 1, 1987, **anyone selling a house in California must complete a state-mandated disclosure form detailing potential problems with the property.** In essence, the form is a general checklist for the lay person of certain things a professional would be likely to notice in the course of house inspection—particularly the "red flags," or bits of evidence which may indicate a major problem. An uneven floor, for example, might be the result of a limited amount of settlement, or it could signal serious subsurface earth movement or structural dry rot.

It was a 1984 California Court of Appeals case, East v. Strassberg, which established that a real estate broker has an affirmative obligation to investigate and report defects to a prospective buyer. As a result, many California brokers, on their own accord, required their clients to complete disclosure forms prior to the effective date of the law.

The 1987 law provides a standard declaration for the owner's signature. It itemizes the systems, machinery and appliances built into the house and questions their condiiton. It also recounts a veritable nightmare of problems and asks if any pertain to the house under consideration.

Since the format encompasses the complete housing market, the disclosure questionnaire includes material extraneous to old houses, like "does the electric garage door opener work?" and "is there a solar heater for the swimming pool?" While such explicit references can easily be dismissed by the buyer of an old house, the implicit message is harder to ignore. The form measures the house against modern expectations and as a consequence, says a local realtor, "old houses usually seem a lot worse than they are." While structural, water leakage and safety problems can be serious and must be corrected, consider the stated deficiencies in the realm of other old houses and whether they share the same problems and to the same degree.

Buyers are encouraged to bring in specialists or home inspectors of their own (see above). The new disclosure law has created a climate in the real estate industry which fosters the revealing of information. As a buyer, you can go beyond the standard statement for areas of particular concern, or seek confirmation of specific line items. The form, after all, was probably filled out by a lay person like yourself. It does not substitute for a professional inspection.

Also, note that the standard form does not call out asbestos insulation or other asbestos-containing materials. The presence of ACMs may influence your purchase decision. (See Chapter 6.)

Copies of the disclosure form are available from your broker, or in bulk from the California Association of Realtors, 525 S. Virgil Avenue, Los Angeles, CA 90020. Similar disclosure requirements are being discussed in other states.

Termite Reports

Wood frame houses are subject to infestation by structural pests, especially if the wood members are in contact with the soil or if moisture has been permitted to accumulate in the wood. The most infamous of these pests is the termite, but fungus, rot, powder post beetles and carpenter ants also pose a serious threat to wood structures. (Refer to the section on wood porches in Chapter 4 for a list of the danger signs.)

A licensed structural pest control inspector will evaluate the property for a fee of about $100. The inspector prepares a termite report which ascertains the presence of structural pests, analyzes the damage, and recommends corrective and preventative measures, or what is commonly called "termite work." Typically, a termite inspection takes place when a property is about to change hands, and is required by the lending institution and/or the buyer. The lender usually requires "termite clearance," which is a form signed by a licensed pest control operator certifying that "no evidence of active infestation, infection or adverse conditions were found." It often takes termite work to arrive at such a determination. The buyer usually requires that the seller pay for correction of the termite damage. The seller may do so directly, by hiring a termite contractor to do the structural work, or indirectly, by reducing the sales price of the house in an amount equal to the cost of correcting the damage.

The City may require a termite report and subsequent termite work:

- in conjunction with a Compliance Letter and the issuance of a Certificate of Occupancy
- to abate a serious safety hazard noted by a housing representative in the course of a general inspection or in response to a complaint
- in a project area that is undergoing a systematic inspection program.

Otherwise, **the City does not require that work itemized by a termite report be undertaken.**

Although some termite work is limited to the removal of debris from the crawl space, or a minor change in grade to allow a 6″ clearance between soil and wood, most termite work is structural in nature and requires a building permit. **A regular contractor, with a B-1 license, is not authorized by law to perform structural pest control work,** and will not be issued a building permit to do so by the City. Nor is a B-1 licensed contractor permitted to issue a termite clearance once the structural work is completed. Only a licensed structural pest control operator may perform these operations, and he must file a copy of the termite report with the permit application. The Inspectional Services Department has records of termite reports dating back to the late 1930s, if you choose to investigate the structural history of your house.

Selecting a structural pest control company requires comparative shopping and powers of observation. Only some pest control companies are licensed in the treatment of wood destroying organisms and appurtenant structural repair. (The others are licensed in either fumigation or general pest control.) Look for the key phrase "termite inspections and structural repair." It is especially important to check around and get recommendations of companies with an honest reputation since the contents of a termite report are a matter of professional judgement. In fact, a discrepancy in the cost of recommended repairs is fairly predictable when two reports are ordered for the same property, especially if one is requested by the buyer and the other by the seller.

Contact the State Board of Structural Pest Control to find out if any complaints have been registered against the operator you are considering, and the disposition of any complaints received. The Board will also provide mediation services, at no cost to the consumer, if there is a marked inconsistency between the reports of two companies. Write to the Board at 1430 Howe Avenue, Sacramento, CA 95825, or telephone them at (916) 924-2291. Likewise, you can file complaints against a structural Pest Control company with them, and seek redress.

For intelligent, alternative approaches to chemical pest control, consult the Bio-Integral Resource Center, P.O. Box 7414, Berkeley, CA 94707, (415) 524-2567. Volume One of their *Common Sense Pest Control Quarterly* addresses in an eye-opening way the major structural pest control problems, including termites, carpenter ants, bees, wood-boring beetles and decay. Volume One can be back-ordered by non-members for $25.00, or included by pre-arrangement as part of a membership package.

CODES AND PERMITS

How to Determine Applicable Code

Construction is regulated by a body of legal documents called codes. Typically, a jurisdiction adopts a generic code, then amends it with accessory local regulations. The Uniform Building Code (UBC) is the standard west of the Mississippi. East of the Mississippi, the Basic Building Code (BBC) prevails in the north, and the Southern Building Code (SBC)

CATEGORIES OF APPLICABLE CODE

Pre-1923

Borderline (Check Date)

1923-1948

in the south. New York City and Chicago have their own building codes.

Certain states, including California, have enacted an additional code specifically for significant older buildings. In California, the State Historical Building Code (SHBC) is mandated for designated historic structures. The SHBC and its applicability to old houses is addressed later in this chapter.

In Oakland, and in most UBC jurisdictions, **single-family dwellings are governed by the code in effect at the original date of construction,** or what is known as the "applicable code." This is extremely important when you REHAB RIGHT because you are permitted by law to rebuild parts of the house exactly as they were originally. With a few exceptions, the contemporary codes are not retroactive and you are not required to change any parts of the house to meet modern standards.

To find out what year your house was built, consult Chapter 2 for a general estimate. In Oakland, contact the Oakland Cultural Heritage Survey, (415) 273-3941. Their records go back to 1905.

Oakland adopted a building code as early as 1906, but it made no specific provisions for residential construction. Thus, the applicable code for single-family dwellings built before 1923 is determined by what was there originally, a handful of retroactive regulations in the 1923 State Housing Act, and the retroactive regulations in the 1981 Oakland Housing Code explained below. This is a real boon to those who want to REHAB RIGHT since the law, in essence, encourages you to respect the architectural character of the house. **Make sure that the building and housing inspectors see what was there before you rip it out and reconstruct.** Take photographs as evidence, in case problems arise later on.

In 1923, the State Housing Act established standards regulating light and ventilation, room size, ceiling height, exits and the like, for single-family dwellings. It also included retroactive regulations governing houses built prior to 1923, pertaining generally to sanitation, plumbing, gas vents, roofing and air space in sleeping rooms. The applicable code for all single-family dwellings built between 1923 and 1948 is the 1923 State Housing Act plus the retro-active portions of the Oakland Housing Code explained below.

In 1948, the City of Oakland first adopted the Uniform Building Code. The applicable codes for dwellings built since 1948 would be the version of the building, electric, plumbing, mechanical and housing codes in effect at the date of construction.

For old houses, present day codes apply to new additions and to buildings which have changed occupancy. Incorporating one additional unit within a single-family house is not considered a change in occupancy for building code purposes, but changing a single-family residential use to three or more units, or to office or commerical use, does invoke the present day code.

The most noteworthy **revision in the 1982 UBC is the limitation on the space between members of a guard rail.** The maximum space allowed had been nine inches; it is now six inches.

The Oakland Housing Code includes several retroactive regulations for single-family houses, regardless of applicable code. It requires:

- fire resistive walls between an attached garage and the dwelling
- a handrail 30"–34" above the nosing on any stairs with four or more risers
- two handrails, as described above, on any stairs that are more than 44" wide
- a smoke detection system, to be installed in conjunction with any rehab work worth $1000 or more, or when the building is sold
- two means of egress (either a stairway or fire escape) from the topmost story to the second story of houses with three or more stories.

Also retroactive is an interpretation by the Housing Conservation Department of Title 25 of the California Adminstrative Code by which **the City may require improvements to electrical and plumbing systems,** even if they do meet the code in force at the time they were installed.

In addition, it is the policy of the Building Department to encourage that **rebuilt stairs conform to modern code.** In some cases this is detrimental to the architectural style, and is worth a firm stand on your part to reproduce the original design. Ital-ianate houses, for example, typically had risers higher than modern code permits, but in perfect proportion to the rest of the building. A precise reproduction of the original is permitted by law. (See Chapter 5, "Staircase.")

Good news for the few people who will be moving a house and continuing its residential use is that thanks to state legislation, relocated houses are now judged primarily by applicable code rather than by modern code, as was the case prior to 1978. Modern standards will only apply to the foundation and the utility systems of relocated structures.

Copies of current codes are available at the Science and Sociology desk of the Oakland Public Library, 14th and Oak Streets. The Oakland Building Code can be purchased at the Permit Counter on the second floor of City Hall.

Compliance Letter

Building codes are used to evaluate older buildings by the Housing Conservation department. **A Housing Representative will prepare a Compliance Letter which enumerates all violations of the applicable code for a fee of $110 per unit.** A Compliance Letter may be initiated:

- by the City for vacant and unsecured buildings
- by the City for all buildings in a project area (like Clinton Park in 1962)
- by the loan applicant in conjunction with an HMIP loan (fee waived)
- by the lender or guarantor, with the seller's approval, as a prerequisite to the Certificate of Occupancy (MGIC, FHA, and VA loans usually require this)
- by tenants or neighbors who suspect code violations
- by the owner him or herself to help direct home improvement.

The law requires that all infractions cited be corrected, but there is no time frame established. The City requires correction of safety hazards first. If a structure has been declared "substandard" by the Housing Official, then either the infractions must be corrected or variances must be granted by the Housing Advisory and Appeals Board before the Certificate of Occupancy is issued.

Permit Fees
For Activities Typically Associated With Residential Rehabilitation
Excerpts from the *City of Oakland Master Fee Schedule*, July 1, 1986

Permit	Permit Fee	Checking Fee (65% of permit fee)
Building Permit		
Application Fee	$25.00	
$1 to $1,000 Construction Value	$20.00	$29.00
$1,001 to $2,000 Construction Value	$27.50–$35.00	$34.00–$39.00
$2,001 to $25,000 Construction Value	$35.00 first $2,000	$41.00–$144.00
	$ 3.50 each additional $500	
Demolition Permit	$150.00 first story	
	$ 10.00 each additional story	
Reroofing Permit	$10.00	
Building Moving Permit	$350.00	
Electrical Permit		
Minimum Basic Fee	$35.00	
Inspection of residential appliances, light fixtures, circuits and outlets	$ .25 to $4.00 each	
Inspection of electrical service	$10.00 (100 amp capacity)	
Plumbing Permit		
Minimum Basic Fee	$35.00	
Inspection of specific fixtures, devices, pipes, service, etc.	$ 5.00 to $10.00 each	
Mechanical Permit		
Minimum Basic Fee	$35.00	
Inspection of specific heating equipment, furnace, range, etc.	$ 5.00 to $15.00 each	
Microfilm Surcharge	2% of building permit fee	
Enforcement Surcharge	15% of building permit fee	

After the Compliance Letter is issued, the owner attends to the repairs through the permit process described below. Following the final permit inspection, a Housing Representative visits the property to make sure that the violations cited in the Compliance Letter have been corrected. If so, a **Certificate of Occupancy** is authorized and issued by the Building Official. The "C.O.," as it is called, is **a statement by the City of Oakland that the building meets all applicable codes.** The fee for the Compliance Letter includes the C.O. as long as the work is completed, or substantial progress is made, within six months.

Building Permits

Before any building project gets underway, the property owner or licensed contractor must secure one or more permits required by City law. The permit process guarantees that work will be done in accordance with code while providing the applicant with a plan check and work inspections by City personnel competent in their assigned fields.

A **building permit** is required for all new construction: for additions, alterations and repairs; for demolition; for swimming pools; for fences over 6' high; for awnings, re-roofing and signs. The permit fee is graduated as the value of construction increases. In addition, there is a 15% surcharge for enforcement of state energy and access regulations, and a fee for plan checking equal to 60% of the permit fee.

A **plumbing permit** or **mechanical permit** is required for all plumbing and mechanical work, except minor repairs.

An **electrical permit** is required for any electrical work other than minor repairs. Either the property owner or an eligible licensed contractor may apply.

If you have any question at all about whether a permit is required for any part of your rehab job, don't hesitate to telephone your presiding Building Department. In Oakland call the **Inspectional Services Department** at **(415) 273-3441** between 8:00 a.m. and 4:30 p.m. They are there to help you.

Permit applications for small jobs are processed at the counter while you wait. Many jobs, however, require a site visit, and even larger projects require that the plans be routed to several City departments for review. Although it may take anywhere from a half-hour to two weeks to issue a building permit, **it usually only takes one or two days to issue a permit for a typical rehab job.** The fee is paid at the time the permit is issued.

Once the permit is issued and work has begun, inspections are arranged to confirm that construction is proceeding according to plan. **Call in for an inspection before any construction is permanently concealed.** Studs, for example, should be inspected before wall covering is installed. A final inspection is required at the conclusion of the job.

There are professional inspectors for each type of permit, and each inspector handles a specific district in the City. When the inspector calls, remember that you will be seeing the same person again as the project progresses, so be as cooperative as you can.

If you have a serious disagreement with the inspector, your recourse is to call the supervisor. This may come up when you are trying to REHAB RIGHT because the inspector may not think that some architectural feature you are set on saving is up to code. The interpretation of the "applicable code" rule is often confusing when it comes to historic house parts. If the inspector wants you to modernize against your will, resort to the person with more authority, and explain the situation calmly. Do not hesitate to demand, in writing, an interpretation of the code in question.

If all else fails, you can bring your issue before the appropriate review board. In Oakland, the Board of Examiners and Appeals hears cases pertinent to the Building Code, and resolves questions regarding construction methods and materials. Contact them through the Inspectional Services Department. The Housing Advisory and Appeals Board hears cases pertinent to the Housing Code, and resolves questions regarding building configuration. Contact them through the Housing Conservation Department. On both boards, the fire marshall sits *ex-officio*, and whichever side of the case the fire marshall and city staff are on, is the side that's likely to win.

MATTERS OF HISTORY

Federal Preservation Tax Incentives

Most old houses are not eligible for the federal tax incentives which are granted to encourage rehabilitation of income-producing historic buildings. Investment tax credits (ITCs) are reserved for industrial, commercial or residential rental properties, so the owner-occupied, single-family house is automatically disqualified. However, **if the old house is used for trade or business, or rented for housing**—and many are, then **it may earn federal tax advantages** if it meets certain additional requirements.

First, the building must be a certified historic structure, that is, it must be:

• listed individually on the National Register of Historic Places, or

• located in a registered historic district and certified by the Secretary of the Interior as being significant to to the district.

Second, the proposed work on the certified building must be a certified rehabilitation project. To be certified, character-defining elements must be preserved. The basis for making this determination is the document entitled "The Secretary of the Interior's Standards for Rehabilitation and Guidelines for Rehabilitating Historic Buildings."

To pursue tax incentives, the owner of a historic property must submit a two-part application to the State Historic Perservation Officer (SHPO). If only part of the building is used for business or rental—a bona fide home office, or an apartment, for example —then the rehab expense devoted to that portion of the building is the basis for determining the amount of the tax credit.

A separate and lower tax credit is available for non-historic buildings over a certain age. However, it is limited to structures rehabbed for commercial or industrial purposes, and residential rental is excluded.

With the revamping of the federal tax system, modifications are expected to the Economic Recovery Act of 1981, which first set forth the ITC provisions. It is likely that under the Tax Reform Act of 1986 the ITC for certified rehab will be 20% and for non-certified buildings constructed before 1936, 10%. For a current description of the tax incentives for rehabilitation, an application for certification and a copy of the Secretary of the Interior's Standards, contact your SHPO or National Park Service (NPS) regional office. Addresses are listed in Chapter 7. The documents are free.

If you proceed, here are **some suggestions from the NPS Western Regional Office regarding certification of the rehab work.**

• Be certain to prepare photodocumentation, exterior and interior, prior to commencing any work. Certification has been denied for lack of adequate "before" photographs. Verbal descriptions do not suffice.

• Contact the SHPO and NPS regional offices at the outset, then keep in touch. They are well-informed and willing to help you to achieve certification. By communicating, you will jointly anticipate pitfalls.

• Ask first. If in doubt, call before pursuing any construction method which may prove detrimental to the historic character. NPS regional staff is always available for advice and clarification. Certification has been denied because well-intentioned owners did not adequately supervise contractors who mistakenly removed entire Victorian porches, sandblasted brick walls, etc. NPS also offers technical bulletins on approved construction methods. (See Chapter 7.)

• The completed project must meet *all ten* of the Secretary's Standards. Nine is not enough. Compliance with the Standards takes precedence over everything, even, believe it or not, building codes. Certification has been denied in cases where measures taken to "meet code" denigrated the historic fabric. (Railings are a common example.) Similarly, steps for energy efficiency may contradict historicity. For the purposes of tax certification, the latter prevails.

• Understand the products and materials brought on the job. Question the supplier about composition and side effects. Harsh cleansers and paint strippers, for example, can damage historic components, pitting wood beyond repair. Be certain that replacement parts which are meant to be visually identical to the originals are correct in all detail. Manufacturer's assurances, especially about prefabricated products, may prove insufficient in the Secretary's eyes.

• Finally, expect fairness but do not expect leniency. NPS must verify compliance with standards and guidelines which themselves have received extensive testing over the years.

Another type of federal tax incentive under present law is the donation of a façade easement to a charitable organization. Owner-occupied, single-family houses are eligible for this provision if they are listed on the National Register, either individually or as significant to a district. The organization which accepts the easement controls in perpetuity all alterations to the façade of the house.

The difference between the value of the house in its entirety, and its value with the façade easement imposed, constitutes the amount of "charitable donation" which can be deducted on the tax return. To pursue this, contact the NPS Regional Office and consult an appraiser, an accountant and a lawyer who have experience with façade donations, as there are many fine points.

State Historical Building Code

The California State Historical Building Code (SHBC) is a great boon to qualified historic buildings. It provides **a comprehensive set of regulations which measure the safety of historic structures in their own terms.**

Previously, in most jurisdictions in our state, all buildings, historic and otherwise, were evaluated according to the prescriptive standards for new construction of the Uniform Building Code (UBC). While the UBC states that it encourages retention of architectural integrity for historic structures, it remains for the building official to determine whether or not the historic design achieves an adequate level of life safety in UBC terms. This can be a very difficult call.

The State Historical Building Code relieves the enforcement official of this burden of judgment by setting forth alternative approaches which can be applied to historic buildings. Topics in this performance code include space and occupancy, structural, plumbing, mechanical and electrical systems, fire protection, handicapped access, historic site considerations and many other sub-topics.

Application of the SHBC was optional when first adopted in 1979, but on July 1, 1985, all California cities and counties were mandated to utilize the SHBC when evaluating "qualified" historic buildings

As for your ordinary old house, it is probably not a historic building as defined by the

SHBC. To qualify, a building must be deemed important to the history, architecture or culture of an area, and so designated by a federal, state, or local authority. Examples include buildings which appear on the National Register of Historic Places, the list of State Historic Landmarks or Points of Historical Interest, or on an adopted city or county inventory of significant sites, landmarks or districts.

In Oakland, and in many other jurisdictions, the absence of historic building designation is usually not problematic for single-family homes because the provisions of the applicable code prevail. The applicable code allows the retention of architectural features as long as they are in compliance with the code in effect at the time of construction. It is usually as good as SHBC. For exceptions, see the above section on codes.

In certain other California locales, however, the rehabilitation of older single-family houses calls into play a system of valuation which mandates present day code for improvements and, in some situations, for the entire building. This can be disastrous for efforts to REHAB RIGHT. For example, in some places, if the value of the rehab work is equal to or greater than 25% of the value of the building, then all the rehab work must be done to meet today's code, even if much of it was meant to be restoration. If the rehab work is equal to or greater than 50% of the value of the building, then the entire building must be brought up to modern code. While this type of language no longer appears in the UBC, it persists in some local regulations.

The owner of an older single-family house may need to call up the SHBC when the Building Official requires compliance with present day code because of valuation, change in occupancy, house relocation, or retroactive life safety provisions of applicable code, and the present day code conflicts with preservation goals specific to that house. How, then, could the house be dubbed "historic" in order to qualify for the SHBC?

Obviously, an outstanding house can earn a place on a sanctioned list. But what about those less exceptional?

One strategy would be to have the local jurisdiction, on the urging of local preservation and political

groups, designate every building beyond a certain age as historic. In cities or counties which have an architectural or cultural survey underway, another method would be to have every building of a certain survey rating be designated as historic for purposes of SHBC qualification or, if the city or county has a study list for buildings awaiting consideration as official landmarks or the like, the governing body could determine that for purposes of SHBC, buildings on said study list qualify as historic. Obviously, it would be better **to pursue this type of comprehensive approach before conflict arises on an individual building.**

While the act of listing is the responsibility of the local jurisdiction, local historians and area architects, the SHBC Board and State Office of Historic Preservation will sometimes assist in indicating if a building appears to qualify for a list. The Board staff may also prepare, for a fee, a letter giving its opinion based on submitted information on how the SHBC should be applied in a given instance. This often satisfies a local building official desirous of technical support in the decision-making process.

Other states do have historic building codes, many of them modeled on California's. Some make the distinction, essential to the typical rehabber, between "old" and "historic." Call your SHPO (see Chapter 7) to determine if your state has a historic building code, and how to apply it when rehabilitating your old house.

Copies of the California SHBC may be obtained from: The State Historical Building Code Board, c/o Office of the State Architect, 1500–5th Street, Sacramento, CA 95814. Enclose a check for $4 payable to the State Historical Building Code Board. For more information, contact C. Cullimore, Executive Director, (916) 445-7627.

The National Register of Historic Places

A listing on the National Register of Historic Places is an honor in its own right as well as the basis for certain privileges. Under the present tax law, it entitles certain buildings to federal tax incentives, as described above. In those states with a historic building code, National Register status is one way to gain access to the provisions of the alternative code, also described above. A listing on the National Register is the criteria for certain preservation grants when funding is available, and a measure of significance in certain planning endeavors. A building can be listed individually on the National Register, or as a contributing member of a historic district.

To find out whether your house might be eligible for the National Register and how to apply, contact the State Historic Preservation Office, or the regional office of the National Park Service, as listed in Chapter 7. Also inquire about the names of consultants who specialize in the preparation of National Register nomination forms.

In Oakland, the Oakland Cultural Heritage Survey can give you a preliminary determination of a building's suitability for Register status. Call (415) 273-3941.

To find out more about the history of your house, for the National Register or otherwise, see the heading "House History" in Chapter 6.

Chapter 4
EXTERIORS

FOUNDATION

A sound foundation is the basis for all rehabilitation work because a weakened foundation threatens the very structure of the house and all of its valuable architectural features. The foundation accepts the weight of the structure and distributes it evenly to the surrounding soil. In Oakland it is typically made up of the masonry perimeter wall which bears most of the load; the interior piers and posts for supplementary support; the sill plate which connects the masonry of the foundation with the wood frame of the house; and in some cases, anchor bolts to secure this connection.

Settlement is the major threat to the foundation. When the ground beneath the building moves, the foundation responds to the movement and adjusts to the new lay of the land. Since solid masonry is not flexible, the change in position causes cracks in the foundation walls. As these imperfections become larger due to more movement or the erosive forces of weather, the foundation loses the strength it needs to support the rest of the house.

Settlement is an anticipated one-time occurrence in new houses. In older buildings, it may be caused by:

● inadequately compacted fill
● landslide, slough or slippage
● flooding
● a clay subsoil which has dried out and shrunk
● deficient drainage or waterproofing
● rotting or drying timbers
● roots of large trees

Running cracks on the foundation, around door tops, sills and window frames are an indication of settlement trouble. To determine whether the movement has stopped, glue a strip of paper across the crack using a contact adhesive. Or, use plaster of paris or two pen marks instead of the paper strip. If the paper tears within two to four weeks, consult an engineer or contractor. Remember that an engineer sells only advice, while a contractor sells both advice and construction services, so the price paid for the engineer's fee is your guarantee of an objective evaluation.

Oakland's earliest homes, built between 1840 and 1870, were constructed with no masonry foundation at all. Instead, a wood "mudsill" was placed directly on a patch of leveled earth, and the frame walls attached directly to it. Sometimes flat stones, without mortar, were used as a footing to raise the wood sill slightly above the ground. If either situation persists, the foundation should be replaced with concrete.

The two common types of masonry foundation in Oakland are brick and concrete. The use of brick began in the 1860s, and its popularity continued through the 1920s. Concrete foundations were introduced about 1906, and their use in various forms continues today.

Brick Foundation

Brick foundations are often cited by termite inspectors or bank appraisers as inadequate, no matter what the condition of the brick and mortar, and irrespective of the foundation's structural soundness. As a result, banks often require the replacement or capping of the brick foundation as a condition of the loan. This is very expensive—approximately $40–$60 per linear foot to cap, approximately $60 per foot to replace—and the loan applicant is understandably disheartened.

Opting for a sound foundation is always a good decision, but with brick it is difficult to know whether the foundation might be adequate as is. The Uniform Building Code (UBC) does not address the question directly; it does not call for the replacement of brick foundations with reinforced concrete. It does require, however, that a structure provide basic life safety, and that structural failure be prevented.

There are two ways that a brick foundation can lead to structural failure. The first is the transmittal of moisture from the ground to the sill plate by way of the mortar. Once dry rot starts in the sill plate, it can travel on up into the cripple wall and from there to the wood frame superstructure. This is most likely to occur where there are only a few courses of brick separating the wood sill from the ground level. Remember, the ground on the outside of the house may have built up considerably over the years. It is the likelihood of dry rot that has made brick foundations a culprit in termite reports. (Detection of dry rot is described later in Chapter 4 under "Porches.")

Failure of the masonry itself is the second way a brick foundation poses a structural hazard. Look for these trouble signs:

● cracks between the bricks, especially cracks running diagonally across the wall
● loose and powdery mortar (scrape the mortar with a screwdriver—it should be firm and solid)
● crumbling bricks
● uneven settlement of the foundation wall (the bricks should be level from one corner to the next).

HOW TO REPOINT

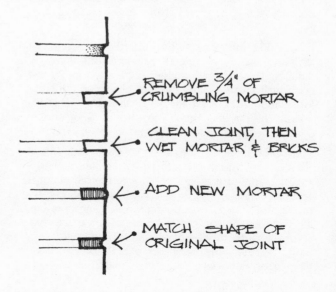

REMOVE 3/4" OF CRUMBLING MORTAR

CLEAN JOINT, THEN WET MORTAR & BRICKS

ADD NEW MORTAR

MATCH SHAPE OF ORIGINAL JOINT

If you find very large cracks or evidence of severe settlement, have a civil engineer, restoration architect or contractor look at the foundation.

Your brick foundation is a candidate for retention if *all* of the following apply:

- It has remained reasonably square and level over the years. Use a transit, or plumb bob and carpenter's level, to describe the foundation line.
- There are three or more brick courses between dirt and wood.
- There are no signs of moisture or deterioration of the sill plate.
- There is good landscape and subsurface drainage away from the foundation.
- The structural integrity of the masonry can be confirmed.

Limited damage to an otherwise sound brick wall can be remedied by repointing mortar and replacing crumbling bricks. On Brown Shingle houses, where a clinker brick foundation is an architectural feature, try to retain the brick and, where needed, replace clinker bricks in kind. Track down the real thing through demolition companies.

Before making a final decision about whether to replace a brick foundation, note that in susceptible soils, brick foundations suffer the greatest damage during earthquakes, and they do not accept anchor bolts to secure the wood frame during seismic shaking. (See "Seismic Retrofit" below.)

If retaining the brick is imprudent for reasons of structural safety or the overall investment in the building, there are two options. One is to remove the brick wall and replace it with a reinforced concrete foundation according to UBC standards. This involves raising the house, so choose a reputable contractor experienced in this particular operation.

The second option is to cap the brick wall with a shell of concrete, a procedure not unlike capping a tooth. Capping requires practically the same steps and amount of precision as complete replacement—raising the house, constructing forms, tying-in re-bar, etc.—and may turn out to be almost as expensive. "Not all foundations are good candidates for capping," warns Jane Spangler, ASHI, of Ask Jane Consulting Services in Oakland. In addition to being

TYPICAL MORTAR JOINTS

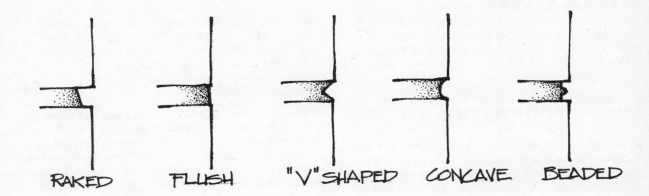

RAKED   FLUSH   "V" SHAPED   CONCAVE   BEADED

fairly square and level, the masonry itself must be in very good condition, with no signs of spalling, or yellow brown fungus in the mortar, as these can be transmitted to the new concrete. There should be a pre-existing subsurface footing and a minimum of one bond course (a course of "headers" or bricks turned perpendicular to the direction of the wall which bond together the two adjacent "wythes" or stacks of brick that make up the wall).

Capping is often pursued in the heat of house buying in order to comply with the bank's demands. "Unfortunately," observes Jim Wilson, City of Alameda housing rehab specialist, "it is not the best long-

BRICK PATTERNS

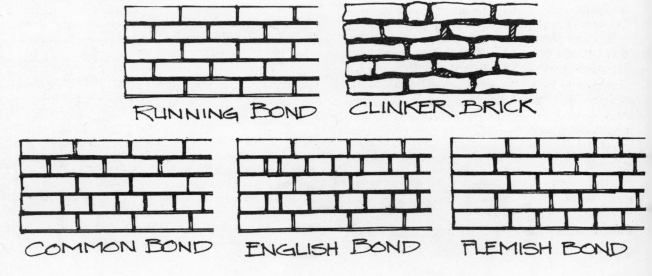

RUNNING BOND   CLINKER BRICK

COMMON BOND   ENGLISH BOND   FLEMISH BOND

term solution." Capping does not provide adequate seismic anchoring, and it can result in a lip which is problematic if there is living space adjoining the foundation, such as a ground-level unit. Also, unless the top of the concrete is tooled to slope away from the sill, water can still accumulate there and do damage. Wilson also points out that raising a house, if smoothly done, is less threatening to the wood frame structure and the plaster walls than a sequential perimeter jacking.

If only a portion of the brick foundation shows failure, then replacement or capping can be confined to that area, but old and new segments must be tied together structurally.

What to do with the salvaged bricks? Save them and lay them on a sand bed to make garden paths. Somewhat soft, irregular and muted, they are far more attractive in the landscape than new brick or so-called "used" bricks. Keep them with the house from which they came.

Concrete Foundation

Look for cracks in a concrete foundation as evidence of uneven settlement. Differentiate between simple cracks and major cracks which are the result of movement in the masonry. Repair minor cracks by scoring the concrete and filling it with concrete patch cement.

If a new concrete foundation is required due to uneven settlement, wood resting directly on the ground, or a thoroughly deteriorated brick foundation, turn the project over to a professional contractor. A new concrete foundation costs $60 per linear foot, and includes raising the house, building forms, excavating and the pour.

Another problem encountered in concrete foundations is **chipped corners.** This is a basic repair which the homeowner can handle, quickly improving the appearance of the house by eliminating a shabby feature.

Posts and Piers

Most Oakland house styles which pre-date World War II have one or more rows of wood posts on

CONCRETE CORNER REPAIR

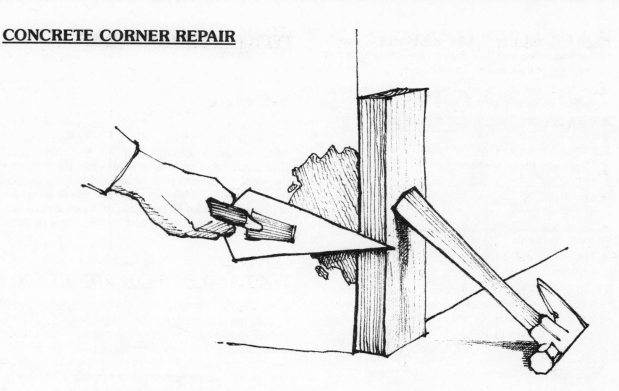

A. REMOVE LOOSE PARTICLES WITH A STIFF WIRE BRUSH.

B. WET CHIPPED AREA THOROUGHLY.

C. PROP A 2×4 AGAINST ONE SIDE OF THE CORNER. FILL CRACK WITH PATCHING CEMENT, THEN SMOOTH FLUSH WITH A TROWEL.

D. PROP THE 2×4 AGAINST THE OTHER SIDE OF THE CORNER. USING THE 2×4 AS A GUIDE, SLICE OFF EXCESS CEMENT THAT MAY STICK OUT BEYOND THE CORNER.

E. LEAVE 2×4 IN PLACE 4 HRS OR MORE.

POST AND PIER ELEVATION

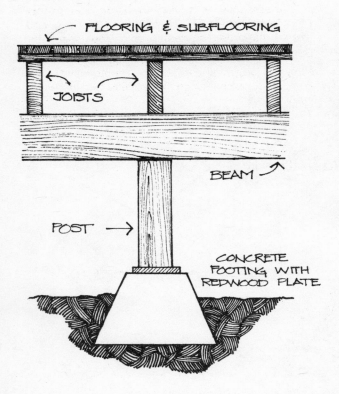

FLOORING & SUBFLOORING

JOISTS

BEAM

POST

CONCRETE FOOTING WITH REDWOOD PLATE

concrete piers for intermediate support underneath the building. **If any of the posts show signs of decay, or if the wood is in direct contact with the ground, then new wood posts treated with a preservative should be installed on concrete piers.** The new posts should be the same size as the older ones.

Wood posts that are exposed to the weather, as on rear porches or front stairs, should be separated from the concrete footing by an air space. Otherwise, this is one of the most common places for dry rot to occur. Without the air space, water sits on the wood plate, working its way into the end grain of the post and rotting it. The construction detail for exterior wood posts and piers is more difficult and expensive to construct than its interior counterpart, but the extra durability makes it worth the trouble and expense.

Sill Plate

The sill plate is a horizontal wood member which acts as an intermediary between the house frame and the masonry foundation. It is the counterpart to the redwood plate which sits atop the concrete piers on interior posts, as illustrated in the previous section. In older buildings, **the sill plate must be replaced if it has been decayed by moisture accumulation or decimated by termites or rats.**

POST AND PIER CONSTRUCTION

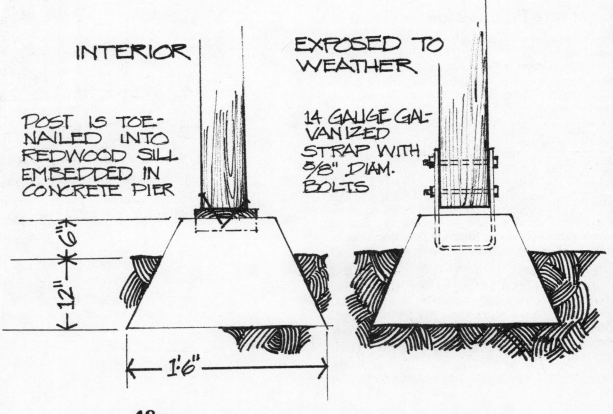

INTERIOR

POST IS TOE-NAILED INTO REDWOOD SILL EMBEDDED IN CONCRETE PIER

6"

12"

1'6"

EXPOSED TO WEATHER

14 GAUGE GALVANIZED STRAP WITH 5/8" DIAM. BOLTS

Seismic Retrofit

The structure of the house must be securely attached to the foundation or the woodframe might "hop off" during the severe shaking of an earthquake. For a newly poured foundation, threaded j-bolts are embedded in the concrete, then connected to steel brackets which are fastened to the studs.

To tie an old house to an existing foundation, expansion bolts are inserted into holes pre-drilled through a sound sill plate into sound concrete. The expansion bolts are installed every four to six feet, and within one foot of corners or the end of a piece of sill. Two bolts are minimum for each piece of mudsill.

ANCHOR BOLT FOR EXISTING FOUNDATION

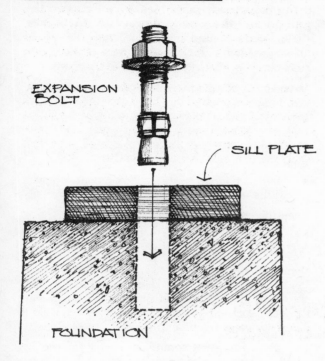

EXPANSION BOLT

SILL PLATE

FOUNDATION

2½″ on center around the perimeter of the sheet, and 4″ on center into all other wood framing members behind the plywood. Drill 1½″ ventilation holes to ventilate each newly enclosed stud cavity. If the plywood obstructs a crawl space vent, relocate the vent to maintain adequate air circulation. (See "Vents" below.)

The installation of anchor bolts requires the manipulation of a rotary hammer and other power equip-

ment in dark and extremely cramped quarters. It has been likened more to coal mining than carpentry. Also, mistakes can diminish the engineering strength of the assembly. It is wise, therefore, to consider hiring a contractor who specializes in this work and has the expertise, equipment and crawl space endurance to guarantee the job.

Plywood shear walls, depending on the crawl space conditions, can be within the scope of the household carpenter.

SEISMIC ANCHOR FOR NEW FOUNDATION

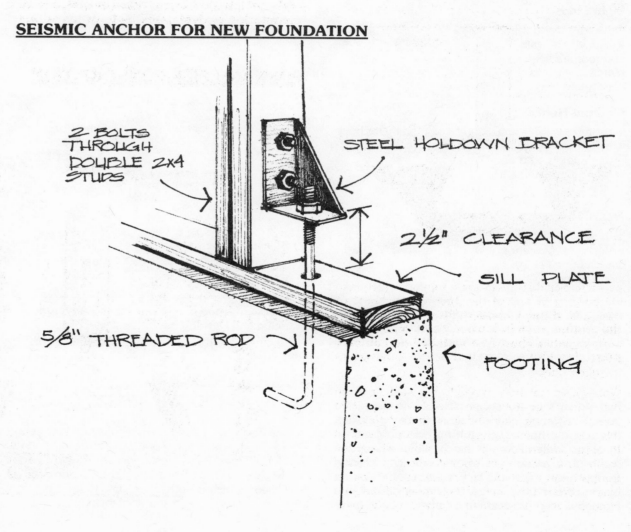

2 BOLTS THROUGH DOUBLE 2x4 STUDS

STEEL HOLDOWN BRACKET

2½″ CLEARANCE

SILL PLATE

5/8″ THREADED ROD

FOOTING

All construction involves some diagonal bracing for rigidity, but there is increased need for shear wall strength in earthquake country to resist heaving and prolonged shaking from the seismic force. Inadequate bracing of the cripple wall—the short stud wall between the foundation and the first floor—is the most common bracing deficiency in older wood frame houses. (Lath and plaster are said to contribute more seismic bracing to the upper floors than sheetrock.)

To provide bracing in the cripple wall, plywood sheets at least twice as long as they are high are nailed to the corners in the basement or crawl space. For best resistance to racking, the plywood must connect the mudsill, the cripple studs and the plates (the horizontal members on top of the cripple studs). This may involve furring out the studs or plates.

The shear wall nailing schedule requires 8d nails at

GENERAL GUIDELINES FOR SEISMIC RETROFIT

In flatland locations, excluding special soils, with sound mudsill and sound concrete foundation

	Size and Placement of Expansion Bolts (Bolts 7"–10" long, depending on foundation. Place bolts within 12" of all corners and ends of sill pieces, plus:)	Minimum Length of Plywood at Corners (5/16" CDX or thicker)	Length of Bracing Relative to Length of Cripplewall (Extend length of plywood at corners to achieve this proportion.)
Light House One-story wood frame, except where walls *and* roof are heavy materials such as stucco, plaster and tile.	½" diameter bolts placed 6' apart	3 linear feet	One-Story: 25%
Medium House Two-story wood frame with lightweight wall and roof materials, and one-story homes with heavy materials.	¾" diameter bolts placed 6' apart	4 linear feet	One-Story: 25% Two Story: 50%
Heavy House Two-story wood frame with stucco, plaster or tile, and three-story wood frame.	¾" diameter bolts placed 4' apart	6 linear feet	Two-Story: 50% Three Story: 80%

This chart was adapted with permission from *Earthquake Hazard and Wood Frame Houses* and *An Earthquake Advisor's Handbook*, published by the Center for Planning and Development Research, College of Environmental Design, University of California, Berkeley, 1982: Mary Comerio, Principal Investigator. See these books for treatment of less typical foundation configurations.

For further information, particularly regarding the great assortment of foundation conditions which occur in old houses, consult the two publications by Mary Comerio cited in the chart. For a Bay Area contractor's account of seismic retrofit, including recommended tools and techniques, read the article by David Benaroya Helfant in the magazine *Fine Homebuilding,* October/November 1985.

CRAWL SPACE

Crawl space is found in buildings without an excavated basement. It is the space between the ground and the bottom of the first floor. **The crawl space is highly susceptible to moisture retention,** a condition which is both destructive to the structure and uncomfortable for the residents.

Clearance

The Uniform Building Code requires that the foundation provide **adequate clearance between the ground and the wood members of the house** so that termites and beetles will not make your home their home. Make sure there is at least:

- 6" of clearance between the ground and any wood sill or siding which rests on the masonry foundation
- 18" of clearance between the earth in the crawl space and the bottom of the floor joists
- 12" of clearance beneath any beam supporting floor joists
- 6" between wood posts resting on concrete piers and the earth.

Keep the crawl space cleared of debris.

Vents

Vents in a crawl space provide **air circulation** which inhibits moisture build up. There should be one vent for every 150 square feet of ground area, placed opposite each other to maximize cross-ventilation. Keep the vents open year round.

For greater moisture control, a layer of roll roofing (15 lb. felt underlayment, at $11.95 per 300 square foot roll) or polyethylene sheeting (6 mils thick at $7.95 per 10' × 25' roll) can be spread across the ground in the crawl space. If so, the number of vents can be reduced to one per 1500 square feet. However, two vents placed opposite each other are the absolute minimum for adequate air flow.

Different vent designs are associated with specific architectural styles and **the original vent should be retained** whenever possible. Victorian homes have ornamental cast-iron vents. Their floral or geometric patterns allow the air to enter the crawl space and at the same time they decorate the building. The vent **design** is often masked by layers of paint and grime which can be stripped fairly easily.

1. Place the grate on a piece of aluminum foil with the sides rolled up. Brush on a paint remover, like Jasco, and let it sit for several hours. The foil does not absorb the paint remover the way other protective surfaces, like newspaper, would.

2. When the Jasco has had a chance to do its job, hold the vent by tongs or with rubber gloves—always protect your skin from paint remover—and hose or scrape off the gummy surface.
3. If paint still adheres, repeat the process.
4. Use steel wool to rub off the final specks.

Now that the crispness of detail has been restored, the vent is ready for a protective primer and a fresh coat of paint.

VENT STYLES

VICTORIAN - CAST IRON

REDWOOD LATHE

METAL SCREENED

CRAWL SPACE CLEARANCE

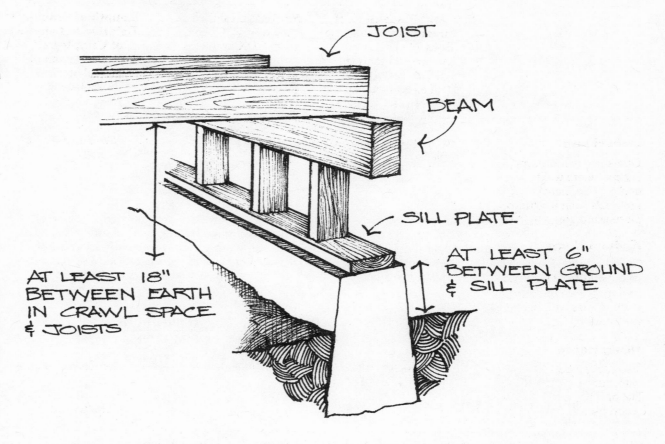

JOIST

BEAM

SILL PLATE

AT LEAST 18" BETWEEN EARTH IN CRAWL SPACE & JOISTS

AT LEAST 6" BETWEEN GROUND & SILL PLATE

Brown Shingle houses and Craftsman Bungalows have vents made of criss-crossed redwood lath. Unfortunately, this design is susceptible to rot and may allow entry to rodents and other pests. Houses with wood siding at ground level have holes drilled through the siding in lieu of a more conventional vent. Air flow there may be insufficient. Wartime Tract houses, and many buildings from the 1920s have galvanized metal mesh vents, and these may rust after several years and require replacement.

Vent openings should be no larger than ¼" square to successfully exclude rodents. To save an interesting vent which exceeds this standard, attach a screen to the inside of the vent. If the vent is neither operable nor noteworthy, use a screen vent alone.

Insulation

The solution of one problem is sometimes the cause of another. **When the crawl space has adequate ventilation, the floor above it may get chilly.** The solution is standard insulation held in place by "lightning rods" underneath. The silvery sheet on one side of the insulation is called the "vapor barrier" and it faces up. Fiberglass batting, 3½" thick, costs about 20¢ per square foot.

CRAWL SPACE INSULATION

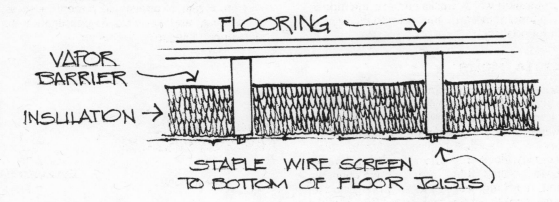

FLOORING

VAPOR BARRIER

INSULATION →

STAPLE WIRE SCREEN TO BOTTOM OF FLOOR JOISTS

Consult the sequel to this book, *Retrofit Right: How To Make Your Old House Energy Efficient,* for more information. Crawl space insulation should be installed as part of a total strategy for weatherization, and may not be the most cost-effective first step.

STAIRS

Outside entry stairs receive constant use and abuse from both pedestrians and the weather. Although more durable materials like concrete and flagstone hold up the best, they are often inappropriate to the architectural style. When repairing steps, don't forget the code requirements.

Wood Stairs

Deteriorated wood stairs are an extremely common problem in Victorian and Colonial Revival houses in Oakland, **yet it is imperative** for the building's architectural integrity **to continue the use of wood** and not give in to the temptation of concrete. After all, the wood steps on many a Victorian have lasted 90 years, so even if new wood steps last "only" another 90 years, they will be perfectly adequate for your needs.

The source of wood step problems is **poor drainage.** Even the smallest accumulation of rain can begin the rotting process. This may result from one or a combination of factors: solid boards installed perfectly flat; worn treads with a depression in the middle; lack of paint and caulk to provide a protective seal; or, adjacent features which pond water on the steps. Look for the symptoms of rot, as described in the section on wood porches.

When repairing wood steps:

- Consider turning worn treads over. A shallow depression switched to the reverse side will have no deterimental effect, and flipping the board will save money and time.

- Install new or recycled boards at a slight angle from front to back, say 1/8″ per tread, as illustrated.

- Design the railing so that the balusters are attached to a handrail on top and a free-standing shoerail on the bottom. This allows a space for the water to run off the edge after a severe storm. Refer also to the handrail illustration.

- Coat the treads with a wood sealer, like Olympic or Rez, prior to installation.

- Make sure the tread nosing projects 3/4″–1¼″ over the riser, to keep the joint water-free, and to afford a shadow that is a definite design asset.

- Do not direct drainage water onto the sill plate underneath the steps.

Brick Stairs

Brick was introduced to Oakland as a stair material in the early stages of the First Bay Tradition and is typically found on Brown Shingle houses and Craftsman Bungalows. **Brick stairs do not belong**

STAIR DIMENSIONS FOR BRAND NEW CONSTRUCTION REQUIRED BY MODERN CODE

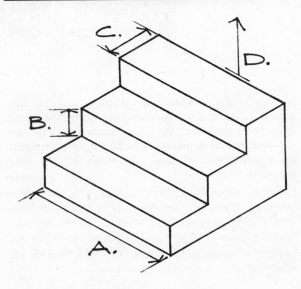

A. WIDTH: AT LEAST 30″ BUT PREFERABLY 36″ OR MORE

B. RISER HEIGHT: 7½″ OR LESS

C. TREAD WIDTH: 10″, MINIMUM

D. HEADROOM CLEARANCE: 7′ MINIMUM

IMPROVING DRAINAGE ON WOOD STEPS

TO FACILITATE DRAINAGE, DRAW STANDARD STRINGER PATTERN ON BOARD, THEN RE-DRAW TREAD LINE SO INSIDE EDGE IS ⅛" HIGHER THAN OUTSIDE EDGE

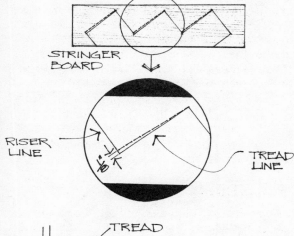

STRINGER BOARD

RISER LINE

TREAD LINE

TREAD

CUT RISER ¼" SHORT OF TREAD, THEN PUTTY THE RESULTANT GAP.

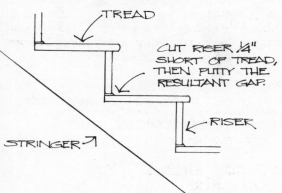

RISER

STRINGER

on a Victorian house; they are as anachronistic as concrete.

One problem encountered with brick stairs is settlement due to shifting soil support. To correct this, concrete must be injected beneath the existing structure, and additional bracing may be required. This is a difficult operation that should be executed by a qualified contractor.

Brick stairs are subject to cracked mortar joints. These require immediate attention in order to prevent water penetration which cracks and rots the mortar further. To repoint mortar joints, refer to the section on brick foundations.

Concrete Stairs

Long concrete stairs are commonly found on Prairie School houses and California Bungalows. Shorter ones, often only a step or two, are typical to the Period Revival style and Wartime Tract. Occasionally, concrete steps are embellished with redwood strips, mosaics or tiles. Mediterranean and Provincial houses are known for their shiny, red, painted concrete steps and matching walks. Green and grey are popular paint colors for bungalow steps. It's valuable to **stick with popular colors** because repetition lends visual unity to the neighborhood.

STEEL NOSING ON CONCRETE STEPS

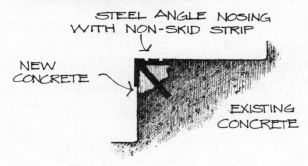

STEEL ANGLE NOSING WITH NON-SKID STRIP

NEW CONCRETE

EXISTING CONCRETE

Another design aspect of concrete steps is the grooves. They may be geometric or abstract patterns, or parallel lines for skid proof purposes. **The arrangement of grooves should be perpetuated** if the concrete is repaired, or reinstated if the stairs are replaced.

Concrete steps are subject to spalling, the chipping off of small pieces from the nose of the tread. This is repaired by using a high strength mortar to bond new concrete to the old. If the damage is severe, consider adding a steel angle plate with an anti-slip surface.

Small cracks in concrete steps are normal and can be repaired with concrete patching cement. Major cracks are a sign of uneven settlement or stress in the concrete, and should be investigated by a professional engineer or contractor.

STAIR RAILING RECONSTRUCTION

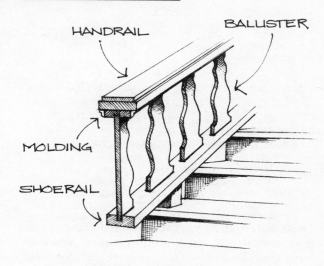

HANDRAIL

BALUSTER

MOLDING

SHOERAIL

RECONSTRUCTED STAIR RAILING HAS FREE-STANDING SHOERAIL (CONNECTED TO EVERY 3RD OR 4TH STEP) TO ALLOW WATER DRAINAGE. THE SCULPTED LOOK OF ORIGINAL TURNED BALUSTERS IS SUGGESTED BY CUTTING FLAT BOARDS INTO A SIMILAR SHAPE WITH A JIGSAW. A HANDRAIL BUILT-UP OF STOCK PIECES OF LUMBER & MOLDING IS CLOSE TO THE ORIGINAL HANDRAIL IN SIZE & APPEARANCE.

STAIR RAILING ALTERNATIVES FOR THE NEOCLASSIC ROWHOUSE

ORIGINAL DESIGN

VISUALLY & PHYSICALLY SOLID, USES CORRECT MATERIAL (WOOD), PROPORTIONS ECHO THOSE OF HOUSE.

ADDING HANDRAILS

WHEN REBUILDING STAIRS TO THE ORIGINAL DESIGN, CODE RE-QUIREMENTS MAY FORCE YOU TO ADD HIGHER HANDRAILS. ON SOME STYLES OF WOOD STAIRS (COLONIAL REVIVAL, CRAFTSMAN, OR WHEN THERE ARE BUILT-UP SIDES WITH OUT BALUSTERS OR HANDRAILS), YOU CAN USE INTERIOR HANDRAIL BRACKETS WITH CLOSET POLES OR 2 X 2 LUMBER FOR RAILS.

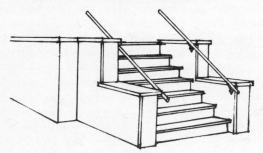

DESIGN INTEGRITY

THINK OF YOUR STAIRCASE AS AN EXTENSION OF THE HOUSE, UNIF-IED IN STYLE, RATHER THAN AS A SEPARATE, REPLACEABLE COM-PONENT. MAINTAIN OR RESTORE THE ORIGINAL DESIGN AND AVOID THE TEMPTATIONS OF READY-MADE WROUGHT IRON RAILINGS OR OVERSIMPLIFIED CONSTRUCTION TECHNIQUES.

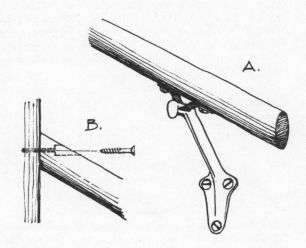

HANDRAIL DETAILS

A. BRACKET WITH CLOSET POLE RAIL. (IF A 2 X 2 IS USED FOR THE HANDRAIL, CHOOSE A SMOOTH-FINISHED BOARD WITH ROUNDED EDGES.)

B. ATTACH THE UPPER END OF RAILING TO WALL OR PORCH WITH A COUNTERSUNK WOOD-SCREW. DRILL PILOT HOLE FIRST.

C. EXTRA HEIGHT CAN BE GAINED, IF NEEDED FOR CODE COMPLIANCE, FROM 2 X 4 EXTENSIONS.

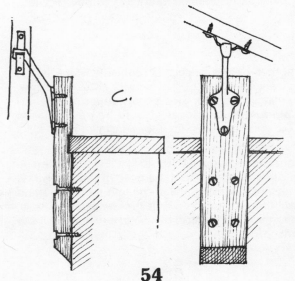

INAPPROPRIATE DESIGNS

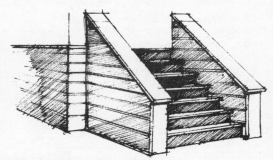

ANGLED SOLID RAILING

PROBLEMS: DOESN'T FIT SQUARE FEATURES OF STYLE, MAKES STAIRS SEEM NARROW & ENCLOSED.

RANCH STYLE RAILING

PROBLEMS: "BACK STAIRS" CHARACTER, INSUBSTANTIAL QUALITY, NO RELATION-SHIP TO HOUSE DESIGN.

WROUGHT IRON RAILING

PROBLEMS: FLIMSY APPEARANCE, WRONG MATERIAL, INCONGRUOUS CURVED "SPANISH" ORNAMENTS.

Handrails

For new front stairs, the Uniform Building Code requires handrails 30" to 34" above the nosing. (Refer to the discussion of applicable codes in Chapter 3 and to the section "Staircase" in Chapter 5.) For rebuilt original stairs with four or more risers, the City of Oakland requires the same. Even if there was no handrail before, **the handrail design should be sympathetic to the architectural style of the house, the material of the original steps and the design of the original porch railing.** For example, on a Victorian house the handrail should be wood with a sculptured feeling. Reconstruct the shapely silhouette by combining standard pieces of lumber and embellishing the composition with cove moldings. Do not use wrought iron. It looks totally out of place, like dime-store jewelry on a well-tailored dress.

The handrail on the Colonial Revival styles should be stepped, not diagonal. Although a stepped railing is more difficult to construct, its right angles and geometric proportions carry out the architectural theme. If you have a two-story Classic Box, use the bannister on the indoor staircase as a guide. It has two balusters per tread, a design feature which could be imitated for the outside railing. (Refer to the "Porch: Railings" section and to the illustration "Downspout Locations" for more examples of railing design.)

PORCH

Every older house style has a front porch. Whether spacious enough for an afternoon nap, or barely big enough to escape from the rain, the porch is the focal point of the façade and deserves the time and effort it takes to repair it properly. It is also a microcosm of the design problems found on the entire building, so **this section is a handy introduction to other repairs you may undertake.**

On any style porch, first **differentiate between ornament and structure.** Then, **determine the extent of damage to each. If damage is limited, repair** the porch; **if deterioration is severe, rebuild.** Consult Chapter 3, or your city's Inspectional Services Department, for the permit and code requirements.

With the structure and ornamentation both, try to **retain as many of the original pieces as possible.** This saves you the expense of purchasing new materials, spares the house the degradation of a porch which has an inappropriate architectural style and keeps valuable antiques from the garbage heap. When the original parts are beyond repair, select new materials that are sympathetic to the design of the house. If exact duplicates of the originals are available and affordable, use them. If not, select counterparts which are the same material as the original, and use a design which is in proportion to the entire building.

Wood Porch

Wood porches belong on houses of the Victorian, Colonial Revival and Craftsman styles. There are so few original wood porches remaining on Oakland's Victorian houses, that it is imperative to save and rehabilitate the survivors. They are an endangered species.

Wood Damage

Wood is very susceptible to decay from moisture. If the wood:
- looks charred, with splits along the grain, or dark veinlike strands
- feels spongy
- shows splits and flaking of the paint

then it has contracted **wet rot.** Wet rot is a fungus that attacks timbers subject to saturation, and it spreads quickly to other wet timbers nearby.

If the wood:
- shows thin white strands
- shows wool-like sheets with spreading tendrils
- feels spongy
- has a multitude of tiny open cells

then it has contracted **dry rot.** Dry rot is a microscopic fungus, transmitted by spores which are airborne or carried on shoes or clothing. Under suitable conditions of moisture and warmth, especially standing water, the fungi germinate rapidly on the timbers where they land. The fungi that cause decay are nature's way of breaking down dead wood and returning it to the earth. Unfortunately, the fungi may be trying to recycle the wood frame of your house.

The properties of strength which are reduced by rot are hardness and toughness. **To investigate the extent of the damage:**
- Prod the wood with a sharp tool, (preferably in an inconspicuous location) and observe resistance to marring. If the wood is sound, the prodding will loosen one or two relativley long slivers, and the breaks will be splintery.
- Pry out a sliver of wood with a screwdriver. If toughness has been greatly reduced by decay, the wood breaks squarely across the grain and lifts out easily. If it is still tough, then it splinters and resists removal.

On the porch, **look for symptoms of decay in these places:**
- on the step treads or deck surfaces, especially those that are checked or concavely worn so they trap water
- at joints in railings
- at the base of the posts, especially if the posts are not raised above the porch floor
- on the underside of the deck and framing.

To detect the presence in wood of harmful insects:
- Look at all areas close to the ground for earthen tubes built over the surface of the foundation as runways from soil to the wood above. Look for swarming of winged adults in the spring and fall, and galleries that follow the grain of the wood. These are all signs of **subterranean termites.** They must return to the ground for moisture, so chemical treatment of the soil is one line of attack.
- Look for sandlike pellets discarded outside the wood, swarming winged insects and tunnels cut freely across the grain of the wood. These are all signs of **nonsubterranean termites.** The Bay Area is the northernmost limit of their range, and they are rare in Oakland.
- Look near the ground for holes the size of pencil lead and borings the consistency of flour, as an indication of **powderpost beetles.**
- Look for piles of coarse sawdust as evidence of carpenter ants.

Refer to Chapter 3 for information on termite reports, structural pest control companies and the Bio-Integral Resource Center.

There are three steps to the repair process which will return the porch to a safe state and attractive appearance. These can be simple or quite time-consuming, depending on the design of the porch and the extent of the wood deterioration.

1. **Remove the ornamentation.** Refer to section entitled "Ornamentation."
2. **Repair or rebuild the porch structure.** The structure of a wood porch consists of the posts for support, the joists and decking for the floor, the railings for safety, the columns for support of the porch roof, and the porch roof itself for overhead protection. If signs of decay and infestation indicate that certain structural parts need improvement, refer to the appropriate sections below.
3. **Repair the ornamentation and install it.** Once the structure is repaired or rebuilt, the ornamentation can be replaced. Refer to the "Ornamentation" section.

Posts and Piers

Decayed posts and piers should be rebuilt using a design which is not susceptible to moisture accumulation. Refer to the section entitled "Foundation: Posts and Piers."

Joists and Decking

The tilt of the porch floor is often exaggerated by settlement. To correct this situation, attach the joists to a new spot on the posts for a more level floor area. If the floor boards are worn, but still sound, they can be turned over for re-use. If the decking is the tongue and groove type, it is less likely to have warped over the years because of the secure fit, and if it has not become decayed, it can last for many more years, with good ventilation. Refer to the section "Crawl Space: Vents" for important considerations on air circulation.

Special coating is available to seal the floorboards against the weather. The safest selection aesthetically is a clear seal that can take paint, like Thompson's or Seal-Treat.

Columns

Wood columns are used on Victorian and Colonial Revival houses as structural members and as ornamentation on the façade. The columns are classic in style, with a base, shaft and capital. The fluted shaft is hollow, constructed in eight parts like an

PORCH BALUSTRADE RECONSTRUCTION

PREFERRED ALTERNATIVE
USES ORIGINAL PARTS INCLUD-ING MOLDINGS & 3 DIMENSION-AL BALUSTERS AND/OR NEW PARTS DUPLICATING ORIGINALS

2ND ALTERNATIVE
USES STOCK LUMBER & MOLDINGS TO APPROXIMATE THE ORIGINAL RAILING. TWO DIMENSIONAL CUTOUT BALUSTERS ARE EASIER TO MAKE THAN THE TURNED ORIGINALS.

3RD ALTERNATIVE
USES PLAIN LUMBER IN THE SAME PROPORTIONS AND WITH THE SAME SPACING AS THE ORIGINAL RAILING

octagon. The capitals, shaped like a collar to fit around the indented top of the shaft, were made of exterior plaster, cheap cast iron or pressed sawdust. Once the seal between capital and shaft is broken, water penetrates the joint and the capital eventually falls off. If the capital is still attached, be sure to keep the seal caulked. If the capital is long lost to deterioration or vandals, it can be replaced with a cast plaster replica. Western Art Stone, in San Francisco, specializes in this. Or, to replace it yourself, see Chapter 5, "Plaster."

If the entire column needs replacement, columns with base and capital can be ordered from the Worthington Group, Atlanta, GA, or A.F. Schwerd Manufacturing, Pittsburgh, PA.

The wood columns on a Brown Shingle porch are repaired like its porch roof members, and like the posts on a cement porch. Refer to those sections. Be certain to support the porch roof at its proper height while working on porch columns.

The wood porches on some Craftsman Bungalows have stone columns, although the stone is usually a veneer over wood. Typically it is this wood support that succumbs to decay. Remove the stone patiently, repair the substructure as described and illustrated under "Stucco Porch" below, and replace the original masonry units. Sometimes, chemical impurities in the air can cause softer stones to decay, as evidenced by flaking and pitting in the stone's surface. Treat this condition with a chemical preservative available from a brick and stone dealer or replace it with a stone that matches the rest of the column. To protect the stones from future chemical erosion, scrub them regularly with plain cold water.

If the mortar binding the stones together is crumbling, restore their strength using the technique described for repointing mortar on brick foundations. Finish the mortar with a concave joint, making sure the stones still project beyond the mortar. Stone columns are important to the architectural character of Craftsman Bungalows and should always be preserved.

Railings

The railing of a porch is structural in that it must support the weight of someone leaning against it, but it is also ornamental because its styling is an important aspect of how the whole house looks. The Uniform Building Code requires that on new porches and balconies which are 2½′ or more above grade, the railings must be 36″ high and the separation between balusters no more than 6″. Most Victorian and Colonial Revival railings are only 24″ or 30″ high. **According to applicable code,** as explained in Chapter 3, **the porch railing may be rebuilt exactly as it was designed originally.** However, you may choose to increase the railing height for safety purposes. If the original railing is substantially intact, and its only shortcoming is its height, the best solution is to raise the entire railing on blocks. The second best solution is to add a very simple rail on top of the more elaborate original. In either case, the crossbars of new and old should line up.

Rebuilding a Victorian or Colonial Revival railing "from scratch" is admirable but painstaking because the turned balusters are costly to reproduce. If salvaged balusters are not available, the most acceptable shortcut is to use cut-out, flat pieces with the same silhouette as the original rounded ones. If even this is too difficult, use conventional rectangular lumber and **retain the proportion and composition of the original railing design.** Whatever you do, avoid the use of wrought iron and horizontal ranch-style railings.

The cap of the original railing was as shapely as the balusters. Recreate this three-dimensional effect with stock lumber and molding, as illustrated in the earlier section on wood stairs.

Roof

On the typical Victorian and Colonial Revival porch, the roof is flat and prone to collecting water. **Proper flashing between porch roof and building wall is a necessity** to prevent decay in the joints. Refer to the section entitled "Roof: Flashing" for more information.

A good temporary solution to rebuilding the porch roof on a Victorian is to install a fabric awning over the front door. Select an awning design whose shape and size is reminscent of the original overhang. Use fabric, not metal or fiberglass, because cloth has a soft texture which sympathizes with the wood

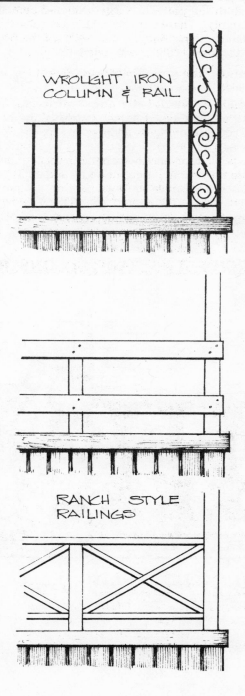

WROUGHT IRON COLUMN & RAIL

RANCH STYLE RAILINGS

STICKWORK REPAIR

REMOVE THE ROTTED END, CUTTING ALONG LINES A, B AND C SUCCESSIVELY. ZIG-ZAG CUT HAS MORE BONDING AREA, MAKES A STRONGER JOINT.

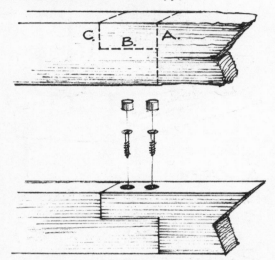

CUT A NEW END FROM EQUAL SIZE LUMBER USING THE ORIGINAL AS A GUIDE. DRILL PILOT HOLES THROUGH NEW WOOD TO OLD WOOD. DRILL COUNTERSINK HOLES HALF A SCREW LENGTH FROM OLD WOOD. APPLY WOOD GLUE TO JOINT, SCREW TOGETHER PIECES. CAP HOLES WITH GLUED DOWEL SECTIONS.

building; a harder metal or synthetic product contradicts it. Besides, this is a temporary solution, so it need not last indefinitely. In fact, avoid building a more permanent compromise, or there will be little incentive to go back and rehab it properly when the time comes.

The roof of the Brown Shingle style porch is actually a trellis. It provides an intriguing shadow pattern on the porch floor instead of continuous shelter overhead. Vines are often trained on the porch and these may be a contributing factor to wood damage, if the lumber was not properly treated with a preservative first.

The individual wood members are typically cut to more generous dimensions than standard lumber today. To **get the right size replacement,** ask the lumber yard for rough-finish wood to the size you desire. Although the wood you get is larger than its standard-finish counterpart, the price of the rough-finish wood is lower. For example, rough finish redwood, $4'' \times 4''$ construction heart, costs $1.08 per board foot. A standard finish $4'' \times 4''$, also construction heart, is $1.15 per board foot and its dimensions are really $3\frac{1}{2}'' \times 3\frac{1}{2}''$.

If only the end of a wood member is damaged, replacement of the entire length is unnecesary. Detach the member in question from the structure for ease in handling, providing temporary support where necessary. Remove the rotted end, plus a few inches for good measure, and splice on the new segment, as illustrated. The holes drilled for the screws will be so deep that they must be refilled with wooden plugs instead of ordinary wood putty. When the bond is secure, treat both segments with a wood preservative. Let it dry, and replace the member in the stickwork porch. Although this technique is more time consuming, the savings in materials may make it worthwhile.

Stucco Porch

The stucco porch is found on stucco style houses, namely California Bungalow, Prairie School and Period Revival. It is also found on houses which initially had a wood porch but have since been modernized. If your stucco porch is in need of repair, and stucco was not the original building

OVERHANG

material, consider replacing the porch with one better suited to the architecture. In most cases the more authentic choice is wood.

Stucco is a many-layered affair. The structural wood frame is covered by rough sheathing, the sheathing is covered by tar paper, the tar paper by wire or wood lath, and the lath by three coats of a stucco mixture which is primarily Portland cement and sand. Any or all of these layers may need repair.

Repairing small cracks or holes in the stucco surface is not a difficult operation, but definitely a time-consuming one. Therefore, it behooves the home-owner to repair the cracks him or herself, because paying for a contractor's time makes this a need-lessly expensive operation. (Refer to the section "Sheathing: Stucco" for more complete instructions.) It is important to **keep cracks patched,** or they will enlarge and allow moisture to seep into the structure underneath.

On stucco porches, **the underlying wood frame is subject to decay from water accumulation and poor air circulation, and to damage from insect infestation.** A deteriorated porch structure is a very common item in the termite report pre-pared prior to sale of a house, but it is difficult to recognize from the outside. The causes of damage are actually the best symptoms to go by. Check for large cracks in the stucco, faulty gutters, inadequate flashing and leaks in the four corners of the flat tar and gravel roof. If damage is severe, the entire porch must be rebuilt and re-stuccoed, with the help of a contractor.

The most important design consideration in the stucco porch of a California Bungalow is the pair of elephantine columns which flank the front steps. The wood members which establish the shape of these heavy set, often tapered posts, are subject to decay due to poor ventilation.

To correct this unsafe condition, the structural stability of the columns must be reinstated. To maintain the proper appearance of the stucco bungalow, **the elephantine columns should always be re-placed in kind.** Never substitute wrought iron posts, a piece of lumber or a steel pipe. These substitutions do not express the weight of the roof above. Their spindly silhouette looks skimpy in

ELEPHANTINE COLUMN REPAIR

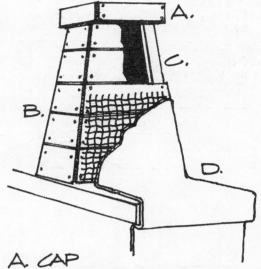

A. CAP
B. BOARD SHEATHING
C. 2×4 (CORNER OF FRAMEWORK)
D. STUCCO

REPAIR

—INTERLOCKING "S" SHAPED WIRE COMMONLY REPLACES BOARD SHEATHING & WIRE NETTING

—MOUND STUCCO SLIGHTLY TOWARDS MIDDLE OF CAP TO FACILITATE DRAINAGE.

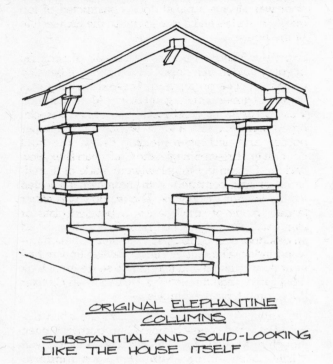

ORIGINAL ELEPHANTINE
COLUMNS

SUBSTANTIAL AND SOLID-LOOKING
LIKE THE HOUSE ITSELF

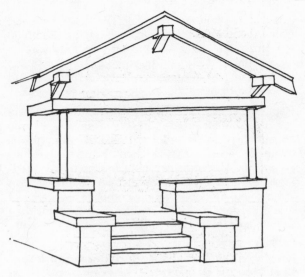

STEEL PIPE COLUMNS

ALTHOUGH STRUCTURALLY ADEQUATE,
THEY DON'T LOOK STURDY ENOUGH TO
HOLD UP THE PORCH ROOF

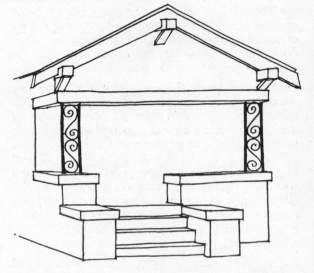

WROUGHT IRON STYLE COLUMNS

CURVY AND LACY IN TEXTURE, THEY
ARE VERY OUT-OF-PLACE ON A
BUNGALOW PORCH. ALSO, THEY MAY
NOT BE STRUCTURALLY SOUND.

comparison to the chunky appearance of the rest of the house. The bungalow has a broad and substantial appearance; it sits solidly on the ground. The elephantine porch columns are in proportion to the rest of the building, and essential to its architectural image. Besides, the substitution may not be sturdy enough to meet code.

Another problem on stucco porches is **rot in the joints between the porch floor and the frame wall of the house due to improper or omitted flashing.** Flashing is a curved strip of building paper and metal which should be installed at this junction to direct the rain water which runs down the wall away from the joint. If there is no flashing, water collects in the joint and deteriorates the stucco above it and the cement-covered wood decking below. Correcting this situation requires removing

the damaged materials prior to installing the protective metal strip.

Flashing is equally important at the joint between the porch roof and the wall of the house. If water is allowed to accumulate here, it can penetrate to the wood frame and cause serious structural damage. (Refer to the section "Roof: Flashing.")

A final problem with stucco porches is more one of function than maintenance. Many homeowners, seeking extra living space, choose to enclose the front porch. Rarely does this accomplish anything, as the effort creates nothing more than a very small and very drafty room. To boot, a gracious entryway, and a place for the front door to swing open without jarring the visitor on the front steps, are lost in the bargain. **If your porch is still a porch, do not enclose it.**

If you absolutely need a windbreak or a sunscreen to make the porch more comfortable for sitting or for growing plants, use a plain transparent plastic or glass panel. This will accomplish your goal without disrupting the rhythm of California Bungalow columns which unify the street scene.

Cement Porch

The original porch on Wartime Tract houses is a cement slab floor, as are modernized porches on almost every other style. The cement may suffer from small cracks. The technique for repairing these is described in the section on concrete stairs. Major breaks in the cement are a symptom of a settlement problem, and a professional contractor or engineer should assess the situation.

Make sure that the porch slab is not draining toward the house. Test this by placing a child's ball on the cement and seeing which way it rolls. If the ball rolls toward the house, then water is being directed toward the building too. If you notice signs of decay where the wood siding meets the porch floor, then ask a contractor about correcting the slope of the slab.

On the tract house the porch roof is a continuous overhang from the main roof, so problems with flashing encountered in styles where the porch roof is a separate plane are not a worry here. However, the wood posts which support the overhang are subject to decay at the bottom if water is allowed to accumulate between the post and the cement slab. Refer to the section on wood porches for the telltale signs of rot. If the base of the post has decayed, it is easier to remove the post to work on it, providing a temporary support for the roof in the meantime.

It is usually unnecessary to replace the entire wood post. Instead, remove the decayed section, plus 4" leeway, and graft on a new weather-treated piece of the same dimension by the mortice and tenon, or the lap technique. Seal the joint between the new and the old sections with wood putty prior to painting it. To prevent recurrence of decay at the base, use a better method of securing the post to the concrete which allows air to circulate, as illustrated in the section "Foundation: Posts and Piers."

Do not replace the wood post with a wrought-iron one. Its garish curlicues look wrong with the frank lines and geometric form of the Wartime Tract house. When repairing the wood post, be sure to retain the short diagonal braces at the top. If your porch posts do not have these v-shaped braces, and you would like some additional ornamentation, add these authentic features rather than anything wrought-iron or prefabricated.

FRONT DOOR

The front door does many jobs. Visually, it catches the eye. Functionally, it protects against unwanted intruders. Symbolically it says, "You're home!" In

CEMENT PORCH FLOOR REPAIR WITH FLASHING

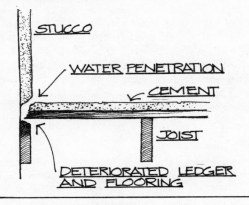

STUCCO

WATER PENETRATION

CEMENT

JOIST

DETERIORATED LEDGER AND FLOORING

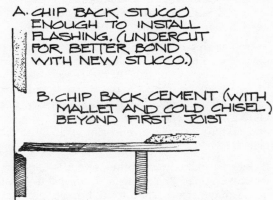

A. CHIP BACK STUCCO ENOUGH TO INSTALL FLASHING. (UNDERCUT FOR BETTER BOND WITH NEW STUCCO.)

B. CHIP BACK CEMENT (WITH MALLET AND COLD CHISEL) BEYOND FIRST JOIST

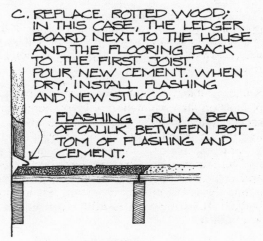

C. REPLACE ROTTED WOOD; IN THIS CASE, THE LEDGER BOARD NEXT TO THE HOUSE AND THE FLOORING BACK TO THE FIRST JOIST. POUR NEW CEMENT. WHEN DRY, INSTALL FLASHING AND NEW STUCCO.

FLASHING - RUN A BEAD OF CAULK BETWEEN BOT-TOM OF FLASHING AND CEMENT.

pre-war houses the importance of the front door was recognized by the care given to its design. The front door was always a panel door, constructed of top quality materials and styled to match the architecture of the house.

Expensive Victorian homes had a pair of centrally opening golden oak doors, with a panel of beveled or flashed glass on top and recessed molding or a veneer of grained mahogany below. More common Victorian and Colonial Revival houses had a single, broad oak door with a large window on the upper portion and decorative molding below. The front door on the Brown Shingle, the Craftsman Bungalow and the California Bungalow were made of fir, redwood or oak, consistent with the material selected for the interior woodwork. The window was either leaded, made of small panes of beveled glass or eliminated altogether. The Prairie School house had an oak door stained to match the finish of the hardwood inside. The fancier Period Revival houses had front doors stained and textured to make them look more rustic. Page through the illustrations in Chapter 2 for some typical examples.

Unfortunately, these valuable doors are often disposed of in the course of home improvement, even though most of the problems can be corrected with a little patient energy. **Substituting a modern, flush door for a beautifully panelled original is a shameful waste of an architectural resource as well as a careless waste of money for the replacement.** The problems with old doors fall into four categories: fit, wear, hardware and security. The subject of fit, more pertinent to interior doors, is discussed in that section.

Wear

The front door gets a lot of use and abuse, from both people and the weather, so some damage is inevitable.

Panels

Oakland houses that pre-date World War II originally had panelled front doors. The shape and number of panels per door varies, but the construction technique is the same: slender panels are enclosed in a heavy structural framework and secured in

HOW TO REPLACE DOOR GLASS

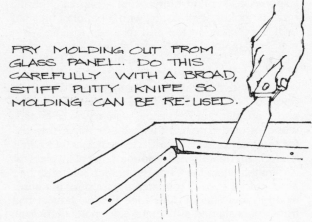

PRY MOLDING OUT FROM GLASS PANEL. DO THIS CAREFULLY WITH A BROAD, STIFF PUTTY KNIFE SO MOLDING CAN BE RE-USED.

GENTLY REMOVE GLASS. CLEAN BED & APPLY A THIN STRIP OF GLAZING COMPOUND IN THE BOTTOM OF THE BED.

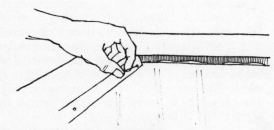

PLACE DOUBLE - STRENGTH PANE CUT SAME SIZE AS ORIGINAL (OR 1/8" SMALLER THAN OPENING IN HEIGHT & WIDTH) IN BED, PRESSING TO FORCE COMPOUND UP AROUND EDGES. APPLY 2ND LAYER OF COMPOUND AROUND GLASS EDGE. RE-NAIL MOLD-ING. FILL NAIL HOLES.

place by moldings for a solid, three-dimensional design. The lower panels, made of wood, usually stay intact, but the upper panels, made of glass, are much more fragile. The glass may be rectangular, round, or oval; it may be a large single window, a matching pair, or a composition of small square panes; and, it may be etched, leaded, stained, or flashed. **If the glass is chipped, cracked, or missing altogether, repair or replace it with glass.** The entry hall depends on the light this window affords.

Veneer

The framework of the door, the portion which surrounds the panel, is typically a solid piece of softwood with a thin veneer of oak, walnut or mahogany on either side. When moisture seeps in between the softwood and the veneer, they separate, and the **veneer begins to fray at the lower edge.**

To repair this condition without it looking like a patch job, make the repair all the way across the bottom of the door. Cut off the ragged piece back to sound wood, using a back saw or an electric router with a straight blade set to a shallow depth. Glue a new piece of veneer of the right size, color, and texture into place, and clamp down until the glue sets.

If only a small corner of the veneer is damaged, it can be chipped back with a chisel. Fill it in with a wood putty of matching tone. Repairs are simpler if the door is already painted, since touch-up paint can mask corrections which are hard to conceal with the natural wood finish.

To ward off future damage from scuffing, a kick plate can be installed quite simply with a drill and screws. Try salvage yards for interesting brass plates that match the other, original features on the door. Otherwise, use a very plain piece of non-ferrous metal or heavy-duty plastic. Do not use aluminum—it is too bright and scratches too easily. Copper and brass are good choices because they acquire a patina or can be shined. The plate should be 2" narrower than the door width to allow for door stops.

HOW TO REPLACE A DOOR THRESHOLD

SWING DOOR WIDE OPEN. IF IT DOESN'T CLEAR THRESHOLD, PULL HINGE PINS AND REMOVE DOOR. USING A PRY BAR, START PULLING DOORSTOP 4" AWAY FROM DOOR-JAMB, FROM BOTTOM TO TOP. THEN RE-MOVE STOP COMPLETELY.

TRY TO PRY UP THRESHOLD INTACT FOR USE AS A PATTERN. IF NECESSARY, SPLIT IT INTO PIECES WITH A WOOD CHISEL. TRACE OUT-LINE OF THRESHOLD ON BOARD OF EQUAL THICKNESS (OR TAKE CAREFUL MEASURE-MENTS FIRST IF YOU MUST SPLIT THE OLD ONE). TRIM NEW THRESHOLD TO SIZE, THEN TAP LIGHTLY INTO PLACE.

FOR HARDWOOD THRESHOLDS (THE BEST CHOICE FOR WEAR), DRILL PILOT HOLES A BIT SMALLER IN DIAMETER THAN NAILS TO AVOID SPLITTING WOOD. COUNTERSINK NAILS (OR SCREWS), FILL HOLES WITH PUTTY.

Paint

A natural wood door is preferable to a painted door because its textured grain lends richness to the appearance of the house. **If the door is in decent condition, and is as yet unpainted, perpetuate the natural finish. If it is severely weathered, however, or if the repairs have left ghastly scars, painting is a much better solution than buying a new door.** If you choose to paint the front door, make sure the surface is treated first with a wood sealer. Otherwise, the paint will be absorbed, and even three or four coats won't achieve a finished look. The seal also provides protection against moisture penetration in the future. (Refer to the section "Paint.")

If the door has already been painted and you want to reverse the process, arrangements can be made to have the door dipped in stripping solvent. This cleans off most of the paint, although the detailed work must still be done by hand. An unduly long bath in the stripping vat risks damage to the wood structure and may make the surface porous and rough, so don't insist on removing every shred of paint by prolonged immersion. Dipping costs between $35 and $45. After stripping, treat the wood with varnish or oil. (Refer to Chapter 5, "Walls: Wood" for more information on stripping.)

Ornamentation

Original Victorian doors have decorative wood pieces applied over the lower panels in a design which matches the ornamentation elsewhere on the building. **Preserve this ornamentation** if it still exists, or try to recreate it if it has been lost to vandals or decay.

Threshold

A worn threshold gives the entryway an unneccesarily shabby appearance, and may present a tripping hazard. It should be replaced in-kind, as illustrated.

Hardware

The doorknobs and hinges on the front door are usually made of brass, steel, or brass-plated steel. Whether elaborately detailed or plain, the brass takes on an elegant lustre when maintained. **Preserving the original hardware on the front door is an example of how important attention to detail is for a satisfactory end product.**

Most older exterior doors are hung on heavy-duty, butt type hinges made of two leaves screwed to the door and jamb, respectively, and held together by a pin. Often, the weight of the front door enlarges the holes which once held the screws snugly. This results in a stubborn door that sticks on one side.

To tighten the hinge attachment, you can try longer screws. Or, you can refill the holes with either putty, plastic wood, a dowel or wood match sticks, and reset the screws. Before you do this, remove the door by knocking out the hinge pin with a nail set and hammer while the door is closed. Then remove the hinges.

If the hinges are covered with paint, let them soak in a coffee can of paint remover to return the brass to its distinctive natural finish. Otherwise, scour the oxidation with Brasso, or another tarnish remover, following the directions on the label. To highlight the detail, polish the brass every few months thereafter. Subsequent polishing can be postponed several years by coating the hinge with a clear lacquer following the clean-up operation. Acrylic spray in an aerosol can, like Krylon, is easy to apply. The same general rules apply to the brass mail slot, if there is one.

Original doorknobs are a luxurious experience to hold and behold. They should be retained for use as a handle, even if their lock mechanisms are no longer adequate for security. Keep the faceplate tarnish-free with a brass cleaner. If the brass plating on the knob has worn off in spots, it can be replated. Meanwhile, the brass cleaner will keep the rust off the exposed steel too.

If the latch bolt is unresponsive, it should be fixed for the convenience of a door that closes properly, rather than for security. Sometimes the latch bolt and the strike plate don't meet because the door itself does not fit properly. To determine if fit is the problem, see if the hinge screws are loose, as described above, and conduct the experiment outlined in Chapter 5 under "Doors." If it turns out to be the latch mechanism, you can detach it form the door and bring it to a locksmith for repair. Of course, do this only after you've installed the auxiliary deadbolt.

Security

Security in the home is a topic on everyone's mind these days, and sometimes the solutions are at odds with a building's architectural style. The recommendations that follow demonstrate that a house can be made secure without sacrificing the quality of its appearance.

Remember that the matter of home security extends beyond the front door. It includes all other openings into the house, the visibility of the house from the street, the presence of street and yard lights, blind spots behind walls, and even the number of neighbors' eyes casually looking out their windows. In fact, according to the Crime Analysis Division of the Oakland Police Department, only 15% of residential break-ins are through the front door. So, **by directing your security concerns to the back door, windows and lighting as well, you need not sacrifice a beautiful front door pointlessly.**

The first consideration is the **vulnerability of the door** itself. There is no debating the fact that modern, flush, solid-core doors are harder to break down than the original panel style. However, the modern ones are so inferior aesthetically, and there are so many aspects to security other than the solidity of the front door, that retention of the original panel door is highly recommended. In fact, the back door is so much more susceptible to break-ins because of its flimsy construction and hidden location, that the homeowner is well-advised to leave an attractive front door intact, and concentrate on the backdoor.

There are a few steps to take which can make an original, paneled door, front or back, very difficult to break through, improvements which **increase security without obliterating the original design:**

- The easiest option is to rely on a twin-cylinder deadbolt with a 1″ throw which cannot be unlocked from the inside without a key even if the glass is broken and the intruder reaches in to open the door. A double-cylinder lock costs $40.
- Reinforce the wood panels, by installing plain metal bars on the outside. Paint the bars so they blend with the color of the door. Or, add a piece

of plywood on the inside of the door behind the panels, and stain or paint it to match the door.

- Reinforce the glass by adding a panel of break-resistant plastic, like Lexan MR 4000, in front, as seen at the Camron-Stanford house. A $2' \times 3'$ piece of virtually bullet-proof Lexan $3/16''$ thick costs about $40. Or, leave the glass as is, and shield it with a woven metal screen of #11 wire on a $1\frac{1}{2}''$ grid. A $3' \times 4'$ piece costs $46 and is available at Howard Wire Cloth Co., Hayward.

DOOR SECURITY: REINFORCED DOOR FRAME

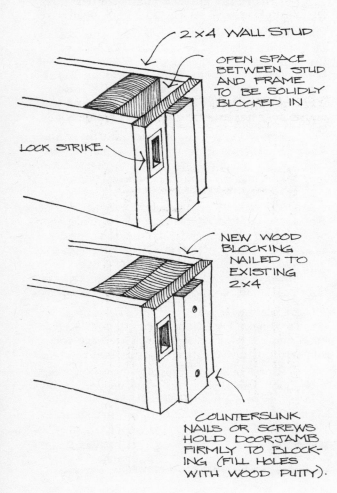

2×4 WALL STUD

OPEN SPACE BETWEEN STUD AND FRAME TO BE SOLIDLY BLOCKED IN

LOCK STRIKE

NEW WOOD BLOCKING NAILED TO EXISTING 2×4

COUNTERSUNK NAILS OR SCREWS HOLD DOORJAMB FIRMLY TO BLOCKING (FILL HOLES WITH WOOD PUTTY).

If a new door is a must, there are secure and attractive options other than the conventional flush solid-core type which looks wrong on every one of the architectural styles discussed in REHAB RIGHT. Made of particle board, the standard $3' \times 6'8''$ solid-core flush door sells for about $50 with a mahogany or birch veneer. For as little as $25, you can get an honest, full-sized

DOOR SECURITY: BRACED STUDS

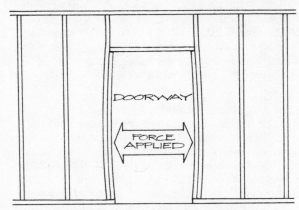

DOORWAY

FORCE APPLIED

A. STUDS IN DOORFRAME ARE VULNERABLE TO SIDEWAYS PRESSURE.

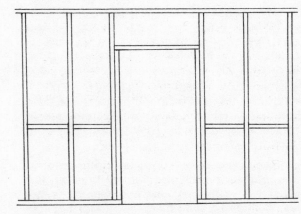

B. ADDING 2×4 BLOCKING BETWEEN STUDS AT THE LOCK LEVEL REINFORCES DOORFRAME.

paneled door at a salvage yard. Prepare for a trip to the salvage yard by measuring the height and width of the doorway from jamb to jamb.

New old doors, that is, new doors that are built in the panel manner, are available at Truitt and White lumber yard. Ask for the catalog to see if there is a design suitable to the house, but make sure the panel portion is at least $\frac{1}{2}''$ thick for security purposes. A paneled door made of fir costs between $100 and $170, depending on the number of raised panels.

DOOR SECURITY: NON-REMOVABLE HINGE PIN

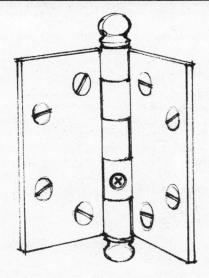

OPEN DOOR. FROM INSIDE OF HINGE, DRILL A PILOT HOLE INTO HINGE PIN. COUNTERSINK HOLE SO SCREW HEAD WON'T INTERFERE WITH CLOSING OF DOOR. INSERT SELF-TAPPING SCREW.

Whatever door you choose, make sure that it is the correct size for the door frame. Victorian door frames are often taller than conventional modern doors, forcing the homeowner to make a dreadful assault on the appearance of the house by blocking in the leftover space. Do everything you can to avoid this mistake.

No matter how secure the door and lock may be, if the **door frame** is vulnerable, forced entry is fairly easy. Many door frames are set into the wall without solid connection to the studs. Since the

FRONT DOOR: DOS AND DON'TS

A.   B.

A. ITALIANATE DOUBLE DOORS. LIKE THE HOUSE STYLE, THEY ARE VERTICAL IN EMPHASIS AND RICHLY 3-DIMENSIONAL. ORIGINAL DOORS WORK WITH YOUR HOUSE'S ARCHITECTURE. IF YOU HAVE THEM, KEEP THEM, IF THEY NEED WORK, FIX THEM AND IF THEY HAVE BEEN REPLACED, IT'S WORTH THE EFFORT TO FIND NEW OR SALVAGED REPLACEMENTS SUITABLE FOR YOUR HOUSE STYLE.

B. BLOCKED-DOWN REPLACEMENT SUFFERS FROM ASYMMETRY, SQUATTY PROPORTIONS AND LACK OF VISUAL TEXTURE. AVOID THIS ALL-TOO-COMMON REHAB ERROR.

DOOR SECURITY: PRECAUTION FOR EXTERIOR HINGE PIN

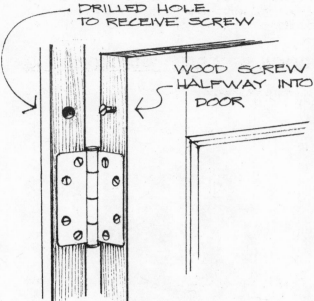

DRILLED HOLE TO RECEIVE SCREW

WOOD SCREW HALFWAY INTO DOOR

lock slides into the frame, the frame, usually a ¾″ thick piece of wood, is all that is holding the door shut. A solid kick to the frame at the lock will rip the bolt out of the frame or the frame out of the wall. Remedy this situation by adding a solid blocking member equal to the height of the door between the door frame and stud. Nail them solidly together.

The frame is also vulnerable to sidewise pressure. Add 2″ × 4″ solid blocking between the studs at lock level, for a much stronger frame.

The **hinges** should be mounted on the inside of the door. If they are already on the outside, they should have a non-removable pin. If the hinges are modern ones, they can be replaced with a special type of hinge that comes with a non-removable pin. If the hinges are original, do not sacrifice the brass and beauty in the name of security. The pin can be made non-removable by drilling a hole

through the hinge pin from the inside and inserting a machine screw.

Another precaution is to install a wood screw halfway into the door near each hinge. Drill a hole into the jamb opposite each screw to receive the projecting screw heads. Then, the door will stay in place even if the hinges are removed.

Old doors have mortise **locks** which are ineffective for today's security needs because their bolt does not have enough throw. The minimum acceptable throw is 1″. However, this is no reason to discard the original brass knob and faceplate. Retain them as an ornamental handle, and supplement them with a twin-cylinder rim lock that has a deadbolt. Be sure to keep a spare key on a hook nearby to use for emergency exits.

DOOR SECURITY: ONE ARCHITECT'S SOLUTION

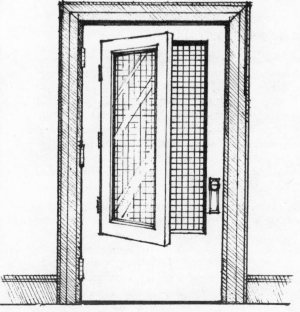

The **glass panel** in the door is extremely valuable for the light it introduces to an otherwise dark hallway. However, it is inadvisable to let people look into the house. Hanging a translucent curtain or shade, sandblasting the glass, or frosting it with a spray can, are all acceptable solutions. An ingenious idea developed by Oakland architect John Campbell and shown here, solves the problem of security and still allows for light, air and controlled visibility.

Some Victorian houses have **double doors** opening in the center. These have the special problem of a weak point where they meet. To secure these doors, use the vertical rod-type lock that effectively latches the door to the floor and the ceiling when operated.

It is a good idea to have a light at the front door, and to keep it on when it's dark. When selecting, **avoid the commercial fixtures which try to look "olde."** While a genuine globe from the proper period at a salvage yard will be a "find," it will not be UL listed or rated for damp locations, as modern code requires. If you must get a new light fixture, select a style that is as plain as possible, one that does not compete with the legitimate features of the house and its architectural style. If you prefer an accurate reproduction, consult Chapter 5, "Light Fixtures" for sources.

Garage Door

While Oakland's earlier house styles were built before the automobile era, many property owners have taken advantage of the raised first floor typical to Oakland cottages and rowhouses to incorporate a garage into the house structure. To keep the garage door from having a jarring visual impact on the façade, **select as simple a design as possible.** Cover it with the same material in the same pattern as the siding on the rest of the house. This applies to detached garages too.

Windows are unnecessary, unless the garage doubles as a workshop. In that case, small square panes are far preferable to long horizontal windows, or whimsical curved ones. Refer to the drawings of the San Francisco Stick style and the Queen Anne Cottage in Chapter 2 for good examples of garages that were added well after the house was built, but which maintain its architectural character.

DOOR SECURITY: ORIGINAL DOOR KNOB AS HANDLE WITH AUXILIARY LOCK

The walls of the garage must be designed for fire resistance. This is a code requirement, imperative for the safety of the residents, and literally essential to the preservation of the architecture. Many garages, converted without benefit of a building permit, lack fire resistive construction. Check to see if there is finished stucco, sheetrock, or other non-flammable surface installed from floor to ceiling on any garage wall that abuts a habitable portion of the house, or on any bearing wall. Also see if the door from garage to house is solid-core, or covered in sheet-metal. If not, correct the situation. The money spent on the fire wall could save you thousands of dollars by preventing the spread of an automobile fire to the rest of the house.

SHEATHING

Sheathing is the weatherproof surface applied to the completed structure of the house. Visually, the original type of sheathing complements the other architectural features of the house, its shape, proportion and ornamentation, so any change to another material has drastic consequences on the appearance of the building. Functionally, the siding protects the wood frame from the elements, and because it takes a lot of abuse from water and temperature extremes, it is commonly in need of repair. **Always repair the sheathing in-kind,** and stick with one kind only. Attempts to save work by changing to a modern, mass-produced siding are not worth the sacrifice in architectural integrity or resale value.

Wood Siding

Wood siding, the most widely used residential weatherproofing, comes in a variety of styles. With the exception of Craftsman houses, on which the finish is left natural, wood siding is always painted.

Design

One type of horizontal wood siding is the drop style, also known as "rustic." It has interlocking panels, and a flat surface which alternates with rounded channels or v-shaped grooves. Drop siding is characteristic of Victorian houses, and was occasionally

TYPES OF WOOD SIDING

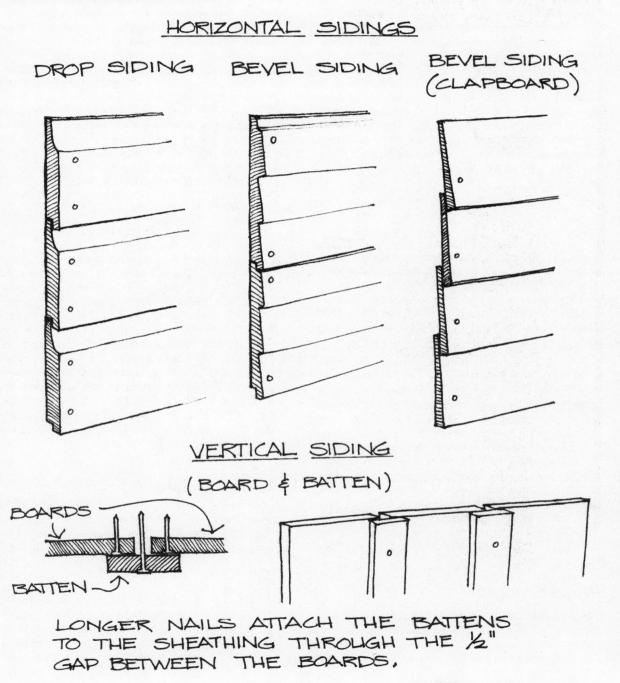

HORIZONTAL SIDINGS

DROP SIDING   BEVEL SIDING   BEVEL SIDING (CLAPBOARD)

VERTICAL SIDING

(BOARD & BATTEN)

BOARDS

BATTEN

LONGER NAILS ATTACH THE BATTENS TO THE SHEATHING THROUGH THE ½" GAP BETWEEN THE BOARDS.

used on the inside too, as the base molding. Half a decade later, drop siding came into vogue again on the Wartime Tract House, although the boards were of skimpier dimensions.

Another type of horizonal wood siding is the bevel style, also known as "lap siding," "shiplap" and "clapboard." (Pronounce it *kla*-bird, with a silent *p*.) In the East, in most home repair books and on some local bungalows, bevel siding consists of single boards, 8'–12' long, about a foot wide and tapered at the upper end. They are nailed to the wood frame in overlapping fashion, through one or two thicknesses. In Oakland, however, the bevel siding characteristic of many Colonial Revival houses has a single unit that looks like three tiers combined. Functionally this allowed more expeditious installation and exposed fewer joints. Visually, it creates a more pronounced line every three slats, a subtle but extremely effective design device to modulate an otherwise repetitive surface.

The most common type of vertical wood siding is board and batten, in which narrow strips are superimposed over broad planks. Board and batten is found on the San Francisco Stick style, the Brown Shingle style, the Craftsman Bungalow and the Wartime Tract.

Damage and Repair

Cracked or decayed wood siding is an invitation to further trouble, especially from water seepage. Use the "pick test" to confirm any suspicions of rot. (Refer to the section on wood porches.) Peeling paint in the room behind the damaged siding is another danger signal.

Small fissures can be filled with putty or caulk. Cracks that are too wide to be sealed with caulk alone can first be stuffed with oakum, a specially treated rope-like material available on spools at plumbing supply stores.

Goad warps back into line with screws. Drill guide holes first, aiming for a stud, and keep the holes far enough apart to avert splitting the board. Countersink the screws and putty the holes. Reunite split boards by butting them together as tightly as possible and securing them with a screw, as just described. Fill the crack with an outdoor caulking compound like butyl. Butyl, both flexible and receptive to any kind of paint, comes in tubes to fit caulking guns, and in cans for application with a putty knife. The latter works best for large gaps.

Major cracks and deterioration require a replacement board. If the entire length must go, remove the nails with a nail puller (rented at $5 a day at Lewis Rental). Countersinking and years of paint usually make the use of a hammer claw alone unfeasible. As needed replace rotted building paper and repair punctures with asphalt roofing compound. Treat the new wood with a "penta" (pentachlorophenol) preservative that can be painted, like Cehrung at $5 a quart. Slip the new slat in place and secure it with aluminum or galvanized nails. Countersink the nails, putty the holes, including those made with the nail puller, caulk the joints and paint.

If less than half of the board's length is damaged, and you prefer to replace that part only, you can remove the entire span, as just described, and conduct surgery on the work table. Or, you can saw off the damaged segment right on the wall. This takes skillful manipulation of a circular saw, and risks damage to adjacent siding and underlying building paper. Consult a home repair book, like *Sunset Basic Home Repairs,* or the *Reader's Digest Complete Do-it-yourself Manual,* for detailed instruction.

Due to the variety in design, it may be somewhat difficult to find drop or bevel siding that is milled precisely like the original. East Bay Lumber Supply and Blackman's Lumber are good places to begin the search. Redwood three-lap bevel siding costs $1.25/foot for $1'' \times 8''$s, and $1.72/foot for $1'' \times 10''$s. Redwood single-lap siding costs 76¢/foot for $1'' \times 6''$s, $1.08/foot for $1'' \times 8''$s and $1.41/foot for $1'' \times 10''$s. Redwood drop siding, with a "V" or cove-shaped channel costs $1.80/foot for the $1'' \times 10''$ size.

Board and batten is a lot easier to repair than horizontal siding. The battens are face nailed, and willingly accept pry bars. Replace damaged pieces in full.

A devastating problem throughout Oakland is the interment of wood siding in a grave of stucco. In some cases this was a voluntary, but throughly misguided effort. In others stucco was the only solution to a code regulation which requires a one-hour fire-rated exterior wall on any hotel or apartment house that is three or more stories tall. Thus, three-story single-family Victorian, Colonial Revival and Brown Shingle houses that are converted to multi-family dwellings must have one-hour rated exterior walls and the only known solution is to bury the wood frame in stucco. This regulation is retroactive to 1948. Buildings converted prior to 1948 are not required to comply with the one-hour rating, and may be left with the wood siding as is. During the 1960s, however, this regulation was interpreted otherwise, and countless three-story, wood frame houses converted to multiple occupancy were stuccoed as a result.

To liberate the architectural spirit of a single-family, wood frame house that has been stuccoed, the stucco can be removed. However, you must first assess the condition of siding and trim underneath as best you can, either from the rear in unfinished areas such as basement and attic, or with exploratory probing. Further, you must be prepared both mentally and financially for extensive repairs to the wood siding and ornamentation once the stucco is removed. If they do turn out to be in fairly good shape, you have indeed discovered a buried treasure.

Starting from the top, attack the stucco a section at a time. With hammer and chisel, make a 2″ wide score in the shape of a square about 3′ long on each side. Pry off the stucco with a crow bar. Use clippers to remove the chicken wire, and gloved hands to rip off the building paper. (Refer to the construction illustration in the section "Façade: Stucco.") Remove the nails with a claw hammer, and you're back to clapboard; but you're far from finished. You must still replace or epoxy damaged portions of siding, patch nail holes and gouges with wood putty and reinstate missing ornamentation in order to prep and, finally at long last, to paint. Read accounts in *The Old-House Journal* for moral support, and see the discussion of removing mass-produced siding, below.

Wood Shingles

Wood shingles are a flexible siding material because they can fit around obstructions, and cover misshapen walls. The standard shingle is 16″, 18″ or 24″ long, made of redwood, or nowadays, cedar.

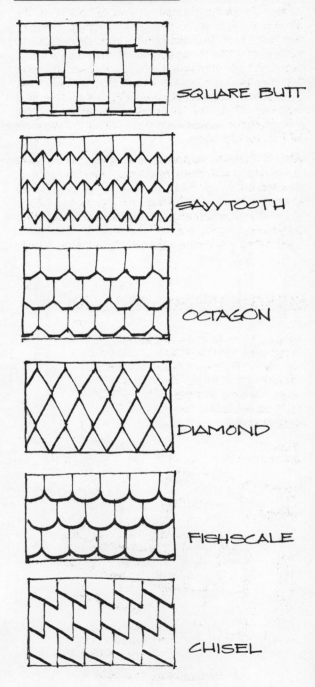

SQUARE BUTT

SAWTOOTH

OCTAGON

DIAMOND

FISHSCALE

CHISEL

Their rustic appearance is essential to the architecture of the Craftsman Bungalow, and of course, to the Brown Shingle style. Shingles of various shapes, like octagons and diamonds, form characteristic patterns in the textural quilt of the Queen Anne façade. Finely corrugated shingles, thinner and more tidy than their predecessors, are common to Wartime Tract houses. Shakes are irregularly shaped shingles exposed 12″ to 24″ beyond the overlap, and are sometimes found as siding as well as on the roofs of Provincial houses.

After decades of exposure, **shingles are subject to rotting, splitting and warping.** Nail split or warped shingles back down with galvanized or aluminum nails. To waterproof the patch, slip a piece of roofing paper of the same size underneath the shingle before securing it. Rotted or badly damaged shingles can be replaced individually, but if

SHINGLE INSTALLATION DETAIL

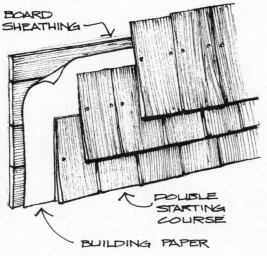

PLACE NAILS ABOVE TOP OF PREVIOUS COURSE & ¾" FROM EACH EDGE, 2 NAILS PER SHINGLE. NO MORE THAN 7½" OF A 16" SHINGLE SHOULD BE EXPOSED.

BOARD SHEATHING

DOUBLE STARTING COURSE

BUILDING PAPER

10% or more in scattered locations need attention, it's time to reshingle the whole wall.

Replacing worn-out shingles is a good job for an amateur. Several hours in advance, soak the bundle in a bucket of water. This wards off swelling in the first rain, and the likelihod of popping. Remove the damaged shingle by slipping a hacksaw blade under the bottom of the good shingle above it, and cut the nails that hold the top of the damaged piece. In the same way, cut the nails at the bottom of the damaged shingle if necessary. Splinter the shingle with a chisel, and pry out the nail stubs with the claw of a hammer or pincers. Slip a new shingle of the same size, thickness and approximate color into the space. The top should be overlapped by the upper shingle course; the bottom should overlap the lower shingle course.

Shingles can be finished with stain, preservative or paint. Painted shingles are appropriate to the Queen Anne and the All-American Ranch styles. For First Bay Tradition houses, paint is the least desirable alternative, not only because it is architecturally out of place, but also because it coats the pores of the wood which allow the grain to expire any absorbed moisture. Some people mistakenly paint shingles in order to conceal discoloration, but this darkening often bleeds right through the paint as well. It is a better idea to apply a fresh coat of stain.

If the shingles on a Craftsman or Brown Shingle house have already been painted, when it's time to repaint the most fashionable color to use is a raisin brown which simulates the appearance of naturally aged redwood. The brown, unlike the pea-green or gray it is probably covering up, provides a visual foil for the rich green of foundation shrubs and nearby trees.

If the shingles are still natural, and have acquired an enviable patina with age, maintain them with a coat of clear preservative. Cedar turns a silver gray, and redwood a raisin brown. If they have already been stained, stick with stain. In contrast to paint, whose pigment is opaque and hides the wood beneath it, stain has only enough pigment to color the wood without concealing the grain or suffocating the fibers. Check the label, or ask the paint dealer for a stain with a preservative in the suspension.

The difficulty of replacing shingles in scattered locations is matching the new slab with the weathered look of the rest of the wall and avoiding the buckshot look. If you anticipate shingle repairs in the next year or so, buy a square of shingles now and leave them in a safe spot outdoors to water on their own.

To match shingles in shorter order, add drops of stain to paint thinner until it tests a tad lighter than the weathered wall. Brush the solution on the new shingles in the same direction as the grain. The pigment darkens the wood enough to camouflage its youth, while the thinner reduces the oil content of the stain which would otherwise deter natural weathering. Use the same staining technique to make cedar shingles blend with redwood originals, as replacement redwood shingles are practically impossible to find. When selecting any stain, remember that the color looks darker in the can or on a swatch than it does in natural light on a large building wall.

Save time by applying the stain to the sides of the bundle before untying it, and to the face of each shingle prior to nailing it into place. While you're at it, stain some extras for future repairs and leave the spares outside to keep pace in color with their counterparts on the wall.

Shingles are sold in packages called squares. A square is made up of four bundles, and a bundle is adequate to cover about 25 square feet. Conventional cedar shingles cost about $72 per square for #1 quality, and $52 per square for #2 quality. The #2 type is not as easy to split in a straight line, nor as flat, as the #1 type. Queen Anne style shingles of distinctive shape are available at State Shingle Company in Oakland and cost about $68 for a bundle which covers 25 to 33 square feet.

Stucco

Stucco is a composition of Portland cement, sand and lime, applied like plaster to the exterior of wood frame houses. In Oakland, stucco belongs on the California Bungalow, Prairie School, Mediterranean, Provincial, and some All-American Ranch Style houses, like those along Malcolm Avenue in the East Oakland hills. Unfortunately, stucco is misused in attempts to modernize Victorian, Colonial Revival, and Craftsman houses, whose rightful weather-proofing is drop siding, bevel siding and shingles, respectively. The section on wood siding addresses the removal of unwanted stucco.

Stucco is prone to surface damage, which begins with hairline cracks, usually near windows and doors, and to structural damage, which begins with leaks in the flashing or inadequate ventilation in the crawl space. The sections entitled "Crawl Space," "Stucco Porch" and "Roof" discuss the problem of structural rot.

The repair of narrow surface cracks prevents more serious damage from getting a start, and is fairly simple to do.

1. Use a knife or a spatula to open the crack to sound stucco. Use a hammer and cold chisel to make the edge of the crack wider on the inside than at the outside edge. This inverted "V" will lock in the new stucco. Brush away all loose material.

2. Prepare a dry mix mortar, adding water until it has a firm yet pliable consistency. Dampen the crack and pack the stucco in tightly with a putty knife or trowel. Overfill the crack if it extends through the stucco to the base material. Let it dry for about 15 minutes, then work it down until flush.

3. Moist cure the fresh stucco with fine spray from the garden hose for about three days, once in the morning and once at night. Dry mix mortar costs $3.50 per 50 lb. bag. A putty knife and trowel cost under $20.

The repair of major patches is a more complicated procedure because it requires attention to the wood framing, sheathing, wire mesh, and to all three coats of stucco, as illustrated. Refer to a home repair book, like the *Reader's Digest Complete Do-It-Yourself Manual* for more explicit instructions.

Make sure the patch matches the rest of the wall in texture and color both. Get a sandy finish, for example, by troweling the stucco with a float as it begins to set up. Get a swirled finish by using an old brush to scrub or jab the surface.

Stucco has a natural color all its own, originally appreciated for the graininess of sand and cement employed without benefit of paint. If the house is

STUCCO CONSTRUCTION

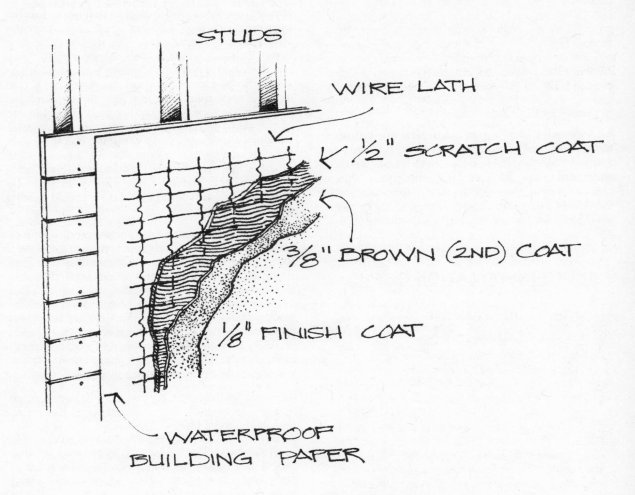

STUDS

WIRE LATH

½" SCRATCH COAT

⅜" BROWN (2ND) COAT

⅛" FINISH COAT

WATERPROOF BUILDING PAPER

still this unadulterated gravelly-gray, leave it as is and perpetuate its distinctive place in the history of building materials.

If the stucco was originally treated with an integral color, then do the same when you patch it. Add mineral pigments to the mortar for the final coat, experimenting in advance, to produce a uniform color. On large jobs, the pigment should weigh no more than 5% of the total weight of the masonry cement. This is a difficult calculation in small quantities, so use a cook's eighth-teaspoon to add a little bit of the powder at a time. Note your final recipe right on the box of pigment for future reference. Available integral colors include pink, yellow, green and tan. Matching an integral color can be difficult and you may wish to consult with a stucco manufacturer, such as Peerless Stucco in Oakland, for assistance.

To maintain natural or integrally colored stucco, hose it down once a year.

Mass-Produced Siding

Beginning in the 1950s, mass production and mass marketing conspired to alter the appearance of the nation's homes by manufacturing and promoting products to "modernize" the house. Because these items were not designed for any particular architectural style, they are so anonymous that they go with no architectural style at all. They were conceived to look enticing in a magazine ad or display case, but not necessarily on the building itself. Off-the-shelf items available by catalog number instead of by design characteristics became the mainstay of the new pastime called "home improvement." They usually did more harm than good. Consumer-oriented house parts, like flush doors, aluminum frame windows, and plastic ornamentation, are discussed in their respective sections. But **the greatest indignity heaped on American residential architecture was modern siding.**

Mass-produced siding invariably pretends to be something it is not: plastic called "stone," asbestos called "shingles," aluminum shaped like clapboard. The imitation is never convincing because the shallow quality of the siding, its superficial aspect, is so patently obvious. In Oakland, modern siding usually defaces Victorian and Colonial Revival houses, Craftsman and California Bungalows. Often a particular brand of siding covers several houses on the block, altogether obscuring their individuality. This is testimony to a persuasive door-to-door salesman who single-handedly destroyed the charm of the neighborhood.

Asbestos shingles are brittle, tile-like slabs made of mineral fibers. Corrugated and thin, they are 12″ high, and broader than the wood shingles they set out to imitate. Asbestos shingles come in nondescript tones like gray-green, gray-pink and speckles. Aluminum and vinyl siding are extruded pieces of metal and plastic, respectively, shaped like shiplap, but much thinner and lighter weight. Aluminum is prone to dents, is noisy in the rain and tends to peel if not properly anodized. Vinyl reacts with light in the atmosphere, becoming brittle and deteriorated if not treated with an ultra-violet inhibitor. Tarpaper brick is like asphalt roofing in composition. The grout is represented by the gray background, and the bricks by rectangles of overly-bright red, with the texture of sandpaper. Other disastrous substitutes include ground stone or brick crumbs suspended in plastic. A fibrous spray that sheathes the building in a filmy cloud, is the worst atrocity of them all. These products are used singly or in combination to cover an entire house, or just the façade or base.

Do not add modern siding to an old house. Aside from the obvious injustice to the building's architecture, modern siding has other disadvantages. For example, there is the hidden expense of adjusting window casing, drip cap and door trim to compensate for the added wall thickness. Visually, the modern siding replaces "line" with "texture" and makes the building look choppy instead of solid. Breaking the façade up into different surfaces also makes the house look smaller than it actually is. The so-called "random" pattern that phony brick and stone sidings promise turns out to be a monotonously repetitive pattern when spread across a wall of any size. Finally, there is something disturbingly dishonest about using a siding which is bogus in its own right and does not belong to the architecture of the house to boot. No matter what modern siding may save you in future maintenance, it can never compensate for the destruction of the building's character.

Unhappily, the addition of mass-produced siding is a miserable process to reverse. **There is no telling what lies below** without serious excavation. For a lucky few, the original siding is still intact. More likely, however, ornamentation has been sheared off, sections of the original siding have deteriorated, and gaps have been filled in with scrap lumber. Therefore, do not remove modern siding until you have well thought-out plans and sufficient funds to confront whatever the removal reveals. Sample exploration at enough different locations gives an experienced eye some clues to predict the condition of the underlayment. Check above windows and doors, near ground level, near the roof liner, and mid-wall. Schedule it so the house is never without siding during the rainy season.

Removal is basically an un-nailing operation, with the difficulty factor depending on the size of the siding unit. Vinyl and aluminum siding are the largest, and therefore the easiest. Tarpaper brick and compressed stone cover less square footage per unit, and so take more time to undo. Asbestos shingles must be removed one by one. Use a crowbar, or chisel the shingle apart enough to get purchase on the nail, and pry it out with hammer. Asphalt shingles are secured at the lower edge through one thickness only, so work from the top down. A dumpster within tossing distance and decent aim simplify the cleanup operation considerably. Textured spray paint is at the bottom of this list because it takes sandblasting to remove.

The choice between repair or replacement of the underlying siding or shingles takes careful evaluation. Calculate labor and material costs for puttying nail holes, caulking seams and repainting the original, compared to removing the old siding altogether and starting again. The latter often proves more economical, though neither could be considered cheap.

ORNAMENTATION

Generic ornamentation is essential to the architectural character of a house. Victorian styles are renowned for their individualized and ostentatious decorations. Colonial Revival houses are more reserved, with a classical motif. First Bay Tradition houses emphasize the structure itself for its ornamental properties. Period Revival houses have stone, tile and wrought iron to accent their foreign flavor. (Real wrought iron is made of flat strips or solid bars of iron, heated and bent or twisted into shape. Imitation wrought iron, the more common product, is a hollow, extruded rod made of steel or aluminum, with riveted, rather than welded, joints.)

The ornamentation on Victorian and Colonial Revival houses is the focus of this discussion. Familiarize yourself with the vocabulary in the illustrations, and determine whether the parts are made of wood, plaster, or pig iron.

ORNAMENTATION VOCABULARY

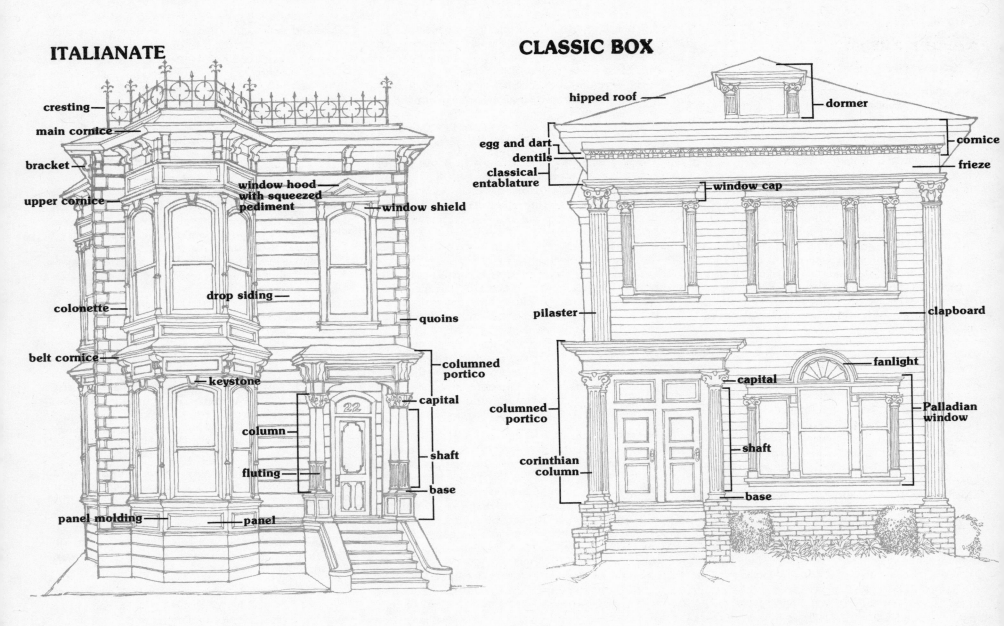

ITALIANATE

- cresting
- main cornice
- bracket
- upper cornice
- window hood with squeezed pediment
- window shield
- colonette
- drop siding
- quoins
- belt cornice
- columned portico
- keystone
- capital
- column
- shaft
- fluting
- base
- panel molding
- panel

CLASSIC BOX

- hipped roof
- dormer
- cornice
- egg and dart
- dentils
- classical entablature
- frieze
- window cap
- pilaster
- clapboard
- columned portico
- capital
- fanlight
- corinthian column
- shaft
- Palladian window
- base

72

QUEEN ANNE

gable

finial

witch's cap

square butt shingles

fascia

flashed glass

turret

scallop or fishscale shingles

bay

sunburst

dentils

patera

non-classical columns

garland

festoon

balustrade

turned baluster

newel post

Wood Ornamentation

Removal

It is often necessary to remove ornamentation in order to repair the underlying structure, or to facilitate repair of the ornament itself. Do so with extreme care and patience. Study the part first to see if it is attached with a toe-nail or a face-nail. Use the broad surface of a prying instrument, like a crowbar, working it in very gradually to loosen the knobs from the supporting post and beams. When space allows, place a piece of wood or corrugated cardboard between the tool and the structural wood to avoid denting the surface as you unnail.

A cedar shingle is a terrific tool for removing ornamentation. It can be split lengthwise so that its width is the same as the part in question, and pressure can be distributed evenly. It is thin enough at its tapered end to allow gradual insertion, and, because it is wood too, it will not scar the ornament the way a metal tool would. The shingle also has a fail safe mechanism: when it bumps into a nail, it will automatically split.

If paint masks the joint between the ornament and its backing, score the seal with a putty knife first. Gently tap the shingle into a crack on an unnailed edge, tapered end first, until the force of the shingle lifts the ornament away from its support. Ease the shingle out, keeping it horizontal. Do not use the shingle as a prying mechanism or it will break off. There should be enough space now to permit purchase on the nail with claw hammer or crowbar. (Refer to Chapter 5, "Trim," for more on removal techniques.)

Put rudimentary labels on the pieces of ornamentation with an indelible marker to help in reassembling the pieces later on. Some people find a sketch a convenient record. Others prefer a "before" photograph. Store the collection of ornamental parts in a vandal-safe and weather-protected place.

Repair

If any of the parts split or crack during the removal process, make them solid again by using a white glue, like Elmer's. Clamp the mended pieces with a vice or with strapping tape.

REMOVING WOOD ORNAMENTATION

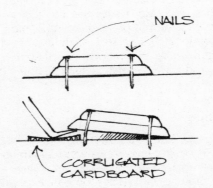

NAILS

CORRUGATED CARDBOARD

WHEN USING A PRYING TOOL, WORK SLOWLY AROUND PERIMETER OF ORNAMENT IN STAGES. APPLY PRESSURE BENEATH NAILS TO PREVENT SPLITTING. SLIP THIN WOOD OR CARDBOARD BENEATH PRYBAR TO CUSHION THE STRUCTURE.

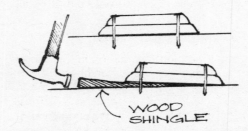

WOOD SHINGLE

AFTER OPENING A SMALL CRACK WITH A PUTTY KNIFE, DRIVE ONE OR MORE PIECES OF WOOD SHINGLE UNDER ORNAMENT, FORCING IT UP. COMPLETE REMOVAL WITH CLAWHAMMER OR PRYBAR, IF NECESSARY.

If a portion of the ornament shows signs of rot, arrest decay with a penetrating epoxy available from a boat supply store. "Git-Rot" encapsulates the wood fibers in resin, and hardens into a resilient adhesive that bonds the wood particles together, making it more plastic than it is wood. A small container costs about $4.25. Marine-Tex, at $2.25, is thicker, like spackle, and can be used to fill in gaps after the fibers have been treated with Git-Rot. For the penetrating epoxy to be effective on a boat surface the wood must be honeycombed with drill holes, no more than 2″ apart. Adjust this requirement accordingly, based on the size and strength of the part in question. These products are available at Marine Parts Company in Oakland.

If the ornamentation came off in one piece, you are spared these preliminaries. Scrape off the ridge of paint, and other loose paint flakes to achieve a fairly even surface. A small scraper suitable for curved surfaces can be purchased for about $3.00 plus blades. Fill any holes and cracks with wood putty.

Replacement

If the ornament is beyond repair, save the pieces and use them as a pattern. Even if the intricate detail is lost in reproduction, combining standard geometric parts in the right proportion is acceptable when the visual relationship among the parts remains the same. For example, perpetuate the appearance of a corner board by using a plain 2″×8″, or keep window trim broad enough by using a 2″×6″. Imply a belt course with a 1″×8″, topped by a 2″×2″ for molding. A rather elaborate proportional reproduction of a cornice is illustrated.

If you prefer an accurate duplication, bring the part, or its pieces, to San Francisco Victoriana, a firm specializing in the reproduction of period house parts. Duplication of a turned baluster in redwood, for example, costs about $10. Or, consult a local carpenter competent in custom work.

Another way to duplicate wood ornament is to make a latex cast, and replace the wood original with a plaster facsimile. Do this in the same manner as making a cast from a plaster original as discussed in the next section.

If you enjoy a hunt, try to locate substitute parts at

PROPORTIONAL REPRODUCTION: A CORNICE

SOME ELEMENTS OF A CLASSICAL CORNICE:
1 EGG & DART PATTERN
2 DENTILS
3 FRIEZE BOARD

PROPORTIONAL RE-CREATION

• UPPER & LOWER BLOCKS ARE CUT FROM STOCK LUMBER

• USE CIRCLE SAW DRILL ATTACHMENT FOR CIRCLES OR JIGSAW FOR OVALS

• USE STOCK MOLDING (QUARTER ROUND, COVE, OR OGEE) UNDER THE FRIEZE BOARD

a salvage yard, like Urban Ore, Ohmega or Berkeley Architectural Salvage. The new acquisitions should match what you've already got, or come in a set. Otherwise the result will be a hodge-podge that would dismay even a Victorian eye. Even though it is more readily available, never use the modern, plastic ornamentation that pretends to look "olde." These products look chintzy because they are more akin to Christmas tree decorations than they are a legitimate reproduction of architectural features of the house.

Re-installation

Treat all the parts, both old and new, with a wood preservative. By doing this before you reassemble, all surfaces receive equal protection. You can be sloppy here. Spread the pieces out on a plastic drop cloth and brush them well. When they are thoroughly dry, and the underlying structure has been repaired, nail the pieces of ornamentation back on.

Tighten pieces of ornamentation which have come loose with screws 4″ or longer. Old wood is pretty tough, so first drill a pilot hole, a little smaller than the screw itself, and lubricate the screw threads with soap. To maintain ornamentation, keep up with caulk in the joints and a decent coat of paint.

Plaster Ornamentation

The yen for sculptural ornamentation in the period of Victorian and Colonial Revival architecture was often satisfied with plaster instead of wood. On the exterior it was used for capitals on classic columns; rosettes, festoons, and garlands at the cornice; and, for oddball accessories on eclectic façades. A striking example is the garish quartet of houses on 16th Street between Market and Brush in Oakland.

Plaster ornamentation is often deteriorated or missing either because the material itself has weathered, or the attachment has failed and the decorative piece has fallen off. If you have at least one original piece of ornamentation left, remove it carefully and make a mold from it to cast replacements for its siblings. Use a special product called Liquid Latex, available at Douglas and Sturgess, San Francisco, for $7.50 a quart or $18.25 a gallon. Follow directions on the

label, brushing on consecutive coats and letting each dry between applications until a rubber mold is formed. Let it cure for a few days, and remove the pattern piece. Cast the mold you have just made with a product suitable for exterior use, like Hydrocal, which costs $19 for a 100-pound sack. If you plan to bolt the new piece to the façade, embed the bolt in the damp Hydrocal before it sets. Otherwise, the plaster ornament can be screwed or nailed to the building, by first drilling holes in the piece with a carbide-tipped masonry bit. For more detailed information on casting plaster reproductions, consult the November, 1985, issue of *The Old-House Journal*.

Prevent the loss of plaster ornament in the future by keeping the seal between ornament and façade well caulked and water-free.

PAINT

A good coat of paint is one of the most important defenses a house has against the elements. It forms a continuous film that sheds

COLOR WHEEL

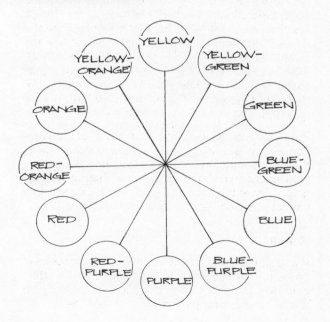

water, and water is the number one source of building damage. Paint is also one of the most important visual choices to make. **The color combination decides the overall appearance of the house, and contributes to the character of the entire neighborhood.**

When to Paint

Trouble signs that point to a new paint job are: alligatoring, checking, cracking and sealing, blistering and peeling and exposed wood. If the paint rubs off like powder, that is quite normal. It is called chalking, and a good outdoor paint is designed to chalk so that rain will wash away the dirt and leave a clean surface. If the paint is dirty or faded but it still provides a protective seal for the wood or masonry underneath, it can be freshened up with a mild detergent. Trim is more vulnerable to weathering than the body of the house, so if the paint shows signs of wear only there, limit the job to repainting the trim this time around. Don't rush repainting, as excessive coats create a thick film that can promote damage.

Do not undertake a paint job until any problems with leaking water have been solved, especially the repair of gutters and downspouts. Many people prefer to leave the paint job for the crowning touch to the rehab process. Others paint early on, finding it easier to get loans and insurance if the house looks presentable. Still others paint the house just to make it look attractive to prospective buyers. As effective as this sales pitch may be, it is somehow unfair to the new owner who has different taste and would like to express it. Even more important is the fact that high quality paint products more than pay for themselves in the long run, but a person about to sell a house has little incentive to use an expensive product. If the buyer does the job instead, he or she would wisely select a top-flight product that would prolong the life of this paint job, and make subsequent paint jobs easier.

The Painting Process

There are four stages to painting the exterior of any house: surface preparation, color selection, paint application and clean-up. Surface preparation is at least half the job, and it is worth every extra day it

PARTS OF A HOUSE TO PAINT

A HOUSE CAN BE DIVIDED INTO FOUR SECTIONS REQUIRING PAINT. A ONE-COLOR PAINT JOB UNIFIES THESE SECTIONS VISUALLY, BUT MAY LOOK DULL ON SOME HOUSE STYLES. DARK COLORS ARE OPPRESIVE WITHOUT THE RELIEF OF LIGHTER-COLORED TRIM, SO SHOULD BE AVOIDED WHEN ONLY ONE COLOR IS TO BE USED.

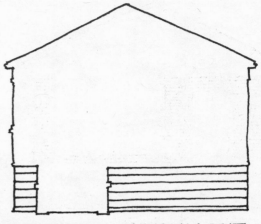

THE BASE. VISUALLY, THE BASE SUPPORTS THE REST OF THE HOUSE. FOR THE HOUSE TO "REST COMFORTABLY" ON THE BASE, THE BASE AND BODY COLORS MUST BE COMPATIBLE. A GOOD CHOICE FOR A THREE-COLOR PAINT JOB IS A DARK SHADE OF THE BODY COLOR FOR BASE AND TRIM, WITH WHITE FOR THE SASH COLOR.

takes because good preparation is the key to the ultimate success and duration of the paint job. Preparation involves:

- removing the loose paint with wire brush, scraper or chemicals (heat is very dangerous)
- fine sanding the scraped surface to feather-out rough edges
- light sanding the smooth base to give it some tooth
- nailing, puttying and caulking, as needed
- cleaning off all dirt and dust.

While lavishing so much attention on the façade and exploring its details with your hands, think

about color selection. Guidelines for this important decision are discussed in detail below.

Paint application is the fun part. Painting involves:

- using a primer as needed
- keeping the paint thoroughly mixed
- brushing or rolling on the color in an orderly way.

On single-story houses it is easier to paint the body of the house first, and then go back and do the trim. On two-story houses, where single-unit scaffolding must be moved with some commotion for each change in location, it is easier to complete both base and trim for a section at a time. Then all that's left

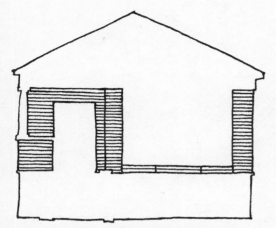

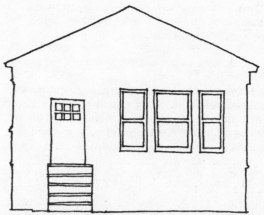

THE BODY. GENERALLY CONSIDERED THE BASIC COLOR OF THE HOUSE, THE BODY MAY HAVE A SURPRISINGLY SMALL SURFACE AREA ON THE STREETSIDE FACADE. IN THE NEOCLASSIC ROWHOUSE EXAMPLE, WHITE OR A LIGHT COLOR WILL EMPHASIZE THE HORIZONTAL SHADOW PATTERN INTENDED BY THE NARROW SIDING.

THE TRIM. TRIMWORK RECEIVES THE SECOND COLOR IN A TWO-COLOR PAINT SCHEME. OFF-WHITE OR LIGHT-COLORED TRIM GOES WITH THE ATTRACTIVE DEEP EARTH TONES. WHEN LIGHT COLORS ARE USED FOR THE BODY, A DARKER VARIANT OF THE BODY COLOR WORKS WELL FOR TRIM.

OPPORTUNITIES FOR MORE COLOR ARE PRESENTED BY WINDOWS, DOORS AND STAIRS. MOVING WINDOW PARTS ARE BEST PAINTED WHITE OR BLACK. WHITE IS PLEASANT SEEN FROM THE INTERIOR AS IT REFLECTS LIGHT INSIDE. STAIRS AND PORCHES ARE TREATED WITH SPECIAL HEAVY-DUTY PAINTS, OFTEN IN A NEUTRAL GRAY. DOORS CAN BE A BRIGHT SPOT, BUT UNLESS YOUR HOUSE IS NEUTRAL (GRAY OR WHITE), PICK A COLOR THAT HARMONIZES WITH BODY AND TRIM.

is clean-up. Refer to reputable home repair books like the *Reader's Digest Complete Do-it-yourself Manual*, and to your local paint dealer, for more detailed instructions on the proper techniques for surface preparation and painting.

The question of paint product selection is summarized in most home repair books. Take advantage of manufacturer's representatives for technical assistance, asking specifically about paint and primer for old wood. Also refer to *The Old-House Journal*, July 1976, on deciphering paint can labels and demystifying the painting process.

The City of Oakland has a special program which offers free paint to eligible property owners. Refer to Chapter 7 for the details.

Color Selection

Paint is the single rehabilitation decision which can unify or destroy neighborhood quality. As a positive influence, color is contagious. It takes only one house to start the trend toward a fresh coat for the whole block. As a potential threat, an odd color selection is like a leper in the local environment. Blending or contrasting colors with

nearby buildings is as critical as choosing compatible colors for the house itself. In case of doubt, assume a low profile. If, for example, the street scene is pastel, stick with pastel. This is especially important if adjacent houses share architectural style because harmony is so easily achieved that cacophony is difficult to forgive. Where there is little landscaping to soften the masses, and few trees to filter view of the façade, considerate color selection is even more critical.

Use the paint palette to help a house assert *its* authentic personality, rather than your own. As with other aspects of appearance, **the historically correct choice is an attractive and safe one.** The further you stray from historical guidelines, the greater the chance of downgrading the general appeal and resale value of your home. For those determined to try something different, or for greater assurance in selecting the precise hue, tone and value for a historical palette, here are some hints.

First, **look at the house as a whole.** Study its shape and proportion, the arrangement of the parts and their relationship to one another. Does the building resemble a square, an upright rectangle, or a rectangle on its side? Discover the role the roof plays. Does it cloak the building or is it out-of-sight? See if the house sits on a base, like a pedestal, or if it is squat on the ground. Appreciate its texture. Is it appliqued and three-dimensional or flat and plain? These observations will make your eye informed enough to proceed with color selection.

Urban houses are seen predominantly from the street, so the façade is the starting point for a color selection equally suitable to the rest of the building. Think of the façade as a picture, a composition of solids and voids. The walls appear as light planes punctured by the dark holes of the windows. The change from one material to another creates a dividing line on the façade, as does the sequence of stories and the bands of ornamentation. **A successful color combination unifies the architectural elements into a single picture, without denying the distinctive features lively emphasis.**

Decide how much of the façade is actually paintable. There is probably a lot more window space than you thought. Do *not* paint: stained shingles, brick, stone, unpainted stucco, untreated wrought iron, the wood stickwork on Brown Shingle or Craftsman houses, the chimney, the roofing, or any of the modern "miracle" sidings. *Do* paint: the base, the trim, the window moldings, the moving parts of wood windows and the previously painted wood siding or stucco body of the house.

VALUE

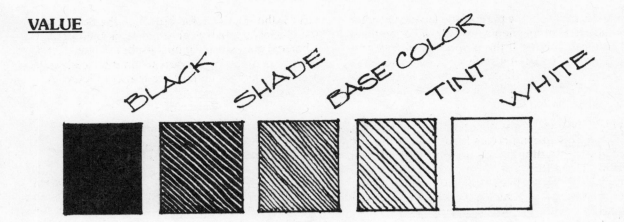

To most people, **color means hue,** an arc of the rainbow. Pure hues are so vivid that they have unpredictable effects when used in their basic state, so the hue is modified. The hue is made into a darker color by the addition of black, and this is called a **shade**. The hue is made into a lighter color by the addition of white, and this is called a **tint**. Or, the hue is muted by the addition of its complement, the hue opposite it on the color wheel, and this is called an **earth tone**. Browns are also made by mixing complementary colors.

Limit the number of different colors on the house to three at most, for economy and appearance both. As a rule of thumb, pick a light or muted color for the body, a compatible darker shade for the base, trim and window moldings, and white for the moving parts of the wood-frame windows. For a two-color scheme, paint the base, body and moving parts of the windows a single light or muted color, and the trim a compatible darker shade. The third option is always a single color for all parts, and once again a light or muted color is the safest choice.

Do not use extremely bright, pure colors, the kind that detergent advertisements describe as "reddest red, greenest green, bluest blue." They're fine for laundry, but disastrous for architecture.

Dark colors are used to advantage to make small areas more intense. For expansive walls, deep earth tones are acceptable because they visually reinforce the feeling of structural stability. Dark colors are also useful as a field for limited amounts of ornamentation painted off-white. There are as many off-whites as there are colors. The one to select for trim is an extremely light tint of the basic hue used on the body of the house. Do not pick a dark color for a single-color paint job.

Light colors do justice to large planes, like the side of a stucco bungalow, because the color reduces the massiveness of the wall. Pastels are tints of pure hues, and are popular in warm climates because they absorb less heat and are cool to look at. The widespread use of pastels on stucco buildings is one reason Oakland has been called "A Mediterranean City." Among pastels, do not use lavender or aqua. While light colors are the safest choice, by the same token then are often the dullest. Do not be shy about the use of contrast to enliven a "blah" façade.

White paint is the best selection for formal building styles whose walls are visually contained around the edges. The clapboard walls on Colonial Revival styles are contained by architectural features: the pilasters on the sides and the pediment on top. The smooth stucco walls on Mediterranean houses are capped by a change in texture; the rough terra cotta of the red tile roof. Both styles look best painted a crisp white.

Contrast is created when dark and light colors are used together, and it certainly perks up a paint job when used in a limited way. Window moldings and doors are good opportunities to create contrast. If contrast is misused, the parts of the façade separate into independent elements, instead of cooperating for a unified picture. If the proportion of light and dark planes is equal, the surfaces seem to advance and recede at will. If contrast is misapplied to ornamentation, the building looks as if it is wrapped in bands, or branded.

A better way to define the form of protuberant parts than contrasting colors is to rely on **a light background to display the shadows.** That is one reason why the clapboard siding on Colonial Revival houses looks best painted white. The profile of the overlapping boards creates a shadow line that is an intentional foil for the building's box shape.

Dangerous **combinations to avoid** are the use of warm and cold colors together, like red and blue, and the use of two colors of the same intensity, like the lights in a traffic signal.

Some highly ornamented Victorian houses are lavished with custom paint jobs in four or five, even six colors, applied in topographic fashion. Although this drama may be an unwarranted extravagence in your budget, the better examples demonstrate how hue, tone and value are used to highlight the architectural features in a unified way. Take a ride by the Camron-Stanford House in Lakeside Park, the DeFremery House in West Oakland or Peralta-Hacienda in Fruitvale. To view an excellent collection of Victorian color schemes condensed in a two-block area of downtown Oakland, walk through Preservation Park. The palettes were selected by REHAB RIGHT illustrator and co-author Blair Prentice.

Notice that the lively effect is achieved, not with vivid colors, but by **careful manipulation of tints and shades.** For example, on the Remillard House, the Queen Ann just within the 13th Street gate to Preservation Park, red and green are the predominant hues, a combination with the potential for garish results. But the hues are not pure, the complementary colors play off one another subtly and the effect is rich, not loud. The body colors, medium and light olive, are defined by a darker green and enlivened by terra cotta sash and cream accents. The whole ensemble is anchored securely to the ground on a base of dark Venetian red.

It is unreasonable to change the roof of the house

just for the sake of color, but when the time comes for re-roofing, color is an important consideration. Charcoal gray is usually the best bet. The eye tends to disregard the roof and focus on the façade anyway, so select a neutral tone that contributes to a low profile.

WINDOWS

More mistakes are made in the rehabilitation of windows than any other part of the house. And because windows are so very important to the appearance of the house—they are the eye to its architectural soul, so to speak—a bad decision on the window has disastrous effects on the appearance of the entire building, and even the neighborhood.

TYPES OF WOODFRAME WINDOWS

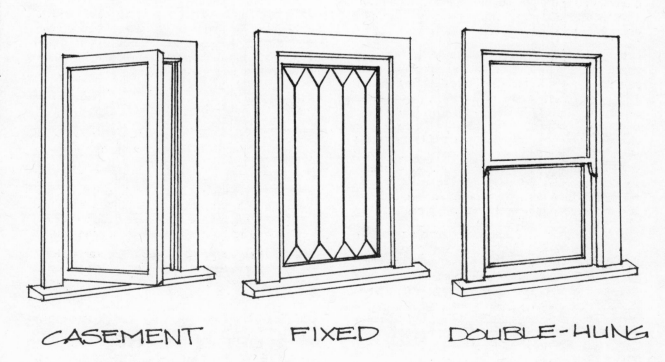

CASEMENT   FIXED   DOUBLE-HUNG

Design

Operationally, there are three kinds of windows appropriate to Oakland house styles. The **double-hung window** opens with an up-and-down movement. It has an upper, outside sash that slides down, and a lower, inside sash that slides up, a design that facilitates air circulation even when there is only one window in a room. The window movement is controlled by cord or chains on pulleys with weights, as illustrated, or by a more modern spring mechanism concealed in the side jamb. Double-hung windows are always made of wood, and belong on Victorian and Colonial Revival houses, the Brown Shingle, Craftsman and California Bungalows.

With age, **double-hung windows are subject to poor fit, broken sash cords, and fouled pulleys. These bothersome defects are surprisingly** simple to repair, and hardly justify the costly switch to an aluminum system just to avoid the problem. All it takes is a hammer, screwdriver, chisel and patience. The Sunset book, *Basic Home Repairs*, offers instructions for correcting problems common to double-hung windows.

The **casement window** opens with an outward movement. It is attached to the frame by hinges along its vertical edge. Wood casement windows came into use with the Craftsman movement around 1905, and their popularity continued with the Prairie School and Period Revival. They seldom need repair beyond occasional tightening of loose hinges and balky sliding rods. Steel casement windows, mass-produced for Wartime Tract houses, are operated by a lever or worm gear, rather than manually like their wood predecessors. These gears sometimes require adjustment, and *Basic Home Repairs* explains how to do it. Also consult *Preservation Brief 13: The Repair and Thermal Upgrading of Historic Steel Windows*, available from the National Park Service (see Chapter 7).

The **fixed window** is a pane of glass enclosed in a rectangular or specially shaped wood frame that does not open. Like a movable window, its dimensions are carefully proportioned to the mass of the house and to the other features on the façade. Fixed windows, either plain or made of stained or leaded glass, are found on all styles. They pose few repair problems, although the leaded bars in leaded and stained glass may become bowed and require straightening. Consult the *Yellow Pages* under "Glass —Stained and Leaded." The Oakland Office of Parks and Recreation conducts stained glass classes at Studio One.

DOUBLE-HUNG WINDOW: DOS AND DON'TS

ORIGINAL DOUBLE-HUNG WINDOW (ITALIANATE).
   DO LEAVE IT INTACT OR REPAIR OR REPLACE IN-KIND. WINDOWS ARE A KEY INTEGRAL PART OF THE ARCHITECTURE.

OPENING BLOCKED DOWN TO ACCEPT STOCK ALUMINUM FRAME.
   DON'T DO THIS. IT LOOKS MAKESHIFT AND MARS THE PROPORTIONS AND APPEARANCE OF THE HOUSE.

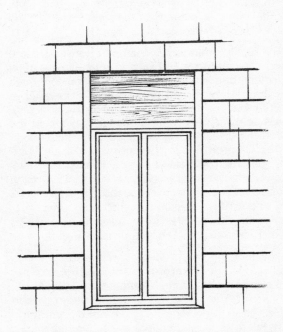

ORNAMENTATION REMOVED TO PUT ON ASBESTOS SHINGLES.
   NEVER DO THIS. TOTAL LOSS OF VISUAL INTEREST RESULTS

PARTS OF A DOUBLE-HUNG WINDOW

DOUBLE-HUNG WINDOW FRAME DETAIL

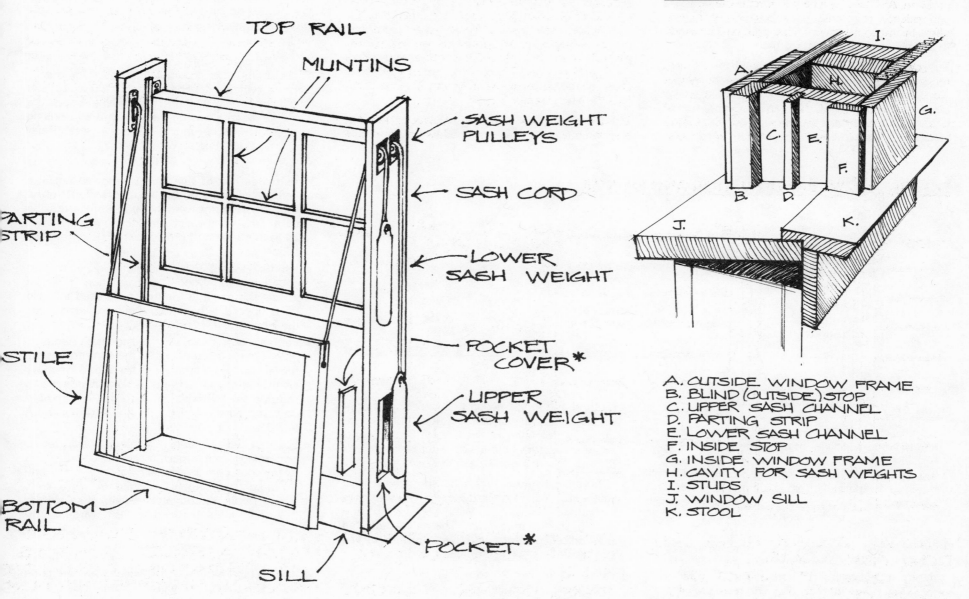

TOP RAIL

MUNTINS

SASH WEIGHT PULLEYS

SASH CORD

PARTING STRIP

LOWER SASH WEIGHT

POCKET COVER *

STILE

UPPER SASH WEIGHT

BOTTOM RAIL

POCKET *

SILL

A. OUTSIDE WINDOW FRAME
B. BLIND (OUTSIDE) STOP
C. UPPER SASH CHANNEL
D. PARTING STRIP
E. LOWER SASH CHANNEL
F. INSIDE STOP
G. INSIDE WINDOW FRAME
H. CAVITY FOR SASH WEIGHTS
I. STUDS
J. WINDOW SILL
K. STOOL

* NOT FOUND ON ALL DOUBLE-HUNG WINDOWS

WINDOW PRICES

	3' × 5'	3' × 4'
WOOD WINDOWS		
Double-Hung (one-over-one)		
Sash and Frame	$175	$170
Sash Only	$ 79	$ 75
Used sash	$ 10	$ 10
Casement (one next to one)		
Sash and Frame	$165	$146
Sash Only	$ 64	$ 56
Used sash	$ 15	$ 15
ALUMINUM WINDOWS		
(Includes Screens)		
Single Hung		
Clear Aluminum	$ 80	$ 68
Bronze Anodized	$102	$ 87
Sliding		
Clear Aluminum	$ 74	$ 62
Bronze Anodized	$ 95	$ 79
Casement		
Clear Aluminum	$ 90	$ 79
Bronze Anodized	$112	$100

Notes on WINDOW PRICES

1. Use this chart after evaluating the extent of damage to wood windows. In many cases, the frame is still in acceptable condition, or needs only a sill repair. Sash (the movable glass portion), can be purchased separately from the frame at window companies or salvage yards. The price of new wood sash can be lower than the price of new aluminum windows.

2. Wood sash and frame show a great range in price because there are optional features available, design subtleties and different methods of manufacturing. When investigating, find out if the price includes any or all of the following: coil spring or spring balances, primer, screens, trim, or glazing. What kind of joinery holds the window together? Mortise and tenon is the traditional and strongest method and a doweled connection is quite adequate, but nailing or stapling does not promise longevity. What type of glue is used? Conventional white carpenter's glue is not water resistant. Ask for glue that is rated for exterior use.

3. The variety in prices shows that shopping around really pays off. Consult the *Yellow Pages* under "Windows—Wood" or "Windows—Metal," and ads in shelter magazines. The price indicated here reflects prices quoted in a telephone survey of several Bay Area companies.

4. According to The Enterprise Foundation Rehab Work Group, window replacement has the lowest payback in terms of improved property value of the 20 most common home improvements. Are you *certain* that those wood windows can't be repaired?

Repair and Replacement

Two problems plague all three window types: broken glass and rotted wood frames. The technique for replacing window glass is illustrated in the section "Front Door."

Wood frames are subject to deterioration from years of use, from water accumulation and from insects. Decay is evidenced by brown or black discoloration near joints or by rippling of the paint. Check the inside for water stains on the sash and sill resulting from condensation running down the glass. (Refer to the section "Porch: Wood Damage" for other danger signs of rot and termites.)

Four times out of five, the verdict to replace an entire window is due to a rotted sill only. Save the cost of replacement by repairing the sill in any one of several ways. The idea in all of them is to fill in the holes and provide drainage toward the outside.

- Use penetrating epoxy marine products, as described under "Wood Ornamentation." Git-Rot arrests the rot, and Marine-Tex is used to build up a slope that will drain. Follow directions on the label.

- For holes and cracks, use the carpenter's standbys. First, scrape away all loose material, then soak the sill with a penta product, like Wood Good, to kill the rot-causing organisms. Give it a day, then saturate the sill with linseed oil. Wait another day, and fill the cracks and holes with putty. A few days later, prime and paint it.

- For bad deterioration, use plastic wood, or its homemade counterpart, a paste of sawdust and waterproof glue, like Sears resorcinol. Apply one or more coats, not more than 1/4" at a time, letting it dry thoroughly between applications. Make sure the new wood slopes toward the outside. Sand, prime and paint.

- For irreparable deterioration, replace the sill entirely. Remove the old sill, being careful not to cut or chisel into the stool, which is the ledge on the room-side of the window frame. Use the old sill as a pattern for the new. Sand it, and bevel the edges slightly to ease installation. Anchor the sill to the window casing with brads, sinking the heads slightly below the surface of the wood.

Putty the holes and seal with shellac. Caulk the joint between sill and frame. Finally, prime the wood and apply two coats of outdoor paint. (Refer to the illustration "How to Replace Door Threshold.")

If the entire window frame is rotted beyond repair, replace it with the same kind of window as the original. **Do not use aluminum frame windows.** Although they are less expensive than wood windows, they cause unbelievable harm to the appearance of the house. On any type of window, the pane of glass looks black when seen from a short distance, say across the street. On a wood window, the frame and trim are flat and broad, providing a visual transition between the glass and the siding. The aluminum window eliminates the valuable window frame, and substitutes instead a shiny filament of extruded metal. The result looks like a grotesque eye without eyelashes.

The shape of prefabricated aluminum windows is not the shape of the window openings on older houses. The Victorian Italianate, for example, was designed for a tall, narrow window. Because the standard aluminum product is not tall enough, the homeowner is forced to block down the window opening. To add insult to injury, this is usually done in a tacky manner, with a scrap of plywood or artificial siding. Similarly, the upper sash of Italianate windows is often curved or indented, and the rectangular aluminum frame just will not adapt.

Another visual problem with aluminum windows is the pattern of the panes. The division of window glass into panes is a conscious design decision integral to the architectural style of the house. On Victorian houses, the double-hung window is the one-over-one style; on Colonial Revival, the six-over-one and eight-over-one arrangement is quite common. Aluminum frame windows do not offer this option, and in fact are designed just the opposite way. The window is divided vertically by a reflective metal strip, instead of being divided horizontally by a substantial wood muntin.

A functional problem of aluminum-style windows is that they are not designed for optimum ventilation. With only a single opening, the air does does not circulate unless there is another open window across

DOUBLE-HUNG WINDOW WEATHERSTRIP PLACEMENT

- THIS SKETCH ILLUSTRATES THE PLACEMENT OF SPRING-METAL WEATHERSTRIPPING. FOAM RUBBER AND VINYL TYPES ARE ALSO AVAILABLE.

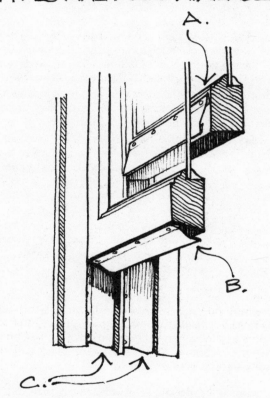

A. INSIDE OF UPPER SASH BOTTOM RAIL (SEALS GAP BETWEEN TOP AND BOTTOM SASH WHEN WINDOW IS CLOSED)

B. BOTTOM OF LOWER SASH

C. SASH CHANNELS (DO NOT COVER PULLEYS)

the room and a decent breeze. Even so, this can prove quite drafty. In contrast, double-hung windows are smartly designed so the top and bottom can be open at the same time. Without a draft, the warm, stale, room air rises and flows out the upper opening, while the cool, fresh air is drawn in at the bottom.

If aluminum frame windows look so miserable on Oakland's older houses, why are there so many of them? The answer is money. There is no arguing the fact that aluminum windows are less expensive to buy, but there is some debate about whether the saving is worth the value lost in the house's integrity and resale attraction.

Instead of looking at the price of an individual window replacement, evaluate the cost in the context of the total rehabilitation project. Say, for example, there are ten double-hung windows on a California Bungalow. Of these, seven are too rotted to repair, two have broken sash cords and one a rotted sill. You are tempted to replace all ten with aluminum frames. Clear aluminum frame windows cost about 45% of the price of a comparably-sized wood window, or the difference of about $95 for a medium-sized window, so replacing all ten with aluminum instead of wood saves you $950. Say your total rehabilitation budget is $15,000. The $950 is only 6% of the total package, a fairly marginal difference economically considering the visual disaster that would otherwise result. In the example, the right way to save money is to repair the sash cords and the rotted sill, instead of replacing three full window assemblies. Prices of comparative-sized windows are summarized in the adjoining chart.

If you must use aluminum, there are compromises which can reduce its negative aspects to some degree.

- Keep wood windows on the front of the house. Replace side or backyard windows with aluminum. This keeps the street scene intact.

- Use anodized aluminum with an integral color, like bronze, or a baked-on color, like white. This minimizes reflectivity, and also cuts down on pitting of the aluminum surface from salts in our marine environment. Anodized aluminum windows cost a third more per unit than clear.

- Leave wood window trim in place.

WINDOW SECURITY: VULNERABILITY OF ALUMINUM FRAMES

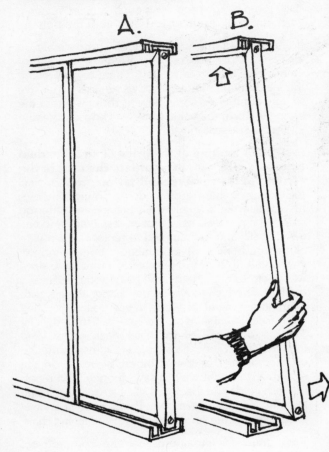

MANY ALUMINUM WINDOWS ARE SUBJECT TO EASY REMOVAL BY INTRUDERS. THE INSIDE (SLIDING) SASH FITS LOOSELY IN ITS TOP CHANNEL (A.) AND CAN BE REMOVED BY LIFTING UP WHILE PUSHING IN (B.)

• Use single-hung aluminum windows because they resemble double-hung wood windows. Never use the sliding type.

Avoid the temptation to install aluminum windows by properly maintaining the wood frame windows you already have. Keep the joints caulked, the holes puttied and the paint protective.

Energy

Heat loss and heat gain occur at the windows. Windows with southern exposures warm a space, while those facing north rob it of warmth. **Three parts of the window contribute to heat transmission:**

• **Frame and sash.** Wood is a better insulator than metal, so wood windows do not lose heat as rapidly as aluminum ones do.

• **Glass.** Conventional glass transmits heat rapidly. Double-glazed panes minimize heat transfer by about half, but cost over twice as much as regular windows. Consider double-glazed glass for very large windows with exposure to extreme weather conditions.

• **Leakage.** Air leaks between sash and frames, between the frame and the wall surface, and where the sash rails meet. Weatherstripping provides a tight seal, eliminating drafts, and is quite simple to install.

Window treatments for energy conservation are addressed in *Retrofit Right: How To Make Your Old House Energy Efficient*, the sequel to this book.

Security

Aluminum windows are much less secure than wood frame windows. Aluminum windows fit so loosely in their frames that they can be removed completely by lifting the window up and pushing in. Wood frame windows can be safely secured with a key-operated window lock. Manually-operated locks are less effective because they are easily dispensed with by any intruder who is willing to break a small area of glass and reach in. If you are considering window bars, the Oakland Housing Code requires that bedroom window bars have a proven interior release mechanism for emergency exits.

WINDOW SECURITY: KEY LOCK FOR DOUBLE-HUNG WINDOWS

ROOF

A leak-proof roof is essential to the longevity of the entire house. If water enters the building it will decay the wood structure and damage exterior siding and interior finishes. Roof repair is an extremely important basic step in rehabilitation.

Roofing

Evaluate the condition of the roofing material by climbing a ladder, taking necessary safety precautions, and checking for:

• missing, broken, warped or worn-out shingles or tiles on a pitched roof

- bubbles, separations or cracking in the asphalt or roofing felt on a flat roof
- loose flashing, especially around chimney and valleys
- sagging ridges
- protruding nail heads.

From the attic, examine the underside of the roof, looking for:
- rays of sunlight
- water stains on the rafters or roof sheathing
- sagging rafters.

Minor leaks in the roof can be repaired with an asphalt roofing compound and liquid roof coating. However, every roofing material has a finite life span, so when the roof starts to leak because of general material failure, it's time to install new roofing.

The selection of new roofing material should take visual and functional considerations into account. Functionally, the questions of durability, slope, fire resistance and cost are important. Visually, the selection relates to the shape of the roof, the amount of roof surface seen from eye-level and the material historically appropriate to the architectural style. When selecting roof color, choose a neutral hue, like charcoal gray, which does not call attention to itself and which sets off, rather than repeats, the exterior paint scheme.

In addition to the home repair books mentioned elsewhere in this manual, an excellent source for roof information is the *Roofers Handbook* by Craftsman Book Company, available at the Oakland Public Library.

If you are considering the addition of a skylight, a good time to install one (or more) is when the house is being re-roofed. For more information on skylights, one place to contact is Skylight and Sun, Berkeley.

Vents

Moist, warm air rises to condense in the cooler attic space. **Proper ventilation of the attic is necessary to allow moisture to evaporate and prevent rot and structural damage to the rafters, especially if the attic is insulated.** Locate and

SOFFIT VENT

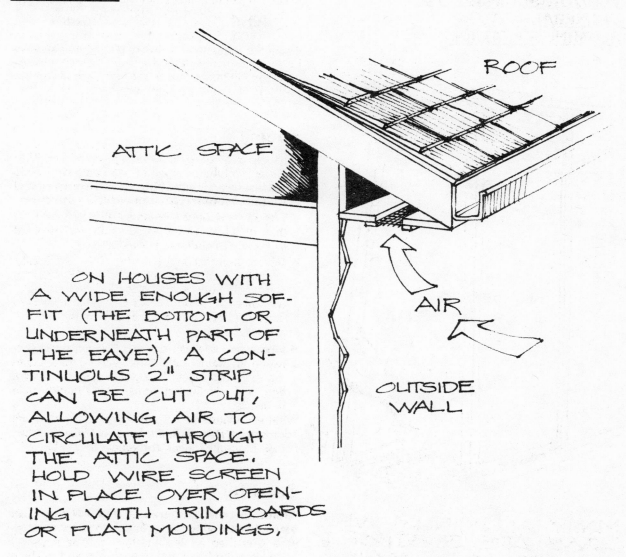

ON HOUSES WITH A WIDE ENOUGH SOFFIT (THE BOTTOM OR UNDERNEATH PART OF THE EAVE), A CONTINUOUS 2" STRIP CAN BE CUT OUT, ALLOWING AIR TO CIRCULATE THROUGH THE ATTIC SPACE. HOLD WIRE SCREEN IN PLACE OVER OPENING WITH TRIM BOARDS OR FLAT MOLDINGS,

reactivate the original vents. The net area for the openings should be about 3% of the ceiling area of the room below. If the original vents are too small or are not arranged to permit adequate air circulation, additional vents may be added.

On architectural styles with an overhang—like Queen Anne, Colonial Revival, and Period Revival—vents under the soffit are easy to install, resistant to leaks, and well-camouflaged.

For buildings with no overhang and inadequate attic ventilation, consider a roof-mounted ventilator. This is a light metal duct with a cap on top which acts like a fan when blown by the wind, and sucks air out of the attic. Prior to cutting the hole for installation,

PORCH ROOF FLASHING

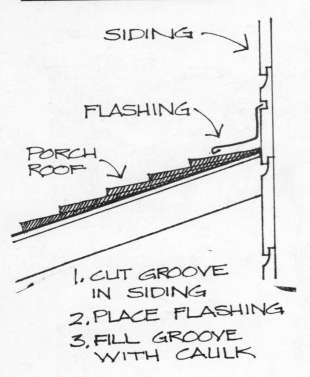

SIDING

FLASHING

PORCH ROOF

1. CUT GROOVE IN SIDING
2. PLACE FLASHING
3. FILL GROOVE WITH CAULK

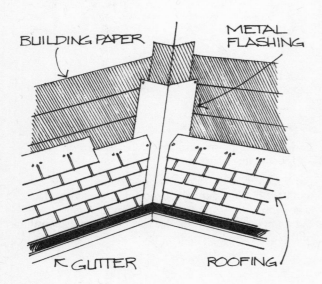

BUILDING PAPER

METAL FLASHING

GUTTER

ROOFING

make sure the roofing is in good enough condition to be sealed up again. **Locate the roof ventilator so it will not be noticeable from the street,** and as far away as possible from the existing vent to ensure air circulation. Paint the vent a neutral color.

Cutting new vent holes into a major façade of the house is the alternative with the greatest visual risk. Carefully consider the style of the house and locate the vent so it blends in with the other architectural features.

Flashing

Flashing is a strip of thin gauge sheet metal which prevents water from entering the building by covering the exposed joints and diverting the water to less vulnerable areas. Modern flashing is typically galvanized steel. On older buildings, the flashing was either copper, lead, terne-metal or zinc alloy. **It is often badly deteriorated, rusted through, or missing altogether.** This is an obvious source of serious leakage and should be corrected early in the rehabilitation process.

Flashing is found at:
- roof valleys, ridges, hips and changes in pitch
- eaves, gutters and parapets
- door and window openings
- expansion joints
- the juncture of building and porch
- vertical projections through the roof, like skylights, vent pipes, chimneys and dormers
- the meeting of building and ground.

At vertical projections, two pieces of flashing are required: the base flashing which keeps water away from the joint, and a cap- or counter-flashing which keeps water from sneaking behind the base flashing. Only one piece of flashing is required for valley, ridge, eave, window and door locations.

To repair small holes in flashing, cut a piece of sheet metal 1″ larger than the hole on all sides. Coat the hole and immediate area with roof cement. Apply the sheet metal to the hole and press for several minutes.

If the holes are widespread, or the flashing is generally deteriorated, replace it. Consult the *Reader's*

GOOD AND BAD DOWNSPOUT LOCATIONS

THE HOUSE ON THE LEFT HAS A DOWNSPOUT LOCATED ON THE SIDE, FAR ENOUGH BACK TO AVOID INTERFERENCE WITH THE PORTICO. THIS IS A GOOD SOLUTION.

THE HOUSE ON THE RIGHT HAS TWO DOWNSPOUT PROBLEMS. A DOWNSPOUT INTERRUPTS THE VISUALLY IMPORTANT STREET FACADE, DIVIDING IT IN TWO. ALSO, IT IS PAINTED A CONTRASTING COLOR, EMPHASIZING THE DIVISION.

Digest Complete Do-it-yourself Manual for instructions. When installing flashing, be certain that all the nails and clips are the same or a compatible metal with the flashing, or galvanic action will result. When dissimilar metals are in contact, a chemical reaction occurs and causes the deterioration of one of the two metals. For galvanized steel flashing, use zinc-coated fasteners.

On houses with a parapet wall, be certain the flashing extends at least 12″ up the parapet, since this area is very susceptible to water accumulation from clogged gutters. On houses with a front porch roof, be sure there is adequate flashing to protect the vulnerable joint between porch roof and house siding.

DRIP STRIP

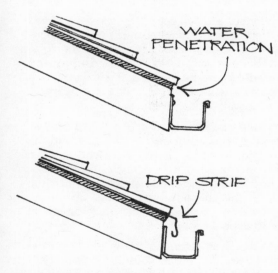

WATER PENETRATION

DRIP STRIP

CAPILLARY ACTION CAN DRAW WATER BETWEEN SHINGLES AND SHEATHING CAUSING DAMAGE TO BOTH. INSERTION OF A DRIP STRIP PREVENTS THIS WATER DAMAGE.

Gutters and Downspouts

Gutters collect the water that drains off the roof and direct it to the downspouts. Victorian, Colonial Revival and some First Bay Tradition houses were equipped with gutters made of redwood. They often had a decorative shape, and became a part of the ornamentation. If the redwood gutter has rotted, but the decay is limited, repair is feasible. Scrape out the rotted material with a sharp tool, until solid wood is reached, and fill the scar with wood putty. You could also try the marine products described in the section on ornamentation. If the rot is more serious but localized, it is possible to remove the bad segment and splice in a new piece to match. Localized rot is common around downspouts or at joints between gutter sections. If the rot is widespread, a new gutter is necessary. One place to find redwood gutters is at Blackman Lumber, Oakland. The 4″ × 4″ size costs $3.50 a linear foot.

Wood gutters should be painted every three years. On the inside, use two coats of asphalt roof paint thinned to a brushing consistency with one part thinner to four parts paint. On the outside, use two coats of appropriate house paint.

Galvanized gutters are available at almost any building supply store, and cost under $10 for a 10′ section of the 4″ size. Reduce the offensive glare of the metal, and help it to harmonize with the architectural style by painting it with a neutral matte finish. Aluminum gutters with a white or bronze finish cost $1.35 a linear foot. Whichever material you select, **choose a gutter shape that relates to the original design in size and cross-section** for better water control and optimum appearance.

Queen Anne houses with towers pose the special problem of curved gutters. Because of the difficulty of replacement, it is not unusual to see towers with partial gutters only, and the deteriorated ornamentation and structure that result. Curved gutters are custom-made out of sheetmetal by sheetmetal contractors for about $10 a linear foot. Consult the *Yellow Pages* under that heading.

Many Brown Shingle houses and Craftsman Bungalows were built without gutters at all. This can cause soil erosion below the roof overhang, and premature blistering of paint on the wall that faces

MAYBECK DOWNSPOUT

ROOFING MATERIALS

Material (In order of durability)	Minimum Slope (Change in vertical distance to change in horizontal distance)	Associated Architectural Styles	Fire Rating
Slate	4" in 12"	Provincial	Non-combustible
Clay Tile	4" in 12"	Mediterranean	Non-combustible
Tar & Gravel	Flat	Prairie, Mediterranean	Non-combustible
Wood Shakes	3" to 6" in 12"	Wartime Tract	Combustible unless fire-rated
Wood Shingles	3" to 6" in 12"	Original to Victorian, Colonial Revival and Craftsman	Combustible unless fire-rated
Composition Shingles (asphalt)	2" to 3" in 12"	Preferred substitute for wood shingles on Victorian, Colonial Revival and Craftsman	Non-combustible
Roll Roofing	2" to 3" in 12"	Budget substitute for composition shingles	Non-combustible

the prevailing wind. If these problems arise, consider adding gutters that are sympathetic to the architectural style.

Check downspouts for leaks, especially at joints, at the gutter connection, and anywhere the downspout is not vertical. If the downspout empties directly onto the ground, place splashblocks at the outflow to break the fall of the water and minimize erosion around the foundation. Use brick, stone, or a pre-cast concrete product, and slope it away from the house. The downspout must not be connected to sewer hoppers or sanitary sewer systems.

When adding a downspout, locate it as inconspicuously as possible, and paint it the same color as the wall behind. The corner, side and back of the building offer much better camouflage than the face. On the other hand, Bernard Maybeck, the most famous Bay Area architect of the Craftsman period, designed custom downspouts as a positive feature of the façade, demonstrating that functionalism and good architecture are inseparable.

Eave, Fascia, and Soffit

The eave, fascia and soffit, all found at the upper perimeter of the building, are parts of the roof structure that are capitalized upon for their ornamental opportunities. Made of wood, they are **subject to rot from faulty gutters, leaking roofs, poor design and deferred maintenance.** If, for example, the gutters become clogged with leaves, overflow will soak the fascia. If the situation persists, the fascia, soffit moldings and rafter ends may decay.

Water is prone to penetrate the eaves at the edge of the roofing. To prevent this, install a metal drip strip between the roof sheathing and the roofing material, as illustrated. A 10' length of metal nosing costs $2.50.

Brown Shingle style houses and Craftsman Bungalows have rafters and brackets which extend well beyond the roof and are normally left unpainted. As water rolls off the gutter-less roof onto the exposed rafters, rot is encouraged. The end grain is the most

susceptible spot of all. Inspect the end of the beam to evaluate the extent of damage. (Refer to the section on wood porches for the signs of decay.) If damage is very limited, remove the tip of the rafter. If the rot has permeated the whole piece, graft on a new section, as illustrated in the section on repair of Brown Shingle style porches. Be sure to protect the end grain of all rafters, new or old, with a clear sealer.

Chimney

The chimney was originally built to match the architectural style of the house, and its character should be respected when improvements are made. Italianate chimneys are straight shafts, with simple corbeling at the top. Corbels are cantilevered tiers that look like upside-down steps. Queen Anne chimneys show more variety in shapes, with terra-cotta inlay and extensive corbeling. Colonial Revival chimneys are plain and square, while Craftsman chimneys used clinker brick, with the very top course corbelled out.

Brick chimneys are subject to the same problems of aging mortar and structural cracks as brick foundations. Refer to that section for the danger signs, repair techniques and design criteria. **Unpainted brick should never be painted.** If you are advised that a coating is necessary for structural reasons, use a sealer with a clear finish.

Chimneys are a potential earthquake hazard because bricks tend to pull away from each other and the structure may collapse. If this is a worry, see a contractor about tying the chimney into the floor and roof framing with metal straps to brace the structure. If the chimney projects well above the roof, ask about a series of steel angle-braces to provide additional support.

For instructions on returning the inside of an old chimney to working order, consult the May 1977 and January/February 1985 issues of *The Old-House Journal.* Also refer to the section on fireplaces in Chapter 5.

Chapter 5
INTERIORS

FLOORS

Floors receive an enormous amount of wear and tear. When you set out to improve the floors, make the job last as long as possible by using good materials and careful workmanship.

Subfloor

The subfloor provides a rough base for the finish floor. In all house styles described in REHAB RIGHT except the Wartime Tract, the subfloor is supported by the joists. The oldest type of subfloor consists of wood planks nailed perpendicular to the joists. Beginning in the 1920s, diagonal sheathing was installed at a 45° angle to the joists, instead. Recently plywood sheets have been used as the subfloor.

The subfloor rarely needs attention. However, as wood dries with age, the joists may sag and members of the subfloor may shrink. The loose fit results in squeaks underfoot. To correct squeaks, consult Sunset *Basic Home Repairs* or the *Reader's Digest Complete Do-it-yourself Manual* for the appropriate technique. The other problem with subfloors is just the opposite of dried wood: rot due to excessive water. This occurs primarily in the kitchen near the sink and in the bathroom near bathtub and toilet. The symptoms can be seen in the finished floor: buckling, discoloration or a spongy texture.

When replacing the subfloor, always locate and correct the cause of the problem prior to replacing the damaged wood. Make sure that the thickness of the new wood matches the old, as the standard dimensions of lumber have been reduced over the years. Gaining access to the subfloor requires careful removal of the finish floor and the baseboard, lest these exposed features suffer additional and unnecessary damage. If the subfloor of an entire room requires replacement, plywood is a good selection. It offers low-labor installation costs, resistance to squeaks, and great strength in earthquakes.

In Wartime Tract houses, the subfloor is the very same concrete slab used as the on-grade foundation. Repairs to the subfloor, therefore, consist primarily of patching concrete that has broken due to uneven settlement. A host of chemical products are available to make concrete repair fairly routine. Ask the hardware salesperson which is the best product for the problem you have: emulsified epoxy concrete, epoxy concrete, vinyl patching compound or latext patch. Consult the home repair books mentioned above for tips on handling these materials.

Finish Floor

The finish floor is the floor you walk on. Unlike the rough subfloor concealed beneath it, the finish floor is a formal part of the room, so the original flooring was intentionally selected to match the interior space. Many Victorian houses do not have finish floors because wall-to-wall carpeting was installed directly over the subfloor. Beginning in the 1890s, finish floor was made of wood in standardized strips, odd-lot planks or checkerboard parquet. Hardwood was typically reserved for living room and dining room; softwood was used for bedrooms, pantries and the second story. Since the introduction of resilient floor covering, dozens of synthetic products have been developed and are available both in sheet and tile form. In new tract developments, the Victorian practice of expeditiously attaching wall-to-wall carpeting directly to the subfloor in lieu of a finish floor has been revived. This absence of finish floor in modern houses is one reason why the finish floor in older houses is a distinctive asset worthy of protection and display.

Hardwood Floor

A hardwood floor is one of the most valuable sales items a house can have. Check the real estate listing in the Sunday paper, and you'll see how eagerly hardwood floors are announced as a special bonus. The image of luxury is well deserved. A handsomely finished oak floor lends an air of dignity to a room, a feeling of warmth, and indisputable character. **It is destructive to paint a hardwood floor, and wasteful to cover it with carpeting, yet both techniques are common remodeling shortcuts.** Usually the only thing cut short is the quality of the final appearance. **Hardwood floors should be repaired as necessary, and refinished to reveal the natural grain.** Then, if a softer surface is desired, area rugs can be placed on top, to complement the resource instead of hiding it.

TYPES OF STRIP FLOORING

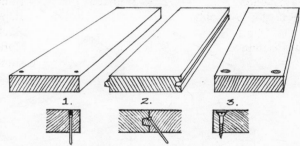

1. COUNTERSUNK FINISH NAILS IN FACE OF BOARD, HOLES FILLED WITH PUTTY,

2. TONGUE & GROOVE BOARDS "BLIND NAILED" THROUGH THE TOUNGE OF EACH BOARD.

3. COUNTERSUNK SCREWS WITH HARD-WOOD PLUGS

In Oakland, hardwood floors are typically made of oak strips. Although dimensions vary considerably, the 2" wide by 5/16" thick size is quite common. The way the sides of the strips are milled determines how the pieces fit together and how they are attached to the subfloor. Strips with a square edge butt up flush against one another, and are secured to the subfloor with facenails or screws. The pattern of nailheads or screw plugs is part of the design of the floor. Likewise, subtle variations in tone and grain in the wood itself contribute to the appeal of the natural texture. Tongue-and-groove strips are inserted one into the next, and fastened to the subfloor with a blind nail through the tongue.

PARTS OF A FLOOR

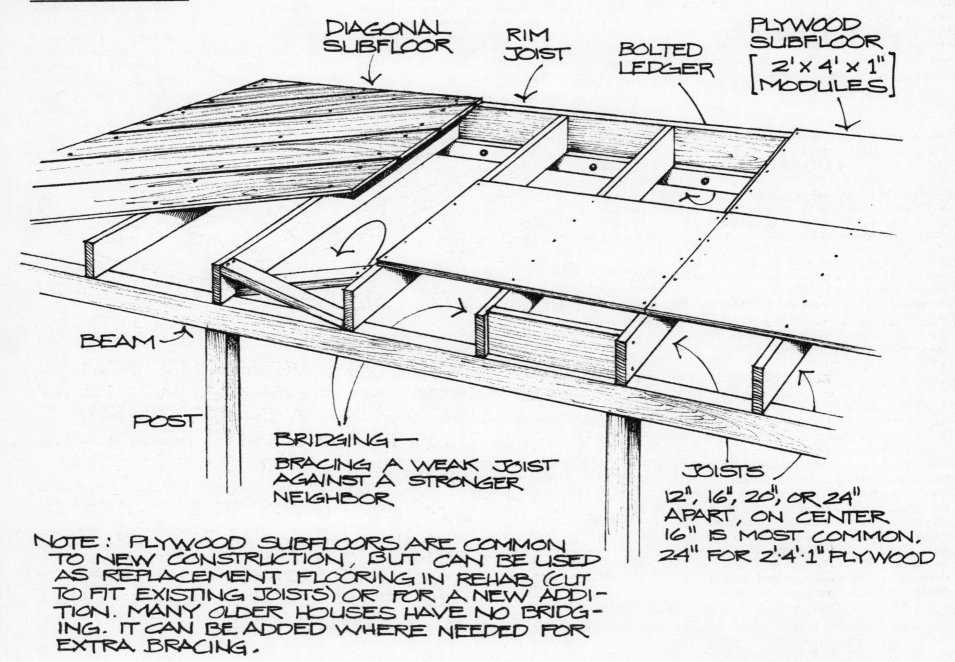

DIAGONAL SUBFLOOR

RIM JOIST

BOLTED LEDGER

PLYWOOD SUBFLOOR [2' x 4' x 1" MODULES]

BEAM

POST

BRIDGING —
BRACING A WEAK JOIST AGAINST A STRONGER NEIGHBOR

JOISTS
12", 16", 20", OR 24" APART, ON CENTER 16" IS MOST COMMON. 24" FOR 2'·4'·1" PLYWOOD

NOTE: PLYWOOD SUBFLOORS ARE COMMON TO NEW CONSTRUCTION, BUT CAN BE USED AS REPLACEMENT FLOORING IN REHAB (CUT TO FIT EXISTING JOISTS) OR FOR A NEW ADDITION. MANY OLDER HOUSES HAVE NO BRIDGING. IT CAN BE ADDED WHERE NEEDED FOR EXTRA BRACING.

Repair. Hardwood floors are remarkably durable, but unfortunately they are not invincible. Damaged wood requires that the boards be repaired or replaced prior to refinishing the surface. Always correct the cause of the damage before making the improvement. The following problems can be easily repaired:

- **Loose boards** can be knocked, nailed or screwed back into place if they are not too badly buckled or warped. Squeaks let you know where the trouble spot is.

- **Water stains** darken hardwood. After eliminating the source of the moisture, a leaky radiator or a potted plant perhaps, the stains can be bleached with a solution of oxalic acid and warm water. Oxalic acid crystals are available without prescription at Longs Drug in Alameda; a four-ounce bottle costs $4.69. Brush the solution on the stain and let it soak into the wood. When it dries, vacuum the crystals and sand the surface by hand or with an orbital sander. If you plan to sand the entire floor anyway, leave the bleaching until you see how much of a stain remains after the major sanding operation.

- **Protruding nails** should be tapped back into the board with a nail set. Otherwise they will chew up the belt on the drum sander, or create a toe-stubbing hazard.

- **Cracks between floorboards** are only an occasional problem in Oakland compared to the East Coast, where the extreme range of temperature combined with high humidity causes floorboards to shrink so dramatically that gaping, drafty spaces are left in between. As the moisture content increases, wood expands, but when abutting floor boards allow no room for expansion, the wood is put into compression and shrinks instead. When dry again, the board is reduced to less than its original width due to the compressive stress. The best way to prevent cracks between first floor boards is with an adequate vapor barrier in the crawl space. (Refer to Chapter 4, "Crawl Space.") Once the cracks have appeared, they can be filled-in with wood putty, sawdust and glue, or wood splines, but because these materials are rigid, and do not adapt top swelling and shrinking of the wood, they may only prove a temporary solution. Felt weather stripping, a more flexible material, can be forced neatly into cracks with a

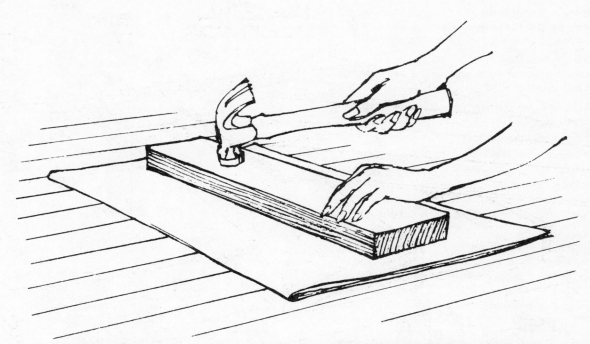

SQUEAKING FLOORS RESULTING FROM LOOSE STRIPS OF FLOORING MAY BE QUIETED BY TAPPING A SHORT LENGTH OF 2×4 (UNDERLAYED WITH NEWSPAPER & PLACED PERPENDICULAR TO THE DIRECTION OF THE FLOORING) WITH A HAMMER. MOVE THE BLOCK IN A SPIRAL PATTERN, CLOSING IN ON THE APPARENT SOURCE OF THE SQUEAK. KEEP THE BOARD ALWAYS AT RIGHT ANGLES TO THE FLOORING. TAP FIRMLY WITHOUT POUNDING.

broad blade knife, and responds to dimensional changes in width of the wood.

Replace. The following problems require **replacement of the damaged or missing wood** with boards to match the rest of the floor:

- severe warping or buckling
- bad nicks or deep scars
- urine stains
- hole left where outmoded floor furnace was removed
- border design interrupted or missing pieces of inlay.

The technique for removing damaged boards and installing the substitutes is discussed in the *Readers Digest Complete Do-it-yourself Manual* and Sunset *Basic Home Repairs.* An electric hand drill is required.

Replacement boards may be available right in the house. Check closet floors, or the portion of an upstairs room where the wall intersects a peaked ceiling and the floor extends onto the eaves. These inconspicuous areas make willing donors. Occasionally salvage yards handle hardwood flooring, but the most convenient source is to buy the boards new. At Blackman Lumber, butt end oak floor boards, 2″ x 5/16″, cost 35¢ a running foot. Also try Golden State Flooring in Brisbane, the supplier many floor contractors use, in the course of comparative shopping. The cost of replacing a few boards will demonstrate the monetary value of the entire floor, and why the investment to refinish it is worthwhile.

Refinish. After the floor is thoroughly repaired, and after all work is completed on the walls and ceiling of a room, it's time to refinish the floor surface. Otherwise loose plaster, splattered paint or dropped tools can be disastrous. During the rehab process, protect the hardwood floor with an old carpet pad and a drop cloth in order to avert unnecessary, additional damage.

A dull finish that does not require a complete overhaul can be rejuvenated with mineral spirits or turpentine. Rub out rough spots with fine steel wool, and use paper towels to distribute and absorb the liquid. **Complete refinishing involves: sanding down the uppermost layer of the wood for a smooth surface, applying a stain if a change**

REMEDIES FOR LOOSE FLOORBOARDS

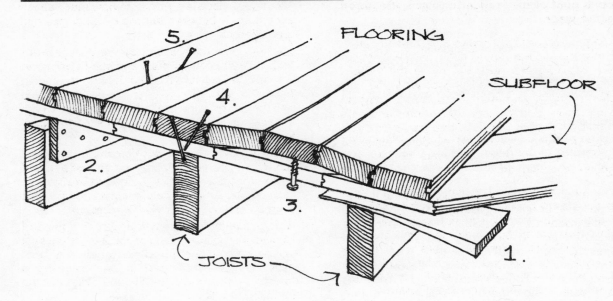

SUBFLOOR

1. IF JUST ONE OR TWO BOARDS ARE LOOSE, WEDGE A SHINGLE BETWEEN THEM AND THE JOIST.

2. IF SEVERAL BOARDS ARE LOOSE, BRACE A 1×4 AGAINST THE SUBFLOOR AND NAIL TO THE JOIST.

FINISH FLOOR

3. LOOSE FINISH FLOORING CAN BE TIGHTENED THROUGH THE SUBFLOOR WITH WOODSCREWS.

4. IF THERE IS A JOIST UNDER A SQUEAKY FLOORBOARD, ANGLE RIBBED FLOORING NAILS INTO JOIST. DRILL PILOT HOLES FIRST.

5. BETWEEN JOISTS, DRIVE 6d FINISH NAILS AT SLIGHTLY OPPOSING ANGLES INTO THE FLOORBOARD CRACKS CENTERED OVER THE SQUEAK. SPACE NAILS ABOUT 6″ APART.

of color is appropriate, and applying a protective coat of oil or plastic to arm the wood against wear.

To prepare for sanding remove all furniture from the room, as well as any drapes or other surfaces which can trap fine dust. Otherwise the waylaid dust may drift back on to the floor while the final sealer is drying and ruin the hard-won smooth surface. Close doors to adjoining rooms and halls in order to contain the dust, and seal them with 2"-wide masking tape. Keep windows open for adequate ventilation. (Here's where double-hung windows really pay off.)

Power sanders are used to remove the old finish and smooth the surface. A drum sander is used for the center of the room; an edger is used around the perimeter where the floor meets the walls. They are available at A-Arrow Rents and Sales at $37 for the pair, plus $2 per belt and 7¢ per disc. An easy-to-follow instruction booklet is included free-of-charge. An average room can be completely sanded in a day by two hard workers.

Sanding is done by making several passes across the floor in different directions. A typical sequence is:

First cut—A coarse sandpaper to break up the old finish (Grit size: 2½-1½)

Second cut—A medium sandpaper to remove scratch marks left by the coarse paper. (Grit size: 1-0)

Third cut—A fine sandpaper to remove scratches left by the medium paper and to leave the floor perfectly smooth. (Grit size: 2/0-5/0)

For more detailed information, a helpful booklet on sanding and refinishing techniques can be ordered free of charge from Pierce and Stevens Chemical Corporation, P.O. Box 1092, Buffalo, New York 14240. Or, consult a home repair manual.

Be attentive to the following:
1. Oak strips that were 5/16" to start with do not allow much leeway for sanding, especially if they've been sanded before. One way to recognize 5/16" boards is by the facenails which are nailed 7" apart. Likewise, tongue and groove floorboards are ruined if they are sanded down to the tongue.

If in doubt, remove a board and see how much "floor" you have left. Also note how much allowance there is between the top of the board and the nailhead.

2. The fine dust that accumulates in the collector bags is highly combustible, and sparks are liable to be sucked up into the bag during the sanding operation. All collector bags should be emptied into boxes or cans and placed outside where they can do no harm should a smouldering spark ignite.

3. Drum sanders draw a lot of current, so make sure when you rent one that the voltage required by the machine matches the output available in your house. A heavy-duty extension cord and a 3-prong plug adapter may be necessary.

4. A drum sander has strength and even a mind of its own, like an automated robot. It takes physical will to control one. To avoid serious damage, never let the sander rest in one place for a fraction of a second or it will grind a crater in the middle of the floor.

5. If you removed linoleum in order to get at the hardwood, additional steps are needed to clean off the mastic and paste before sanding begins. (Refer to the section "Asbestos" in Chapter 6, and to the January 1977 issue of The Old-House Journal.)

6. Clean-up after sanding is critical to the success of the finish. Vacuum the floor, baseboards, window sills, bookshelves, and everything in the room that could possibly sequester dust.

After sanding, **the color of the floor can be left as is or made darker by the use of stain.** Remember that even a clear finish without stain will make the floor look darker than it does as raw wood. As this is difficult to envision, test it by spreading mineral spirits (benzine) or turpentine over several square feet. The wood will have about the same tone when wet as it will when finished. If you decide to use stain, don't forget that stain appears darker on a small sample than it will look on the floor. An overly colorful commercial stain can be diluted with turpentine for a more subtle effect, but keep a record of the proportions used, in case you run out between coats. Be certain that the stain you select is chemically compatible with

the finish you have in mind. **Never use a varnish stain.** Instead of enunciating the grain, this product obscures it like a sheet of formica.

The next decision is a very important one: which finish to use. There are two basic types. The surface film type (shellac, varnish, quick-dry varnish, polyurethane) is a traffic tolerant coating on top of the floor. The penetrating type (penetrating sealer, oil) seeps into the wood, filling the spaces between the uppermost fibers. It offers the soft lustre associated with old wood floors, but not the abrasion resistance of surface film.

By and large, **the best floor finish for the average household is polyurethane.** Its advantages are: resistance to abrasion, easy maintenance, and the choice of gloss or satin sheen. Although at $27 a gallon it is the most expensive of the floor finishes by a few dollars, it has the longest floor life of them all. For best results, apply the polyurethane in several thin coats, rather than a single thick one. Polyurethane is incompatible with certain stains, but generally oak and fir floors typical to older houses look better without stain anyway. If you are undecided between satin and gloss, satin is recommended. It shows less dirt, and it offers the option of switching to gloss later on by waxing and buffing the polyurethane (which otherwise does not require waxing).

The Old-House Journal, a special interest periodical "published monthly for people who love old houses," is an excellent source for advice on refinishing floors. Much of the information offered here was derived from back issues dated February, May, July, December 1974, January 1975 and April 1977. Also see the May 1981 and December 1985 issues. The journal is available at the Oakland Public Library, main building and Rockridge branch. (See Chapter 7, "Publications," for subscription information.)

If you are stymied by the time and skill involved, but are anxious for the results of a refinished hardwood floor, you can hire a flooring contractor with a C-15 license issued by the State of California to do the work for you. Most offer free estimates. Make sure the estimate includes everything you want done, like boards replaced or nails countersunk, as well as the quality of materials and performance you deem satisfactory, like the number of sanding cuts, or the type of finish. Then make sure the estimate is firm.

For a complete refinishing job, flooring contractors charge about $1.50 a square foot for small rooms, and a little less for larger rooms. Installing hardwood in the space left by the grill of a disconnected floor furnace, and feathering the edges so it does not look patchy, costs about $50-$75 for a 3′×3′ spot. This is a common situation in Craftsman and California Bungalows with FHA financing. (See "Utility Systems: Mechanical.")

Some flooring contractors might agree to let the homeowner do a portion of the job and reduce their prices accordingly. Persuasion may be difficult, however, because State law and professional reputation govern the quality of the completed product.

Softwood Floor

Softwood floors found in kitchens, pantries, bedrooms and second stories of older Oakland homes are typically made of tongue and groove Douglas fir strips, although pine boards and square edge joints are seen too. Unlike oak, softwood boards are as broad as 4″ wide, and run right up to the wall without a border.

Fir may not appear promising to the uninitiated eye, but it produces startlingly good results when refinished because for a "soft" wood it is very hard. The open grain is so pronounced you can actually feel it with your hand. This is a good way to differentiate fir from pine which is smooth to the touch. Also, fir is reddish when stripped, while pine is white to yellow. Pine is much softer than fir and does not refinish as successfully. Unfortunately, fir is often misidentified as pine.

Repair, replace, sand, stain and finish a fir floor in the same way you would an oak floor, as described in the preceding section. Since the fir is a softwood, take extra care to sand delicately. Unless there is a heavy coat of paint to remove, start with a medium grade sandpaper. Try to limit the total number of cuts. Polyurethane is a good finish for softwood because it lends additional strength to the floor.

Ceramic Tile Floor

Ceramic tile is the original flooring for practically all bathrooms. The bathroom itself was introduced during the Victorian era, with the creation of a separate room for bathing instead of just a zinc tub in front of the fireplace. At first, the bathroom floors were softwood, splatter-painted in five colors. But with the fashionable concern for hygiene at the turn of the century, tiles were quickly incorporated into bathroom floor and walls. Pastel tiles were not common until the 1920s.

Small, white hexagonal tiles are a distinctive asset in many Oakland houses dating from about 1910-1930, like California Bungalows. These tiles should not be replaced with modern square ones, but rather repeated in-kind if repair or additions are needed. They are available at Tile Town in Oakland for $3.89 a square foot. Usually, no special tools are needed for installation since their size makes them a flexible unit. White hexagons are also typical to kitchen counters of the same houses. Give a remodeling job an air of authenticity by using the original tile selection in a modern context.

Quarry tile is the finish floor in the entry hall of some Mediterranean style houses. Replacements should always be in-kind. Quarry tile is available at most tile stores in Oakland. Select a store that offers competent instruction and free loan of tools with a refundable deposit, if you are a novice.

Resilent Flooring

Resilient flooring is made of pliable materials such as vinyl, asphalt, linoleum, rubber, cork and various synthetic compositions. It comes in tile or sheet form. When it is time to replace worn-out linoleum, or when, for maintenance purposes, you have decided to switch to a resilient floor covering, no historical rules really apply, since the selections are all modern. Use the following design guidelines to aid in the selection of color, pattern and style.

The floor should provide a neutral background. Each of Oakland's older house styles has architectural features of interest in the kitchen. If you REHAB RIGHT, these should be the focus of attention, not the floor. Select a restrained solid color. Patterns

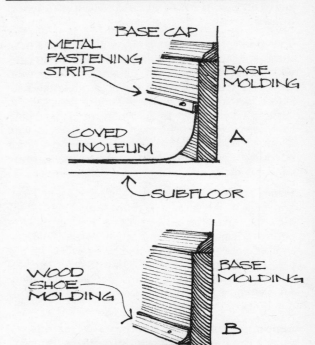

SHEET VINYL: DOS AND DON'TS

AVOID THE SITUATION SHOWN IN "A" ABOVE WHERE LINOLEUM OR VINYL FLOORING "CLIMBS THE WALL", HALF-HIDES THE SUBSTANTIAL BASEBOARD AND GIVES UNDUE PROMINENCE TO THE INCONGRUOUS METAL STRIP. IF "A" EXISTS, CORRECT IT BY CUTTING THE FLOORING ALONG THE MIDPOINT OF THE CURVE WITH A LINOLEUM KNIFE. HOLD THE EDGE FLAT WITH COVE OR QUARTER-ROUND WOOD MOLDING, AS SHOWN IN "B". USE THIS METHOD FOR NEW FLOORING AS WELL.

make small rooms look smaller, and generally give the kitchen an unsettled feeling.

Resilient tiles are somewhat easier for an amateur to install than sheetvinyl, but the sheets offer better hygiene. There are no seams to collect dirt, and the edges can curve up the wall 3″ or 4″ for a coved base. While excellent where concealed under cabinets, **coved bases are highly inappropriate when they cover up shoe molding** or when it looks as if the floor is climbing up the wall. Along these boundaries, install the sheet vinyl flat so it abuts the wall in the same manner as a tile would.

For a finished edge where the resilient flooring meets the wall, use an ample strip of wood molding. (Refer to the section "Walls: Trim.") Do not use the thin metal strip more commonly associated with modern floor covering. The metal strip looks shiny and skimpy in a location where something with a subdued finish and substantial mass is appropriate.

WALLS

Walls are more than the flat sides of a box. They have three dimensions of their own. The quality of the wall surface, the quantity of trim and the proportion of blank surface to shapely ornamentation, all determine the character of a room. If the rehabilitated wall treatment is consistent with the original design of the house, then the room will be interesting to look at and comfortable to be in. If the original treatment of the wall is disregarded, the room can become incredibly boring and cold.

Plaster

Plaster is the universal wall surface for old houses. It provides a plain but not bland background to offset architectural details, like molding and beams. Plaster frequently needs repairs because it is a rigid material applied over a flexible framework. As the house settles, the wood members shift, including lath strips nailed to the studs, but the plaster attached to the lath does not. Its recourse is to crack. Plaster is also prone to brown spots from leaky water, to chips from picture

fasteners which pull away and to holes from plumbing and electrical work.

The good news is that these mishaps are easily repaired by the amateur. Cracks and chips do not justify the expense or esthetic travesty of switching to another wall surface. Most home repair books include instructions on plaster repairs. An excellent reference is the four-issue series in *The Old-House Journal,* December 1973 through March 1974, and more recently, selected issues in 1984 and 1985. Note the similarity to the repair of stucco, as discussed in the chapter on exteriors. **Always correct the cause of plaster damage,** like leaky plumbing or rotted wood, **before repairing the plaster itself.**

There are two new plaster repair products to look for. Backer rods made of closed-cell foam for mending large holes, and metal cups to uplift sagging ceilings.

Very large holes and extensive deterioration of a plaster wall call for complete re-plastering and the help of a plastering contractor. The alternative and more modern solution to major plaster problems is sheetrock. Gypsum board, another name for it, is like a solid sheet of plaster. It comes in 4′×8′ panels, in varying thicknesses. A ½″ thick panel, for example, costs $5.80. The installation of sheetrock, unlike the art of plastering, can be handled by the average handyperson.

Sheetrock should be used to fill in large areas where plaster is dilapidated, in consort with other architectural features appropriate to the room. Instead, sheetrock is often mistakenly used like panelling, projecting out from the wall and covering up or eliminating architectural details. When the job calls for sheetrock, do the following:

1. Carefully remove any molding, cornice work or other trim from the wall area where plaster will be replaced by sheetrock, and store it safely aside. (See "Walls: Trim.") It may be possible to leave the shoe molding in place if the plaster can be cut below the top of the molding and the sheetrock installed behind it.
2. Pull off the bad plaster and its lath back to the studs. As with many demolition jobs involved in rehab, it doesn't take much skill to rip something

out, just time and aggression. This is a dusty operation, so remove all furniture and drapes from the room, close the door, sealing the cracks with 2″-wide masking tape, and open the windows. Wear an inexpensive fibre mask and, at the end of the work day, sweep and vaccuum the dust that settles.

3. Install the sheetrock so that it fits into the space once filled by plaster. It should not make the wall any thicker than it was. Think of sheetrock as solid plaster, not as paneling.
4. If the surface texture of the sheetrock is not the same as the existing plaster, special spackling compounds are available so the sheetrock can be coated to match. Practice first on a scrap. Matching surface finishes is noteworthy in Period Revival houses where the plaster is heavily textured.
5. Replace the molding or trim in its original position on the wall. This is extremely important. Blank sheetrock walls look rather insipid; when combined with architectural features they are suddenly meaningful. This is particularly noticeable in Victorian houses with high ceilings. An uninterrupted expanse of sheetrock on a wall 10′ or 12′ high can resemble a drive-in movie screen if the trim is not returned to its rightful place.

Wood

Judging by the walls of modern tract homes, you'd never know that wood is a wall surfacing material. Yet in older houses, **wood walls and interior features** are quite common. In fact, they are one of **the main reasons these vintage residences feel so warm and welcoming inside.**

A skirt of wood on the lower 3′ to 4′ of the wall is called wainscotting, and the design varies with the architectural style, as illustrated. Other wood architectural features inside include ceiling beams, archways, columns, platerails and moldings. The concept of preservation and the technique of restoration described here for wood wall surfacing applies equally to these features. (Refer also to the section "Walls: Trim.")

If wainscotting is still in place, leave it in place. If the wainscotting has been removed, it can

PLASTER REPAIR

A. <u>HAIRLINE CRACKS</u> CAN BE FILLED WITH A THIN MIXTURE OF PATCHING PLASTER OR WALLBOARD JOINT CEMENT. RUB THE CRACK LIGHTLY WITH VERY COARSE SANDPAPER, THEN BRUSH OUT LOOSE MATERIAL, FORCE THE FILLER DEEP INTO CRACK WITH FINGERTIPS, THEN SMOOTH SURFACE WITH "V" STROKES OF A PUTTY KNIFE.

B. <u>SMALL CRACKS</u> SHOULD BE OPENED AND UNDERCUT WITH A SPECIAL TOOL OR A CAN OPENER. THIS PREVENTS THE CRACK FROM REAPPEARING AFTER FILLING AND PAINTING.

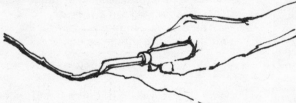

CLEAN OUT LOOSE MATERIAL FROM CRACK. FORCE FILLER DEEP INTO CRACK FROM 2 DIRECTIONS, THEN LEVEL SURFACE WITH "V" STROKES.

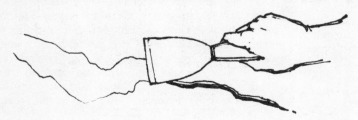

C. <u>WIDE CRACKS AND HOLES</u> LARGER THAN A FEW INCHES IN DIAMETER SHOULD BE FILLED WITH 3 LAYERS OF PATCHING PLASTER. UNDERCUT THE EDGES OF THE HOLE OR CRACK BACK TO THE LATH, MAKING SURE THAT THE LATH IS FIRMLY ANCHORED TO THE STUDS. (IF NOT, OR IF THERE IS WATER DAMAGE, SEE ILLUSTRATION ON EXTENSIVE REPAIR.) DAMPEN CRACK WITH SPONGE. ADD FILLER TO HALF THE DEPTH OF THE CRACK, SCORE THE FILLER COAT WITH COMB OR PUTTY KNIFE, THEN ALLOW TO DRY. BRING 2ND COAT TO WITHIN $\frac{1}{8}$" OF THE WALL SURFACE. LET DRY, APPLY FINAL COAT WITH TROWEL OR WIDE-BLADED PUTTY KNIFE.

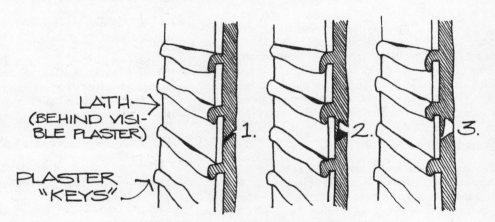

LATH→
(BEHIND VISIBLE PLASTER)

PLASTER "KEYS"→

1. CRACK IN PLASTER
2. CRACK OPENED & UNDERCUT
3. FILLING COMPLETE

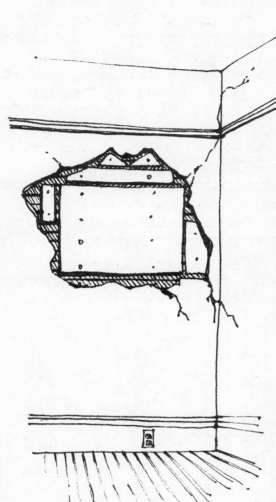

WHEN AN EXTEN-SIVE SECTION OF PLASTER IS LOOSE OR CRUMBLY, PULL THE LOOSE MATER-IAL OFF THE WALL, SA-VING LATH IF POSSIBLE. NAIL SHEETROCK TO STUDS, FILLING IRREG-ULAR GAPS WITH SMALL SCRAPS NAILED TO LATH. SHEETROCK SHOULD BE SAME THICKNESS AS OLD PLASTER OR A FRAC-TION LESS.

APPLY TWO OR MORE LAYERS OF THICKLY-MIXED PATCHING PLAS-TER, PRESSING FIRMLY INTO CRACKS AND LATH AND STOPPING JUST SHY OF THE ORIGINAL THICKNESS. LEVEL PATCH WITH A FINAL THIN COAT OF PLASTER.

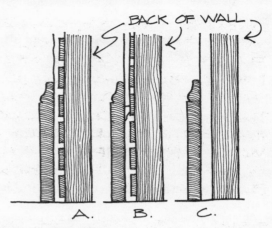

BACK OF WALL

A.   B.   C.

CORRECT

A. ORIGINAL PLASTER AND BASE MOLDING.

B. THIN SHEETROCK OVER ORI-GINAL LATH, INSERTED BE-HIND OLD MOLDING (CLEAR OUT PLASTER BEHIND TOP OF MOLDING FIRST).

C. THICKER SHEETROCK DIRECT-LY ON STUDS. MOLDING CARE-FULLY PRIED OFF, THEN PUT BACK OVER SHEETROCK.

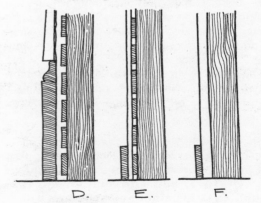

D.   E.   F.

INCORRECT

D. SHEETROCK ON TOP OF PLASTER.

E & F. SHEETROCK APPLIED CORRECTLY, BUT ORIGINAL MOLDING DISCARD-ED FOR SKIMPY NEW MOLDING.

be recreated as shown, and interest returned to an otherwise defaced wall. Wainscotting can be ordered at Bartley Milling Co., Oakland.

If the wood wall surface is unpainted, by all means leave it that way. If it is a rare remaining example of graining—a 19th century skill by which one wood was artfully painted to look like another—then too it should be left intact.

If the wainscotting has been painted, you can repaint it, strip and refinish it, or if the house is a Victorian, you can arrange to have it grained in the traditional manner. Two San Francisco craftsmen who specialize in this kind of work are John L. Seekamp and Nat Weinstein. In no case should original wood wall surface be "antiqued" or made to look old by a two-tone paint and glaze job. Absolutely shun the process called "distressing," by which wood is brutally marred with chains and hammers to simulate age and wear.

Existing woodwork may require repair prior to refinishing. To replace damaged pieces, bring a sample to a big lumber yard that stocks a variety of interior finish lumber to match type, grain, size and stain. Redwood, fir and mahogany are fairly easy to find, but the gum wood (eucalyptus) so typical of Prairie School, Period Revival, and some turn-of-the-century houses is no longer available. A good substitute is birch. The grain of birch approximates the gum, and it is a light enough color to allow staining to match. If the original pieces are thicker than standard replacement stock, you may have to buy an even larger piece and have it cut to size. A less costly alternative suitable for camouflaged location is to buy the thin standard piece and back it with inexpensive plywood until the thickness matches the original stock.

Refinished woodwork can make a dramatic improvement in the character of a room. However, **stripping is a tedious commitment that should be undertaken selectively and with forethought. It is advisable to strip paint or varnish from woodwork when:**

● The architectural style calls for natural wood.
● There's fine hardwood underneath, and you have the time and patience to do the job right. Delinquent specks of paint or haze of color negate

the improvement. As with floors, hardwood was usually reserved for the formal rooms, and softwood used for the family rooms and service areas.

● There's softwood underneath, and stripping would make repainting easier and more effective because accumulated layers of paint are so thick that the detail of carving or molding has become obscured.
● There's softwood underneath, but the paint is so alligatored that stripping is more expedient than scraping.
● There's a varnish or shellac finish that has darkened unattractively with age and a fresh clear finish is desired.

The art of stripping and refinishing interior woodwork is a subject of much debate among energetic restorationists. The technique is similar to refinishing furniture, but offers the advantage of relatively flat surfaces, and a stationary surface to bear up against without additional bracing. Stripping is unavoidably messy and either clouded by unpleasant fumes, or accompanied by a piercing noise. Familiarize yourself with the options described below. Choose your weapon, save up old newspapers, and be sure to ventilate the room.

Chemical removers are applied with a brush and left in place long enough to buckle the layers of unwanted paint so that they can be scraped off with a wide-bladed putty knife in a continuous ribbon. There are at least seven different types of compounds available for this purpose. The most appropriate to interior woodwork is a non-flammable heavy-bodied water rinsing remover. It is thick enough to hold on vertical or irregular surfaces and it contains methyl chloride to minimize the fire hazard. A typical brand is Jasco, available for about $20 a gallon.

The most important rules for successful chemical stripping are:

● **Don't be stingy with materials.**
● **Let the remover sit for a long enough time to cut through all the paint.**

While most home repair books recommend stripping only a small area at a time, professionals do large sweeps (as much as 50 square feet) with great efficiency. This is advisable for the amateur once the knack is acquired. If any of the large soaked

WAINSCOT STYLES AND VOCABULARY

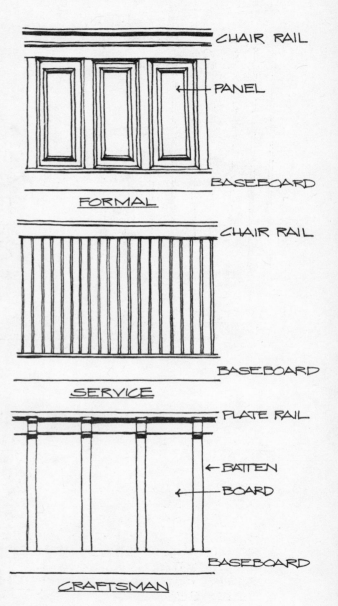

CHAIR RAIL
PANEL
BASEBOARD
FORMAL

CHAIR RAIL
BASEBOARD
SERVICE

PLATE RAIL
BATTEN
BOARD
BASEBOARD
CRAFTSMAN

RE-CREATING A WAINSCOT

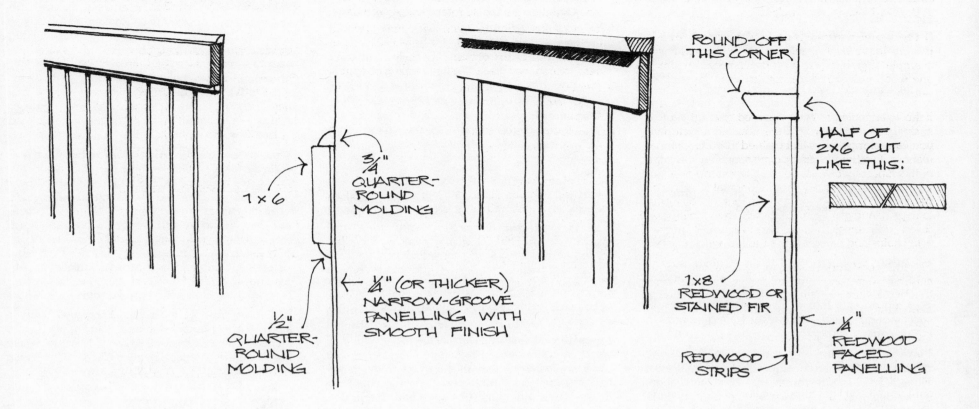

1 × 6

3/4" QUARTER-ROUND MOLDING

1/2" QUARTER-ROUND MOLDING

← 1/4" (OR THICKER) NARROW-GROOVE PANELLING WITH SMOOTH FINISH

ROUND-OFF THIS CORNER

HALF OF 2×6 CUT LIKE THIS:

1×8 REDWOOD OR STAINED FIR

REDWOOD STRIPS

1/4" REDWOOD FACED PANELLING

A. RECREATING A <u>SERVICE STYLE</u> WAINSCOT: CHOOSE A STRAIGHT-GRAINED WOOD PANELLING WITH REGULARLY SPACED GROOVES 2"–4" APART. IF PANELLING COMES IN 8' SHEETS, USE 4' SECTIONS TO SAVE WOOD. PLACE SECTIONS ABOVE BASE-BOARD MOLDING AND NAIL TO STUDS. BUILD UP TOP MOLDING FROM QUARTER-ROUND MOLDINGS & 1×6 BOARDS, AS ILLUSTRATED. FILL NAIL HOLES, THEN STAIN MOLDING TO MATCH PANELLING. SEE SECTION ON PAINT STRIPPING FOR HINTS ON FINAL FINISH

B. RECREATING A <u>CRAFTSMAN STYLE</u> WAINSCOT: NAIL HALF SHEETS (4'×4') OF SMOOTH-FINISH REDWOOD FACED PANELLING ABOVE BASEBOARD, WITH GRAIN POINTING VERTICALLY. CUT 2×6 LUMBER IN HALF LENGTHWISE AT A 60° ANGLE (YOU WILL NEED A CIRCU-LAR SAW FOR THIS) AND BUILD TOP MOLDING AND PLATE RAIL AS ILLUS-TRATED. PLACE SMOOTH-SANDED STRIPS OF WELL DRIED REDWOOD LATH (BUY 6" LATH AND CUT INTO 3" STRIPS) AT 1 OR 2 FOOT INTERVALS OVER PANELLING, COVERING JOINTS BETWEEN PANELS.

areas should dry out before you get there with the blade, wet them down again with more remover.

Heat removers are appliances that literally melt the paint away. Several kinds are available. A semi-enclosed electric coil, like the heating element on top of a stove, is available at Mark's Paint Mart for about $50. Or, it can be rented from the Alameda Rental Center for $7 a day. Another type is the heat gun that resembles a blowdryer for hair, but is actually an industrial tool. It can be ordered via *The Old-House Journal* for $78, including shipping. A propane blow torch should not be used for interior work due to the likelihood of scorching and the high fire hazard.

Another option combines **heat and chemicals.** Use a wallpaper steamer to accelerate the effect of a water-rinsable paint remover. Apply the stripping compound, preferably one with a high methyl-chloride content, and let it sit for 15 minutes. Apply the steam through the pan of the steamer, moving it slowly across the wall, about a square foot a minute. Follow it with a wide-blade scraper, and you can remove four or five coats promptly with success. Do not use steam with chemical removers which contain carbon tetrachloride or benzene.

Manual stripping of woodwork involves more physical effort than heat or chemical methods. Nonetheless, health constraints, poor ventilation, or personal preference may preclude other methods, as nothing short of a gas mask can prevent some intake of the noxious fumes they engender. Also, successive layers of old, rock-hard enamel may not yield easily to chemicals. Manual scraping can cut clean through multiple paint layers and into the pristine wood lying below the paint impregnated outer wood fibers.

A hook-type scraper is the basic tool required. Get a 2½″ bladed scraper for wide surfaces and fast cutting, plus another small enough to fit into the tightest spot you must deal with.

Here's the technique:

- **Use two hands** when you can. One hand pulls on the end of the handle, controlling speed and cutting angle, while the other pushes on the blade end, controlling pressure. Determine the most efficient blade angle and use only as much force as necessary to conserve your energy.

- **Sharpen blades often** for easier, smoother scraping. Replacement blades are usually available, but most blades accept repeated sharpening with a fine-tooth flat file. When using the file, maintain the original bevel of the blade.

- **Scrape with the grain,** especially on woods with pronounced grain, like fir. Scraping across the grain or on the end grain will result in splintering and gouging. (Resort to coarse sandpaper here.)

- **Wear earplugs and goggles,** and spare yourself. The sound of the manual scraper at work is a chilling, high-pitched vibration. Paint flecks scatter upward toward your face as you draw down on the tool.

Once the wood is stripped, a stain and/or finish must be applied to protect the wood. **Stain selection is a matter of architectural style and interior decor.** The dark stains historically appropriate to Colonial Revival and some First Bay Tradition houses are truly sombre, and a slight divergence from accuracy may be warranted for modern taste.

For the finish, select among the film-forming types (varnish, lacquer and shellac) **and the oil types** (boiled linseed, Danish and tung oil). The secret to using film finishes is to thin them. Thin coats dry faster and harder than thick coats, and a thin first coat seals the wood properly. Varnish is thinned with turpentine (4 parts varnish to 1 part turpentine), lacquer with lacquer thinner and shellac with denatured alcohol. An old nylon stocking is a good applicator that leaves no bristle marks. Oils are typically applied with a piece of soft cotton, but for large surfaces a brush can be used if each of the three coats is very thin. Whichever finish you select, always work with the grain of the wood, and always allow plenty of drying time—usually 24 hours—between each application. Adequate ventilation is crucial when using these volatile fluids.

The Old-House Journal offers detailed advice on stripping woodwork. Refer especially to the issue dated January 1976 for the problem of paint specks and haze and to the June 1985 issue. For answers to specific questions, write to: Refinishing Clinic, *The Old-House Journal,* 69-A 7th Avenue, Brooklyn, N.Y. 11217. Enclose a stamped, self-addressed envelope.

Lincrusta-Walton

Lincrusta-Walton is a heavy, embossed cardboard wall covering, imported from England and Belgium in the late 19th century as wainscot and wall covering for Victorian and Colonial Revival parlors and hallways. It came in large rolls and was soaked in water for several hours before installation. Unfinished, lincrusta-Walton is beige, but when in style, it was usually coated with a glossy brown varnish. Subsequently, as Victorian taste lost favor, the modeled surface was made unintelligible by layers of paint.

A house that has lincrusta-Walton boasts a real antique. The original embossed cardboard is extremely valuable and should be retained and shown off. Patches deteriorated by water can be mended by making a plastic mold from an unharmed portion, and filling the mold with papier-maché compound. This ingenious technique was developed by Agnes Pritchard, plasterer, in association with San Francisco Victoriana. Complete instructions are available from that firm, or can be found reproduced in the October 1975 issue of *The Old-House Journal.*

It is even possible to replace lincrusta-Walton in kind. Due to popular demand, Crown, an English manufacturer, has reissued its line of lincrusta panels. For literature, contact Bentley Bros., 918 Baxter Avenue, Louisville, KY 40204.

LINCRUSTA-WALTON

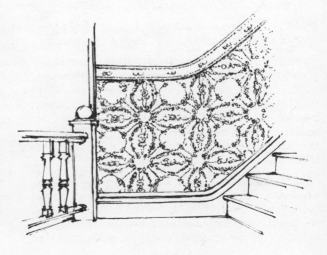

Paneling

Paneling is a modular wall surface which, with dubious thanks to modern technology, comes in an untold number of designs and offers an astounding range of natural and special effects. Paneling falls into three basic categories: (1) solid wood, (2) plywood with wood veneer (by far the most popular), and (3) non-wood, like polystyrene, plastic laminates, fiberglass, hardboard and cork. **Modern paneling was not the original wall surface for any of the architectural styles in this book,** although a non-manufactured version of solid wood wall panels is found in some Victorian, Colonial Revival and First Bay Tradition houses.

Paneling is a gruesome mistake when it is used to cover up original architectural features that are still substantially intact. If, however, a wall in a less important room has been devastated by earlier misguided remodeling efforts, paneling can be an acceptable solution if certain guidelines are followed:

- Always use real wood products. Imitations look cheap even if they cost dearly.
- Select paneling with regular spacing between the vertical grooves. So-called "random" spacing looks contrived rather than interesting.
- Select a wood with a color and grain sympathetic to the original architecture, as indicated by other features in the room.
- Avoid flamboyant grains, like birdseye maple or pecky cedar, that compete with original features in the room rather than working with them.

Paneling can also be used to recreate the proportions of long lost wainscotting, as illustrated previously.

Equally pertinent here is the removal of unwanted paneling in hopes of recapturing the original architectural character of a room. Paneling is either nailed to the studs, or glued in place with a contact cement. Some panels are additionally attached to each other with tongue-and-groove joints. Look for the nails hidden in the tongue or recessed in the V-groove.

To remove paneling, you'll need a pry bar, a hacksaw blade and brute strength. Work the pry bar under the edges of each panel to loosen it. Cut nails you can reach with the hacksaw blade. Be prepared to make a complete renovation of the wall behind, as

CROSS-SECTION OF A PLYWOOD PANEL

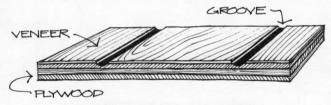

GROOVE

VENEER

PLYWOOD

THIS SECTION OF STANDARD PANELLING IS EXAGGERATED IN THICKNESS TO SHOW THE PLYS. (ACTUAL THICKNESS IS ABOUT 3/16"). GROOVES ARE CUT THROUGH THE WOOD OR VINYL VENEER INTO THE FIRST PLY. GROOVES ARE OFTEN STAINED DARK TO SIMULATE A SHADOWLINE BETWEEN "BOARDS". IF YOU USE PANELLING, CHOOSE STRAIGHT-GRAINED, REAL WOOD VENEER WITH EVENLY SPACED GROOVES.

damage to the original plaster is almost certain. The most practical replacement is to install sheetrock against the studs and reinstate the trim as needed.

Paint

Paint is properly applied to plaster, sheetrock, and in some cases, wood. The advent of latex paint has markedly simplified the painting process. Latex, a water-based as opposed to oil-based paint, thins with water, spreads easily, dries in about an hour, and has little or no paint odor. A full spectrum of colors and finishes is available.

Use a flat latex for walls and ceilings. Use semi-gloss latex enamel, also called satin finish, for trim, doors, shelving, woodwork and kitchen or bathroom walls. A new product from the Dutch Boy company and others is a flat latex enamel that is ideally suited to kitchen and bathroom walls because it is washable but not at all shiny. **Do not use high-gloss latex enamel.** It catches and reflects light in a distracting way and accentuates imperfections in the painted surface, without offering any additional advantages of longevity or maintenance.

Color selection has an enormous impact on the way a room looks and feels. Use color to highlight architectural features, but not to create a carnival atmosphere. **See "Paint" in Chapter 4 for a basic lesson in color, and follow these additional guidelines for interiors:**

- It is generally best not to use more than two colors in a single room. The safest combination is a light color for the walls, and a somewhat darker shade of the same color for the molding and trim.
- If at all in doubt, use a single light color only, preferably a white or off-white.
- When selecting an off-white, pick the one that is tinted with a color that goes with the other colors, or woodwork, in the room. Hints of color, like blue, green or brown, are what make the off-white "off."
- Light colors make a room look more spacious. Dark colors make an average room look small and a small room look cave-like.
- Paint the ceiling white for more light and the feeling of more air. Almost all rooms can benefit from this.
- Warm colors (yellow, orange, red, brown, warm gray) make rooms with a northern exposure feel more inviting. Both warm colors and cool colors (blue, green, cool gray) are appropriate to sunny rooms. It is difficult to combine warm and cool colors successfully.
- Historically accurate colors are a safe selection and a conversation piece.
- Where one room merges visually with the next, use blending colors. If in doubt, use the same color.
- For wainscotting that needs to be repainted, use a light, warm earthtone like beige, ivory, straw or eggshell. Do not use a pastel.
- To dramatize a stairway balustrade, use the wall behind it as a foil. If the balustrade is natural wood, paint the wall a light color that matches the rest of the decor. If the balustrade is to be repainted, select a color contrasting but compatible with the wall. A dark wall calls for a light balustrade, and vice versa.
- *Do not* paint unpainted wood surfaces, brick or stone, fireplaces, ceramic tile or floors.

PARTS OF A ROOM TO PAINT

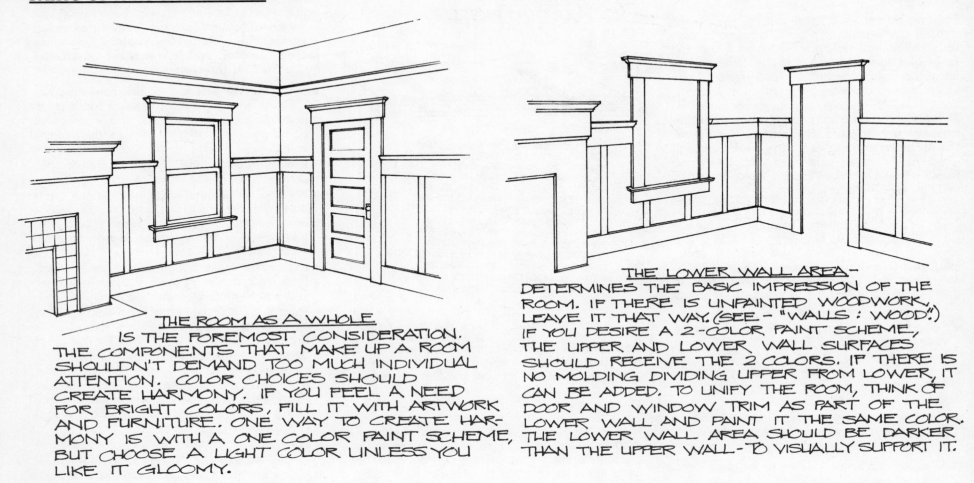

THE ROOM AS A WHOLE

IS THE FOREMOST CONSIDERATION. THE COMPONENTS THAT MAKE UP A ROOM SHOULDN'T DEMAND TOO MUCH INDIVIDUAL ATTENTION. COLOR CHOICES SHOULD CREATE HARMONY. IF YOU FEEL A NEED FOR BRIGHT COLORS, FILL IT WITH ARTWORK AND FURNITURE. ONE WAY TO CREATE HARMONY IS WITH A ONE COLOR PAINT SCHEME, BUT CHOOSE A LIGHT COLOR UNLESS YOU LIKE IT GLOOMY.

THE LOWER WALL AREA—

DETERMINES THE BASIC IMPRESSION OF THE ROOM. IF THERE IS UNPAINTED WOODWORK, LEAVE IT THAT WAY. (SEE - "WALLS : WOOD".) IF YOU DESIRE A 2-COLOR PAINT SCHEME, THE UPPER AND LOWER WALL SURFACES SHOULD RECEIVE THE 2 COLORS. IF THERE IS NO MOLDING DIVIDING UPPER FROM LOWER, IT CAN BE ADDED. TO UNIFY THE ROOM, THINK OF DOOR AND WINDOW TRIM AS PART OF THE LOWER WALL AND PAINT IT THE SAME COLOR. THE LOWER WALL AREA SHOULD BE DARKER THAN THE UPPER WALL—TO VISUALLY SUPPORT IT.

- *Do not* use sickly colors like pale olive green, mustard or chartreuse. *Do not* use garish colors like pink, violet, lavender, aqua or purple.
- *Do not* paint over wallpaper with an oil base paint.
- *Do not* paint over wallpaper unless it is properly hung, and not brittle with age or about to peel off.

For instructions on selecting paint and tools, consult a home repair book, like the *Reader's Digest Complete Do-it-yourself Manual,* and your paint dealer.

As with exterior paint jobs, **proper surface preparation is essential to success,** although it is rarely as difficult on the inside as out. First, repair any damage to the wall. (Refer to "Walls: Plaster.") Scrape off loose paint flakes and peeling wallpaper. Clean the surface with a common pre-painting solution to remove years of grime and oil. Feather edges created by chipped paint or old wallpaper. If the existing paint is enamel, it must be hand-sanded in circular motion with a coarse paper to give the surface enough tooth for the latex to adhere. If layers of old paint are so thick that they obscure the detail of shapely wood features, it is advisable to strip the accumulated coats before repainting. (Refer to "Walls: Wood.") Since the surface will be repainted, the stripping need not be meticulous. Cabinet doors can be removed and dipped in a commercial stripping vat for about $15-$20 apiece at the Strip Shop in San Francisco.

If there is mildew on bathroom walls or ceiling, it must be eradicated before repainting. Scrub the offending black shadow with a commerical mildicide, or a Clorox and water solution (1:5). Repaint with a mildew resistant product.

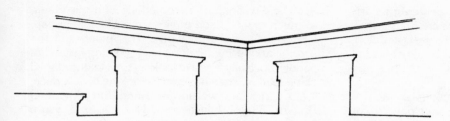

UPPER WALL AREA — THE CORNICE MOLDING SIGNIFIES THE END OF THE WALL AND THE BEGINNING OF THE CEILING, EVEN IF THERE IS MORE VERTICAL WALL SURFACE ABOVE IT. IN OLDER HOUSES WITH HIGH CEILINGS, THE POSITION OF THE CORNICE MOLDING KEEPS THE EXPANSE OF WALL SURFACE AT A MORE HUMAN SCALE. ACKNOWLEDGE THIS FUNCTION WHEN SELECTING PAINT BY REGARDING THE CORNICE MOLDING AS PART OF THE UPPER WALL AREA AND USING THE SAME COLOR FOR BOTH.

LEAVE THE CORNICE MOLDING UNPAINTED ONLY IF THE OTHER WOODWORK IS UNPAINTED OR THE CEILING AND UPPER WALL ARE DIFFERENT COLORS. OTHERWISE, THE MOLDING WILL LOOK LIKE A BOLD STRIPE INSTEAD OF THE JUNCTION BETWEEN CEILING AND WALL.

ACCENTS ARE OPTIONAL. WHEN USED, THEY SHOULD BE SUBTLE AND CHOSEN TO ADD INTEREST TO THE COLOR SCHEME, NOT COMPETE WITH IT FOR ATTENTION. A DARKER OR LIGHTER VARIANT OF THE BASIC WALL COLOR IS A GOOD CHOICE. ACCENTS SHOULD BE SMALL IN AREA (FOR INSTANCE, THE MOLDING AROUND THE FIREPLACE TILE AS OPPOSED TO AN ENTIRE DOOR).

CEILING — PAINT IT WHITE OR A LIGHT EARTH COLOR FOR REFLECTIVITY. DON'T PAINT NATURAL WOOD BEAMS.

DOORS AND MOVING WINDOW PARTS SHOULD BE LEFT NATURAL IF THEY AREN'T ALREADY PAINTED. OTHERWISE, PAINT THEM THE SAME COLOR AS THE LOWER WALL AREA OR OFF-WHITE. OFF-WHITE REFLECTS LIGHT INTO A ROOM AND, ON DOORS, SHOWS OFF THE SCULPTURAL QUALITY OF THE PANELS. DON'T HIGHLIGHT THE DOOR PANELS WITH COLOR — IT LOOKS "SPOTTY". LET SHADOWS DEFINE THE PARTS.

TILE AND BRICK SHOULD NOT BE PAINTED. IF ITS ALREADY PAINTED AND BEYOND YOU TO STRIP, PAINT THE BRICK OR TILE AN EARTH TONE WHICH COMPLEMENTS THE BASIC WALL COLOR.

Wallpaper

In the mid-19th century, the first wallpaper color-printing machine was brought to the United States from England, and with that thousands of geometric and floral patterns became commercially available.

The art of wallpaper making peaked in the late-19th century, and in most Victorian and some Colonial Revival and Craftsman houses, wallpaper was used to strengthen the composition of the room. The lower walls (below the picture molding and above the wainscotting) usually had a consistent pattern, applied in vertical strips of paper, as is the custom today. The frieze area (between the picture molding and ceiling) usually had a single horizontal band of paper, often in patterns derived from actual frieze designs in Classical, Renaissance and Baroque buildings. The effect of this treatment is to give the portion of the wall above and including the picture molding the appearance of a single huge cornice. Sometimes, too, a much smaller horizontal band of paper was applied directly below the picture molding, giving the molding the appearance of a secondary cornice. Wallpaper was also used on ceilings. Sometimes it was applied in successive strips, as on lower walls, and sometimes in borders around the ceiling rim.

Victorian and Colonial Revival patterns varied greatly. Frequently, they were used to create lavish effects similar to those associated with much more expensive materials such as wood, carved plaster and marble. Interestingly, in contrast to the architectural exuberance typical of the period, many of these wallpaper designs were rather delicate, derived from Art Nouveau or Far Eastern motifs. Authentic Victorian wallpaper used in the restoration of the Camron-Stanford house can be ordered through the Camron-Stanford House Preservation Association. Bradbury and Bradbury specialize in elegant reproductions of authentic Victorian patterns. Their catalog is $4 (P.O. Box 155, Benicia, CA 94150).

Wallpaper was often supplemented in the Victorian house by stenciling, particularly for border effects, such as around the rims of chandelier rosettes, above and below moldings, and within frieze areas. Stenciling consists of tracing a pattern from a template, repeating it, and coloring it with paint. To do this yourself, select a design from a reprinted Victorian pattern book, like the one published by Dover, and make a template from a rigid material, like cardboard. Further instructions are available in *The Old-House Journal*, June and July 1983.

In rehabilitation, wallpaper is properly used to add texture and interest in consort with the architectural features of a room. It is often mistakenly used as the focus of a room or as a substitute for valuable woodwork and trim erroneously removed. Serious restorationists try to duplicate the precise pattern of the original paper, or at least replicate a pattern popular during that era. For the purposes of REHAB RIGHT, a sensitive selection of a modern paper is perfectly acceptable and generally more economical.

Selection of the right wallpaper design starts with **color,** and the considerations are the same as those for paint, described previously. In addition, use the following guidelines to aid in the choice of pattern:

1. The **direction** of the pattern influences the way the room feels. A strongly vertical pattern can make a low ceiling seem higher. A dominant horizontal pattern can make a narrow room seem wider. Generally, a vertical pattern anchors the wall visually and gives it more solidity than a horizontal or random pattern does.

2. The **texture** of the pattern determines the general impact of any wallpaper selection. Fine-grained patterns give an impression of overall color, while coarse patterns call more attention to the form of the individual shapes. Remember that on the test swatch of wallpaper, the pictograph seems all-important, yet on the wall, it is the cumulative effect that really matters. The eye tends to blend the colors and designs together. If in doubt, choose a fine-grained pattern with muted colors, rather than a large pattern with bold colors.

3. Stylized **patterns** are more effective than naturalistic patterns because abstracted designs create a textured surface, while realistic representations call attention to themselves like a painting.

4. For the area above wood wainscotting, and generally for high-ceilinged Victorian houses, a paper with a vertical emphasis complements the architectural features and the interior space. The Victorians had exceptionally busy taste in wallpaper design, but there is no need to abide by their precedent unless it appeals to you.

5. **Do not use theme papers** to try to make a house look old. Representations of Colonial America with horse and buggies do not belong in a Colonial Revival house. Likewise, red flocked wallpaper that connotes the Gay Nineties in a pizza parlor is not at all suited to a large Victorian residence.

6. **Do not use contact paper.** It looks shoddy and harms the plaster. There are an ample number of wallpaper products which are just as convenient. You can buy wallpaper that is washable, prepasted, scuff-resistant, pre-trimmed and strippable, in addition to the standard product.

Actually, "wallpaper" is something of a misnomer, as much of it is made of vinyl, metallic foil, burlap, fabric, cork and even wood. This points out the possibility of using fabric as wall covering instead of paper, especially if you're looking for a textured solid color. Burlap, stretched taut across the wall surface, looks particularly well in Craftsman Bungalows and Brown Shingle style houses. Rice paper is also a wallcovering original to these styles.

Trim

A basic tenet of REHAB RIGHT is **respect for architectural features.** The architectural features are what's left in a room after all the furnishings have been removed. They stay with the house, from one owner to the next, and make a room look complete. **Architectural features contribute to the resale value of the house.**

An architectural feature easy to identify is the original wall trim. **It is extremely important for esthetic and economic reasons to retain the wall trim.** Fortunately, if the trim is missing, it is fairly easy and inexpensive to replace. Trim includes door frames and caps, window frames and caps, cornices, baseboard, chairrail and assorted molding. Visually, trim breaks up the mass of the wall and adds sculptural interest to an otherwise flat plane. Functionally, it conceals seams and joints.

The words "trim" and "molding" are often used interchangeably because trim is typically made of one or more pieces of molding. In Early American houses of the 18th and early 19th-centuries, elaborate wood moldings, hand-carved with simple tools, constituted the personal signature of the carpenter. By the Victorian period, standardized molding was milled commercially. Eight classic shapes derived from Greek and Roman precedents formed the basis for molding design, and do to this day. Victorian builders took advantage of the great variety and convenience of mass-produced molding and combined the patterns into imaginative wall decorations. Although taste became more simplified in subsequent years, molding itself persisted as an essential part of the wall in all of the architectural styles described in REHAB RIGHT.

BASIC MOLDING SHAPES

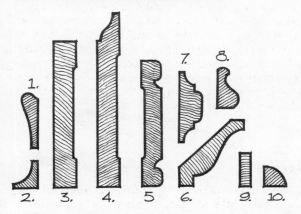

1. PICTURE: OFTEN USED ALONE AS A SIMPLE CORNICE
2. COVE
3. BASE
4. BASE WITH INTEGRAL "OGEE" CAP: SOMETIMES USED UPSIDE DOWN AS PART OF A CORNICE
5. CHAIR RAIL
6. CROWN
7. ASTRAGAL
8. BASE CAP
9. LATTICE: CUT INTO SECTIONS TO CREATE DENTILS
10. QUARTER ROUND: OFTEN USED AS SHOE MOLDING

If the molding is still intact, preserve it. **Repairs to the walls, floor or ceiling may involve temporary removal of the molding. Remove molding carefully, and only when absolutely necessary.** If the molding is painted, sand the surface enough to locate the nailheads. Gently work a stiff, broad-bladed putty knife behind the molding, lifting it enough to insert a small, flat prybar or the claws of a hammer. Put the end of the prying tool into the gap made by the putty knife, placing it as close as possible to where a nail passes from molding to wall or woodwork. Pad any spot where the prybar presses on visible woodwork or plaster with thick cardboard.

Pry the molding away just far enough to allow insertion of the prybar at the next nail. When the last nail is reached, the whole molding should stand away slightly from the surface behind. Now work back from nail to nail, increasing the gap a uniform amount each time. After two or three passes in this manner, the molding should be loose enough to pull off by hand. Wood wedges or scraps of shingle may be helpful to keep the moulding from springing back and closing the gap.

Sometimes molding is secured by nails in opposing directions. Check to see if this condition exists before pulling molding off in one direction, as it will probably split. In this case, or if a molding begins to crack, drive nails all the way through the molding into the surface behind with a nailset and hammer. This works with finish nails only. (Consult the *Reader's Digest Complete Do-it-yourself Manual,* and Chapter 4, "Ornamentation.")

Some portion of the molding may be damaged and require replacement, or all too often, the molding may be missing due to a previous misguided improvement effort. Molding does not self-destruct; loss or damage is due to active interference by remodelers. Occasionally there will be a replacement right in the house, if the molding was saved when a wall was removed or a closet added. Otherwise, a trip to the lumberyard is called for. **A simple molding can be replaced outright. A more complicated pattern requires the combination or two or more basic moldings,** a technique used by the Victorians themselves.

Always buy wood molding, either pine or redwood. Never settle for extruded metal molding with a wood veneer, or wood molding with a layered vinyl veneer. Nor should you allow a hurried or unimaginative salesperson to tell you that what you want is "impossible" or "not done that way." Determine the size and shape of the moldings you need based on the original, as illustrated.

In 1957, a system called the WP/Series was introduced to categorize the vast number of stock molding sizes and styles. A $5/8'' \times 5/8''$ quarter round, for example, is called WP 107. This classification replaced a numbering system, probably developed in the 1880s, which identified molding styles by a four-digit number, beginning with a 4000 series and continuing into the 8000s. A catalog illustrating high volume, stock molding designs and sizes with WP numbers can be ordered for $2.50 from: Western Wood Molding and Millwork Producers, P.O. Box 25278, Portland, Oregon, 97225. Standard molding costs from 25¢ to $1.35 per foot, depending on its complexity.

If the trim is missing altogether, it is advisable for esthetic and investment purposes to put it back in place. A pattern for an exact duplicate of the original molding can sometimes be deciphered by looking for old paint profiles at the edge of door frames or in the corner of walls. Authentic copies of Victorian molding are available in stock at San Francisco Victoriana, 2245 Palou Avenue, San Francisco. Ask for their catalog. Custom-made molding for Victorian and other house styles can be ordered from the Bartley Milling Company, 8515 San Leandro Street, Oakland. For recycled trim, try Berkeley Architectural Salvage, 2741–10th Street, Berkeley.

MOLDING TO AVOID

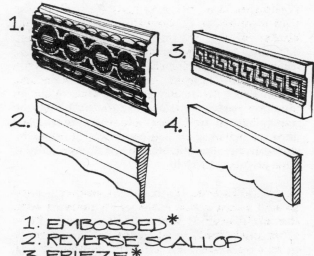

1. EMBOSSED*
2. REVERSE SCALLOP
3. FRIEZE*
4. SCALLOP

* MAY BE PLASTIC, WOOD OR METAL

If it is impossible to surmise the silhouette of the original molding, or precise reproduction is too costly, a perfectly adequate replacement can be installed using standard parts as long as the proportions are correct. Baseboard, for example, must be thick enough and high enough to visually anchor the wall to the floor. For baseboards in Colonial Revival houses, consider using a piece of exterior drop siding, with a base cap on top. That's what the original builders did. (Refer to the illustration "Do's and Don't's for Sheetrock" under "Walls: Plaster" for proper size and placement of baseboards.) Picture molding must be at the proper location on the wall to relate the height of people to the height of the ceiling. Remember, it was originally used to hang picture wire from.

Trim can be used with great success to make a plain house look a little more fancy as long as it is within the bounds of the architectural character. Supplement plain window or door frames with caps. Be certain the caps are consistent with one another. Add a chairrail or platerail to the top of wainscotting, or add cove molding where wall and ceiling meet. A piece of molding about 4"–6" wide, about 3½' from the floor on a 9' high wall, can create a valuable visual line for different wall surface or paint colors. (The bottom section should always be darker than the top.) If you're stuck with a modern, flush door, use molding to imitate the patterns of a real paneled door.

When adding new molding, **always choose classic designs that are suitable to the architectural character of the house.** Do not use scallops, inverted scallops, fake friezes, heavily embossed Spanish styles, or any other decorative pattern that calls attention to itself.

Some original trim is made of plaster instead of wood. Plaster cornices are found in Italianate, Colonial Revival and Prairie School houses. If the plaster has deteriorated, it may be expedient to use a combination of wood molding pieces to construct an acceptable replacement. Four basic shapes make up the forger's palette: the one-inch square, cove, half-round and quarter-round. Use plywood and/or masonite as a base and for projections.

Otherwise, a plaster cornice can be reproduced by a process called "running the molding." This involves

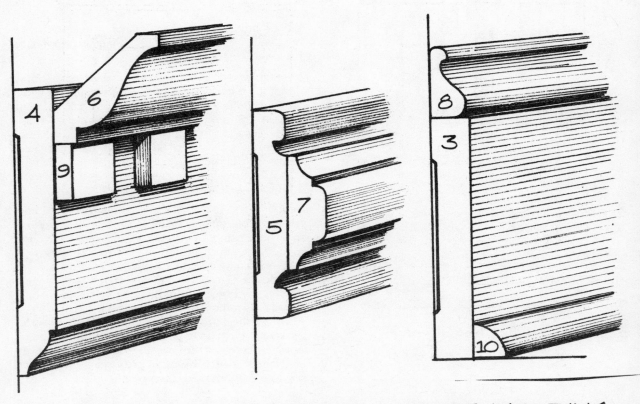

CORNICE   CHAIR RAIL   BASE MOLDING

TRIM MAY CONSIST OF A SINGLE MOLDING OR IT MAY BE BUILT-UP FROM 2 OR MORE OF THE BASIC SHAPES. THE COMPLEX TRIM PIECES SHOWN ARE NUMBER CODED TO THE PREVIOUS ILLUSTRATION TO REVEAL THEIR INDIVIDUAL COMPONENTS.

PLAIN, FLAT DOOR & WINDOW TRIM
CAN BE ENHANCED BY ADDING CAPS
OF THE PROPER PERIOD. THE WIN-
DOW CAP SHOWN WOULD BE SUIT-
ED TO A CRAFTSMAN OR COLONIAL
REVIVAL WINDOW. BE CONSISTENT:
ADD CAPS TO ALL THE DOORS &
WINDOWS IN A ROOM AT ONCE.

making a template that is the exact reverse of the cross-section of the molding you want to duplicate, throwing wet plaster up on the wall, and running the template over the wet plaster to shape. This is how it was done originally. Techniques for replacing plaster cornices are described in detail in *The Old-House Journal*, December 1984. An example of restored "run" plaster moldings can be seen at the Camron-Stanford house.

Removing Walls

The floor plan of a house can sometimes be improved by removal of a wall. A Victorian kitchen, for example, consisting of a trio of small rooms—one for cooking, one for washing, one for storage—may be converted to a single large room with a convenient work triangle and space for the family to gather. Or, in a Bungalow, two small bedrooms might be combined for a master suite.

When planning, **envision the shape of the space that will result.** Keep in mind the proportions of the room, the relationship of height, width and depth. More floor area is not the only criterion. A room that is made longer must be wide enough not to feel like an alley. A room that is made bigger must be high enough not to feel like a cellar.

Never remove a wall before its structural role is determined. Walls that are load-bearing support the ceiling above them. The overhead weight must be transferred to another support before the wall is removed, or collapse is likely. Non-load-bearing walls are more like floor-to-ceiling partitions. They separate one room from another, but play no part in the structure of the house.

Consult an architect or a builder for a professional evaluation of the wall's structural role, and recommendations regarding transfer of loads. Removal of a wall requires a building permit. The field visit by the building inspector is a valuable check on the safety of your plans.

Before the wall is demolished, salvage architectural features from it for use in other parts of the house. Molding, wainscotting, doors, doorframes and caps are especially useful for clothing a stripped wall elsewhere as well as for incorporating a new addition sympathetically.

THE DIFFERENCE BETWEEN A STRUCTURAL WALL AND A PERMANENT PARTITION

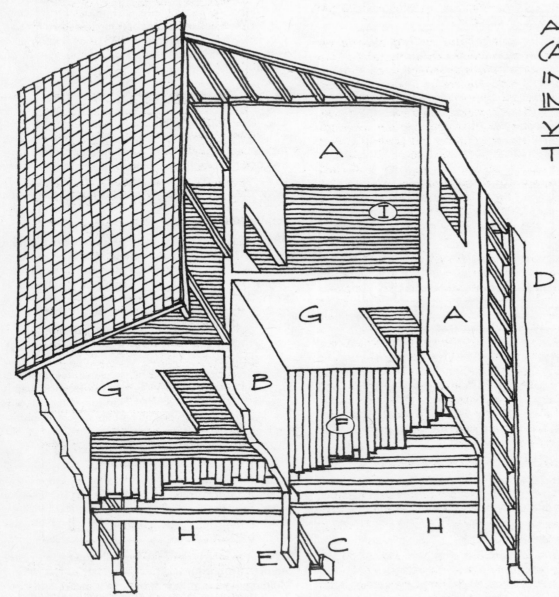

ALL EXTERIOR WALLS (A) ARE LOAD-BEARING. IN ADDITION, THERE ARE INTERIOR LOAD-BEARING WALLS (B) WHICH HELP TRANSMIT THE WEIGHT OF ROOF AND CEILING TO THE INTERIOR FOOTINGS (C) AND THE PERIMETER FOUNDATION (D). INTERIOR LOAD-BEARING WALLS SIT ATOP A FOUNDATION BEAM (E) AND ARE PARALLEL TO THE:
- SUBFLOOR (F)
- CEILING LATH
- CEILING CRACKS.

NON-LOADBEARING WALLS (G) ARE LIKE FLOOR TO CEILING PARTITIONS. THEY ARE USUALLY PARALLEL TO THE:
- JOISTS (H)
- FINISH FLOORING (I).

CEILING

The height and surface of the ceiling have a powerful influence on the way it feels to be in a room. A high ceiling, for example, suggests formality, and provides a setting that seems spacious enough for groups to gather, even if the dimensions of the floor plan are not that generous. A low ceiling suggests informality, and provides a more intimate setting for conversation or privacy. The height from floor to ceiling should be in proportion to the length and width of the room to ensure that the interior spaces will not seem awkwardly squat or elongated. Often, the ceiling heights within a house will differ from one room to the next to offer the residents a variety of living environments. The ceiling height original to each room in a house was intentionally selected to express the function of a room and the mood of the architecture, and this should be respected in the course of rehabilitation.

Whatever ills befall an old ceiling—and they are prone to cracks, for the ceilings, like the walls on pre-World War II houses, are made of plaster—**never change the original ceiling height.** The so-called "solution" offered by most home repair books to the problems of deterioration posed by aged plaster ceilings is to install a modern, dropped, acoustic tile surface overhead. This is no solution at all. It is an unnecessarily costly cosmetic cover-up that clashes with the architectural character of the house. Such measures reduce the appeal of the house rather than increase it.

Surface

Ceiling damage is not impossible to reverse and the repair process is generally less expensive than conversion to a modern, inappropriate ceiling style. Plaster ceilings are subject to cracks and holes due to settlement, water leakage and improper installation of hooks or fixtures. Always correct the cause of damage, like faulty plumbing, before correcting the symptom. Use the same techniques described for the repair of plaster walls, with the additional help of a sturdy ladder or two. Plaster dust from the ceiling can blanket a room, so cover floors and furniture, or remove the furnishings entirely.

Occasionally, plaster ceilings begin to sag because over time the lime in the plaster may corrode the lath nails. The bulging surface can be pressed back into place by drilling a hole through the plaster and installing a ceiling anchor, or by using a metal cup designed for that purpose.

For extensive damage, **the ceiling can be replastered, or sheetrock can be installed** by a technique similar to replacement of a wall. Refer to the *Readers Digest Complete Do-it-yourself Manual* for more detailed instructions. If the ceiling has ornamental trim, take the steps necessary to remove, save, and replace it. After attaching the sheetrock and taping the seams, prime and paint it. Unless there is an original plaster texture on the walls in the same room that warrants repetition, **do not trowel on an additional texture.** The use of a paint roller with thick pile is perfectly adequate. It will lend very subtle relief, and mask small imperfections in the sheetrock surface in the course of painting.

Compare material costs for resurfacing the ceiling of a small room measuring 8' by 12'. The preferred sheetrock method would cost about $52, complete. (This includes 3 sheetrock panels, $4' \times 8' \times \frac{1}{2}''$ at $5.30/sheet, sheetrock tape and joint compound at $10, one gallon of Lucite ceiling paint at $13, one hi-pile paint roller with a 9'' frame at $7.50 and one or two paintbrushes for $5.) The acoustic tile method would cost $112, more than twice as much. (This is based on 96 square feet of acoustic tile at 75¢/square foot average, 96 linear feet of $1'' \times 3''$ furring strips at 20¢ a linear foot and staple gun and staples at $20.) The larger the ceiling, the greater the price differential will be.

If you must use a modern ceiling surface:

- Select a modern product that is plain white, without patterns, glitter or volcanic eruptions. Respect the fact that the original plaster was flat and entire.

- Select as neutral a surface as possible. The ceiling is not a planetarium.

- Install it at the same level as the original ceiling. If the plaster is in place, smooth it out by the same techniques described for plaster repairs, and glue the tiles directly to the plaster with a special contact adhesive manufactured for that purpose. If the plaster and lath have been removed, nail

CEILING: DOS AND DON'TS

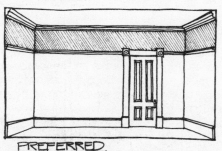

PREFERRED
ORIGINAL CEILING AND WALL TREATMENT OR SHEETROCK CEILING WITH MOLDING REPLACED.

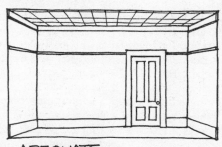

ADEQUATE
NEW MATERIALS BUT PROPORTION AND LOCATION OF ORIGINAL ELEMENTS ARE RETAINED. PLAIN ACOUSTIC TILES ARE PLACED DIRECTLY UPON THE CEILING, ABOVE A MOLDING OF ADEQUATE WIDTH.

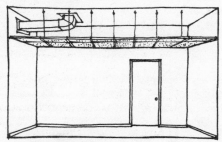

OBJECTIONABLE
LOWERED CEILING WITH HOLES OR HEAVY TEXTURE ON THE SURFACE OF THE PANELS. DECORATIVE ELEMENTS AND PROPORTIONS OF THE ROOM ARE DISREGARDED.

furring strips no more than 1″ thick directly to the joists of rafters above, and staple the tiles to them.

Space

Never suspend the ceiling. In addition to the questionable purposes of cosmetic concealment and outright modernization, dropped ceilings are also misused as a way to hide new wiring or plumbing, as acoustic mufflers and as heat conservers. There are alternative approaches to each of these situations that are much more sensitive to the architectural style.

To reduce fuel costs, consult *Retrofit Right: How To Make Your Old House Energy Efficient*, described on the last page of Chapter 7. Note well: insulating the interior walls or ceilings of a house does not save fuel or money, as explained in detail in *Retrofit Right*. To muffle sounds, use rugs, drapes, upholstery, or fabric "wallpaper" to absorb the reverberation. To isolate sounds from other rooms, install fiberglass batt insulation between studs in situations where the lath and plaster have been removed on at least one side. To conceal new plumbing and wiring, plan modernized utility systems in advance of other improvements so that closets, shafts and floor space can be used to their best advantage. (Refer to "Utility Systems.")

Special Features

Where special architectural features distinguish a ceiling, **these assets should always be retained.** If the features are missing, but belong to the style, it is to the building's advantage to replace them.

Rosette

Victorian and Colonial Revival houses are fortunate to possess a rosette in the middle of the ceiling as a highly decorative surround for the chandelier. A rosette is a circular plaster sculpture shaped like a flower, hence its name. Small rosettes are molded in a single piece as small as 6″ in diameter, while others are assembled in several sections, or wreaths, and are as wide as 4′ in diameter. The rosette design is in proportion to the size of the ceiling, the volume of the room and the shape of the original light fixture.

In Victorian times, the rosette was integrated in the

ROSETTE CROSS-SECTION

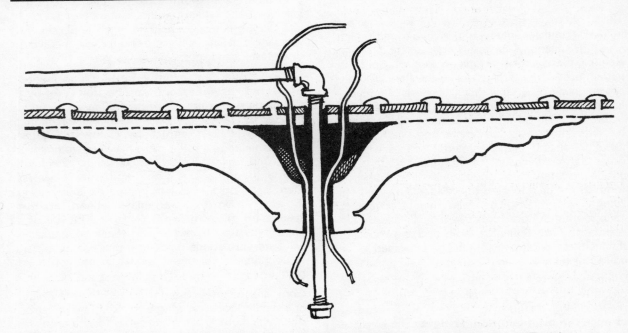

THIS IS A CROSS-SECTION OF A PLASTER ROSETTE, APPLIED TO THE CEILING WITH PLASTER OF PARIS (AND WIRE TIES FOR THE LARGE, SEGMENTED ROSETTES). A HOLE WAS PROVIDED FOR A GAS PIPE AND THE CAPPED PIPE OFTEN REMAINS DESPITE THE REPLACEMENT OF GAS FIXTURES WITH ELECTRIC ONES. ELECTRIC WIRES WERE RUN THROUGH THE PIPE HOLE.

ceiling plaster. Segmented rosettes were additionally supported by tie-wires, threaded through the lath to the structural member above. Thus, major repairs to the rosette require cutting it out of the ceiling. Saw through the lath around the perimeter of the rosette, supporting it as you do so. Use a long chisel to loosen it from behind, and a hacksaw to sever the tie-wires. This may be easier from the floor or attic above it.

Once the rosette is off, you can strip accumulated paint by dipping the rosette in a pan of very hot water right on the stove and scrubbing with a toothbrush. The difficult layer is the calcimine, closest to the plaster. Fill in small cracks and holes with plaster. If necessary, rebuild missing sections with a self-mold and casting plaster. When sanding, be very careful not to smooth sharp edges, or you will destroy the detail instead of resurrecting it. Prime and paint, as you would a new rosette.

Re-install the rosette in the original way by replacing it in the hole in the ceiling and securing it with tie-wires and a fresh coat of plaster. Or, secure the rosette with bolts and screws to the joists.

A much simpler solution, if the rosette is missing, broken, or obscured by countless layers of paint, is to buy a new one. San Francisco Victoriana has a selection of 42 different styles, averaging in size from 20″ to 28″ in diameter. The average price is $2.00 per diameter inch. Complete instructions are provided to guide installation.

Even if the original light fixture is missing, you can still take advantage of the rosette. Select another pipe-type chandelier that looks appropriate, even if it is not an accurate reproduction. (Refer to "Utility Systems: Electrical" for guidelines on fixture selection.) If the gas line is not yet sealed, have the line capped off by a qualified plumber. Amateurs should not handle gas lines that may still be active.

Trim

Victorian and Colonial Revival houses have ceiling moldings made of wood, or more commonly, plaster. **Ceiling molding, cornices or other trim should be retained, or removed and replaced if necessary, in the course of ceiling repair.** (Refer to "Plaster Ornamentation" and "Walls: Trim.")

COVED CEILING DETAIL

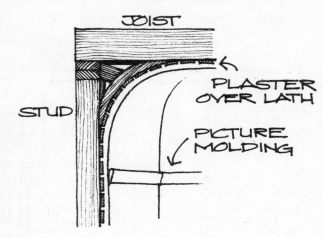

JOIST

STUD

PLASTER OVER LATH

PICTURE MOLDING

Half a century or more of paint jobs can result in a nasty accumulation that blurs the crisp juncture of ceiling and wall. To correct this, use a manual paint scraper to score and remove the build-up. Sand the edge of the newly exposed layers of paint so that the transition from thick paint to scraped corner is as smooth as possible. To conceal the build-up instead of correcting it, paint the corner as is, then add a strip of suitable cove molding around the perimeter of the ceiling where it meets the top of the wall.

Beams

First Bay Tradition houses and some Colonial Revival houses boast exposed or boxed beams on the living room and dining room ceiling. Or, they may have imitation coffered ceilings which are made of stepped planks, combined to resemble timbers and criss-crossed to suggest recessed panels. If wood ceiling ornamentation has been painted so many times that the angular corners have become rounded, or if you choose to reveal the natural wood as is so well-suited to the Craftsman styles, strip the paint by one of the techniques described under "Walls: Wood." **Natural wood beams are dramatic,** and a real architectural asset since they are a rarity in new residential construction.

Coved Corners

Coved ceilings curve down gracefully at the edges to meet the wall. They are found in selected Victorian houses and in some examples of the Colonial Revival, First Bay Tradition and Period Revival styles. Coved ceilings were created by attaching the lath strips above the cornice or picture molding to a curved framework instead of to the studs. This framework usually describes a quarter circle between the wall and the ceiling surface. Repair techniques for a coved ceiling are identical with those for conventional plaster walls, as the basic construction technique is the same. However, if damage is severe enough to call for replacement, the surface must be replastered because sheetrock is inflexible and cannot be nailed to a curved surface. The plasterer will probably use expanded metal lath for backing instead of the original wood strips. If coved corners are intact, keep them in place. If they are in disrepair, it is worthwhile to attend to them because **coved corners give a room a special sense of enclosure that makes the space particularly nice to be in.**

DOORS

Style

Classified by construction method, there are three types of interior doors: the panel door, the solid core door and the hollow core door. **The panel door is the type original to all house styles discussed in REHAB RIGHT,** except the Wartime Tract. The panel door is made of a wood outer frame inset with recessed wood panels or with glass which is often frosted, stained or leaded. Panel doors are three-dimensional by nature, and they distinguish a room the same way a fine piece of handcrafted furniture does.

In sorry contrast, the solid core and hollow core door are plain, flat and mass-produced. The solid core door is made of layers of wood laminated together with glue. The hollow core door is made of a wood frame filled with honeycomb cardboard and covered by sheets of lightweight veneer.

TYPES OF DOORS

PANEL DOOR

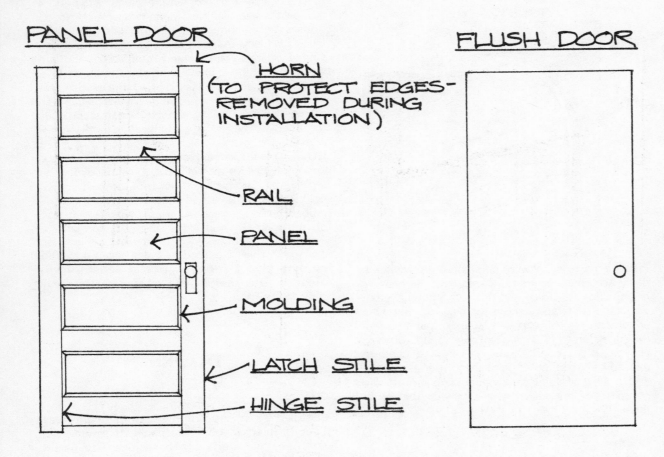

HORN
(TO PROTECT EDGES—
REMOVED DURING
INSTALLATION)

RAIL

PANEL

MOLDING

LATCH STILE

HINGE STILE

FLUSH DOOR

- Thanks to their solidity, panel doors offer more effective sound insulation than hollow core doors.
- Panel doors are usually outfitted with more attractive hardware. The knobs and hinges available for core doors do not compare in execution of detail.
- Panel doors are architectural features that stay with the house and add to its resale value, contrary to what a core door salesman may tell you.

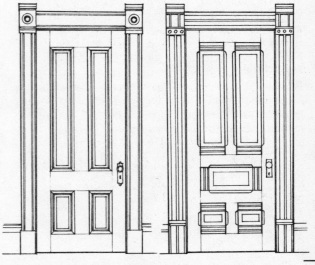

VICTORIAN DOORS ARE PANEL DOORS WITH A VERTICAL EMPHASIS. THEY DISPLAY SUCH A VARIETY OF MOLDINGS AND EMBELLISHMENTS THAT IT IS HARD TO ASSIGN SPECIFIC DOORS AND DOORFRAMES TO EACH RECOGNIZED VICTORIAN ARCHITECTURAL STYLE.

DOORS WITH VERTICAL PANELS WANED IN POPULARITY AFTER THE VICTORIAN ERA AND THE HORIZONTAL PANEL DOOR, COMMONLY WITH FIVE PANELS, WAS THE DOMINANT FORMAT DURING THE CRAFTSMAN PERIOD. THE FIVE PANEL DOOR YIELDED TO THE SINGLE PANEL DOOR ABOUT 1915. RUSTIC DOORS OF VERTICAL BOARDS, FOUND IN PERIOD REVIVAL HOUSES, WERE AN EXCEPTION TO THE PANEL DOOR TREND WHICH ENDED WITH THE PROLIFERATION OF FLUSH DOORS IN THE 1940's AND 1950's.

It is a grievous error to replace panel doors at the entry to a room or a closet with solid or hollow core counterparts, or to camouflage a valuable panel door under a sheet of plywood in imitation of its arch rival. Here's why:

- Panel doors match the architectural features of older rooms, and core doors do not. The molding that outlines the recesses, the proportion of the panels, the sturdiness of construction and the solidity of appearance, all look right with the other architectural features in the room. A core door is woefully out of place.

- Panel doors match the door frame, itself a composition of molding, trim cap and baseboard. A core door in this context looks like the piece of cardboard in a fancy picture frame before the work of art is mounted.

- Replacing a worn or damaged panel door with a "carefree" modern door is wasteful. Most problems experienced with panel doors can be repaired at practically no expense, and the result is a door that is far more durable than a core door—particularly a flimsy hollow core door—will ever be.

Fit

All doors are subject to binding or looseness, but panel doors more so, simply because of their years of service. Usually this is not a fault of the door itself, but a matter of poor fit at the hinges or lockset, or excessive layers of paint. **Correcting a balky panel door is so inexpensive that no justification exists for switching to a modern door style.**

There are three common causes of balky doors: a set of improperly adjusted hinges, distortion of the door so that it no longer fits the frame, and distortion of the frame so that it no longer fits the door.

To determine which is the cause, stand so the door opens toward you, but keep the door closed. Take a coin, or a piece of wood 1/16″ thick, and slide it along the space between the door and the jamb. Pinpoint the sticky spots where the coin won't slide. If there is a large gap at the opposite side of the door from the stubborn spot, then the problem is a loose hinge. If the door fits too tightly all the way around, and you can't fit the coin on the top and bottom, then the door has probably swelled from dampness or paint and the troublesome edges require planing. If the coin hits several sticky spots at random locations, and if there are telltale cracks in the plaster around the doorframe, then the house has probably settled and caused the doorframe to shift position and press on the door at several points. This too requires planing. It is far simpler to fix the door than the door frame.

Consult a home repair book, like the *American Handyman* or Sunset *Basic Home Repairs Illustrated*, for the specific techniques necessary to tighten loose doors and loosen tight doors, like planing, shimming, door removal and door hanging.

Damage

Worn panel doors may have a kicked-in panel or a loose rail. Thanks to its construction, **the panel door can be dismantled and the damaged piece repaired or replaced,** as illustrated. Compare this to the flush or solid core doors which, once damaged, offer no repair options and require costly replacement.

Often, after a succession of occupants over the course of half a century, panel doors become swaddled in

PANEL DOOR CONSTRUCTION

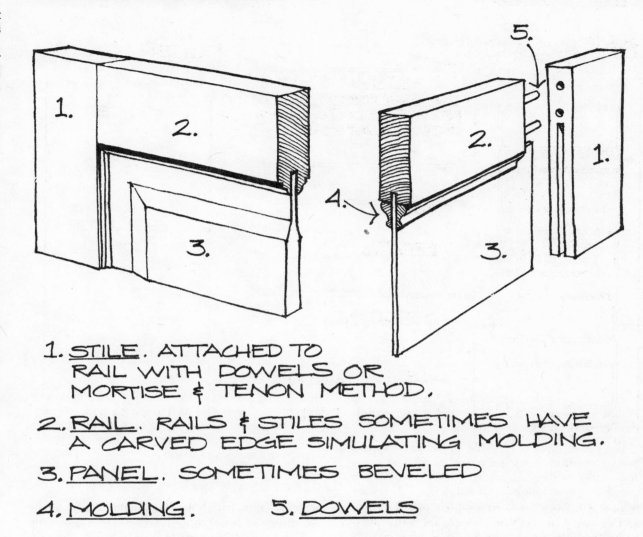

1. STILE. ATTACHED TO RAIL WITH DOWELS OR MORTISE & TENON METHOD.
2. RAIL. RAILS & STILES SOMETIMES HAVE A CARVED EDGE SIMULATING MOLDING.
3. PANEL. SOMETIMES BEVELED
4. MOLDING.   5. DOWELS

coats of paint. The crisp edges and recesses lose their definition, and the angular corners become rounded. To resurrect the geometric form of the door the paint should be stripped, even if you plan to paint it again. (Techniques for stripping wood are discussed under the heading "Walls: Wood.") Or, you can arrange to have the door dipped, as des-

cribed for front doors in Chapter 4. If the house is in the First Bay Tradition style, you may choose to leave the natural wood exposed, using an oil finish or clear varnish.

If it is appropriate to repaint a painted door, use a semi-gloss latex enamel, as described under "Walls:

FLUSH DOOR CONSTRUCTION

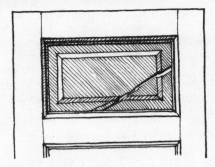

VENEER

AIR SPACE

HOLLOW CORE

CARDBOARD HONEYCOMB

SOLID CORE

SOLID WOOD BLOCKING

PANEL DOOR REPAIR

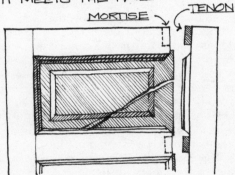

MORTISE   TENON

- REMOVE DOOR.
- CAREFULLY WORK A PRY BAR BETWEEN TOP RAIL & STILE. PRY OFF STILE GRADUALLY, WORKING DOWN ALONG THE STILE AT THE POINTS WHERE IT MEETS THE RAILS.

- PRY OFF TOP OR BOTTOM RAIL IF TOP OR BOTTOM PANELS ARE DAMAGED, OTHERWISE REMOVE SECOND STILE ENTIRELY.
- REMOVE DAMAGED PANEL. REPLACE WITH MATCHING PANEL FROM SALVAGE YARD OR LESS PROMINENT DOOR. IF THE PANEL IS FLAT, ¼" PLYWOOD MAY DO AS A REPLACEMENT.
- CLEAN DOWELS OR TENONS AND APPLY A THIN COATING OF WOOD GLUE. RE-ASSEMBLE DOOR, ALLOWING GLUE TO DRY BEFORE HANGING. FASTEN ANY LOOSE MOLDINGS.

Paint." Prepare the surface by lightly sanding to assure adhesion, and fill nicks and gouges which mar the surface with wood putty.

If the panel door is missing or broken beyond repair, replace it with a panel door that suits the style of the house as indicated by other panel doors, or trim designs still in place. You may be able to relocate a closet door for use to better advantage as a room door. Otherwise, go to a salvage company. At Berkeley Architectural Salvage a 4-panel door costs about $25. Before you go to the salvage yard, jot down the dimensions of the door opening, from the inside of the hinge jamb to the inside of the latch jamb, and from top to bottom. A door that appeals to you and suits the house but is too large by 2″ or less can be planed down to fit.

New panel doors can be ordered through any local lumber yard. Compare manufacturers' catalogs to find the style that best suits the architecture of your

house. A 1″ hemlock door with six raised (beveled) panels costs about $190. For the sake of comparison, solid core interior doors cost about $66 and hollow core doors about $46, with the price depending on the species of wood.

Doorframe

The doorframe is as much a part of the doorway as the door itself. The style of the trim goes with the design of the door so **it should always be left in its original form** and repaired or replaced as necessary. Doorframes, like other types of architectural trim, are constructed of components. The Victorian examples are often quite elaborate, the Colonial Revival style, refined, and the First Bay Tradition, straightforward. Often the design of the door and frame is held over from the preceding architectural styles, so it is not uncommon to find Victorian doors and frames in Colonial Revival houses and

TYPICAL PROBLEMS ON INTERIOR DOORS

5. STOPS : WARPED DOOR OR STOP
SOLUTION : MOVE STOP

6. DOOR JAMB : MAY SHIFT DUE TO
SETTLEMENT OF HOUSE.
SOLUTION : WORK ON DOOR
ITSELF, NOT DOORJAMB.

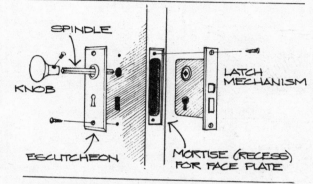

SPINDLE

KNOB

ESCUTCHEON

LATCH MECHANISM

MORTISE (RECESS) FOR FACE PLATE

7. KNOBS : KNOB MISSING OR RE-
PLACED WITH ONE INAPPRO-
PRIATE TO DOOR & HOUSE
SOLUTION : FIND KNOBS MATCH-
ING OR IN CHARACTER WITH
ORIGINALS. OR, USE KNOBS
FROM LESS CONSPICUOUS LOCA-
TIONS SUCH AS CLOSETS.
IF KNOB IS JUST LOOSE :
TIGHTEN MACHINE SCREW THAT
HOLDS KNOB TO SPINDLE (OB-
TAIN REPLACEMENT IF SCREW
IS STRIPPED OR MISSING).

8. ESCUTCHEON : MAY BE TARNISHED
OR PAINTED (ALSO HINGES, KNOBS,
FACE PLATES & STRIKE PLATES).
SOLUTION : USE PAINT REMOVER
(TAKE OFF OF DOOR FIRST) & BRASS
POLISH. REPLATE IF NEEDED.

9. LATCH MECHANISM : CAN HAVE
MECHANICAL MALFUNCTIONS.
SOLUTIONS : CLEAN & OIL. IF
THIS FAILS, CONSULT A LOCK-
SMITH OR FIND AN OLD LATCH
THE SAME SIZE WHICH WORKS.

10. STRIKE PLATE : MAY BE OUT OF
ALIGNMENT WITH LATCH, PRE-
VENTING PROPER CLOSURE.
SOLUTION : ENLARGE MORTISE
ENOUGH TO MOVE STRIKE PLATE
UP OR DOWN AS NEEDED.

1. EDGES : MAY SWELL.
SOLUTION : PLANING. (DON'T
PLANE ON LATCH SIDE.)

2. HINGES : CAN CAUSE STICK-
ING WHEN LOOSE.
SOLUTIONS : ADD CARDBOARD
SHIMS, REMOUNT SCREWS
AFTER PACKING HOLES FOR
A TIGHTER FIT, OR SET MOR-
TISES DEEPER.

3. BOTTOM : MAY SAG (BIND)
ON LATCH SIDE.
SOLUTIONS : SHIM OUT
BOTTOM HINGE, RESET SCREWS
OF TOP HINGE, OR DEEPEN
MORTISE OF TOP HINGE.

4. DOOR PLANE : MAY WARP
SOLUTIONS : TRY HOME REPAIR
BOOK METHODS TO STRAIGHTEN,
RESET STOP, REPLACE DOOR.

Colonial Revival doors and frames in Craftsman houses.

The doorframe is a good opportunity for embellishment. A simple doorway can be made much more interesting by the simple and sensitive addition of a door cap on the head trim, or an extra strip of molding on the jamb. Make sure the embellishments are in keeping with the trim style in the room, and the general character of the house. Use the exterior window ornament, for example, as a guideline on a Victorian house. Refer to the sections "Walls: Wood" and "Walls: Trim" for additional information on sources of molding and creative ways to combine standard parts. See especially the illustration "Adding a Window Cap" as the technique is equally applicable to the doorframe. The windowframe and doorframe should be embellished at the same time.

Hardware

Like the door and the doorframe, **the hardware original to the panel door is architecturally valuable for its appearance and economically valuable for its material.** Original knobs and hinges should always be retained, yet, like the door and the doorframe, the hardware is often needlessly plundered in the name of modernization. Do not replace a fine brass, brass-plated or glass doorknob with an ordinary cylindrical handle. A latch that malfunctions can usually be repaired by a locksmith. Make sure to check the alignment of the strike plate before faulting the latch mechanism.

If the latch is diagnosed as beyond repair, then try salvage yards, antique stores or specialty shops. Sometimes locksmiths are privy to desirable doorknobs sacrificed by customers less enlightened than you. The design of a replacement knob or hinge should be consistent with other hardware in the room, if possible. You may choose to swipe a doorknob from another, less obvious location, like the inside of a closet door.

When remounting door hardware, use solid brass screws to remount brass or brass-plated hardware. Likewise, use bronze finish screws for bronze hardware. Refer to Chapter 4, "Front Door: Hardware," for the improvement and care of brass or brass-plated door hardware.

FIREPLACE

Throughout history, the hearth has been a romantic symbol of the happy home, a warm fireside that beckons the world-weary. As such, the fireplace is an architectural feature valuable for the sensual enjoyment it offers as well as for the visual focus it provides.

An attractive and functional fireplace definitely adds resale value to a house. Some realtors estimate as much as $5000. Do not board up an old fireplace in an attempt to modernize. Doing so drastically alters the character of the room, needlessly sacrifices an economic asset, and otherwise deprives your family and future residents of creature comfort, not to mention a hitching post for Christmas stockings. Besides, in these days of energy conservation, what could be more "modern" than an auxiliary source of heat?

Exterior Appearance

Style

The style of the fireplace is dictated by the architecture of the house. It could even be said that the fireplace sums it up, since the features prototypical of the building design—proportion, mass, materials and ornamentation—are incorporated in the mantel, surround, firebox and hearth. If the original fireplace is intact, keep it by all means. If the original mantel, surround or hearth are missing or irreparably damaged, replace them in a manner sympathetic to the architectural character of the house.

Basically, there are two kinds of fireplace designs: the **built-in mantel** and the **add-on mantel.** The latter is typical to Victorian houses. During construction, a hole would be roughed in the wall, a firebox, damper and flue installed, and the surround surfaced with fire resistant tile. Only much later was the mantel added on. Thus the Victorians could select whatever mantel design appealed, as if choosing a piece of furniture.

Although mantel designs usually echoed the houses' other architectural features, they were nevertheless quite varied due to the assortment of construction materials, mail-order catalogs and the Victorian esthetic. The earliest examples were carved from marble, but this costly stone was soon replaced with its economic counterpart, slate. By the 1880s, carbon copies of the marble mantels were hewn from wood. In San Francisco Stick style houses, an elaborate overmantel with mirrors and what-not shelves was incorporated in the fireplace design. The distinct disadvantage of the add-on method is that it facilitated removal of mantels in subsequent years by misguided modernizers and well-informed vandals.

Most Victorian fireplaces were the primary heat source and generally burned coal. With the introduction of central heating, fireplaces were redesigned as an auxiliary heat source. They were made larger to accommodate wood as fuel, and the mantels were built in. In Colonial Revival houses, both types of fireplaces can be found. The predominant mantel design is a pair of classic columns with a pediment on top, in a darkly stained or painted wood.

The built-in wood-burning fireplace is a hallmark of First Bay Tradition houses. Typically, the mantel is flanked by built-in bookcases, with glass doors, and the stack by a pair of fixed windows, often leaded or stained. The hearth is made of brick, or square tiles in gray, tan or brown. The mantel may be built entirely of clinker brick or it may be wood, with the hearth tiles incorporated as the surround. To determine whether the wood was originally painted, look at the abutting cabinet shelves. If their undersides are painted, the mantel usually was too, and the wood probably does not warrant stripping.

The fireplace is essential to the interior of the Period Revival house because it helps to carry out the fanciful architectural theme. Again, the mantel is built in. In fact, it is so ensconced in a massive silo of stucco that it is a protuberant continuation of the wall. The hearth and surround may be tile, rough stones, or brick laid in the herringbone pattern. The stack, and the walls to either side, have arched, recessed niches, or else darkly stained wood beams to reiterate half-timbering elsewhere in the house.

On the Wartime Tract house, the bulk of the fireplace structure is outside the building, as seen in the drawing in Chapter 2. The brick facing, and the

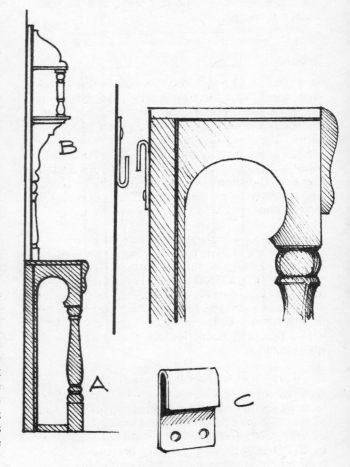

INSTALLING AN ADD-ON MANTEL

ADD-ON MANTELS (A) AND OVERMANTELS (B) CAN BE SECURED TO THE WALL WITH FLAT HOOKS (C). USE 2 OR MORE SETS OF HOOKS. PATIENCE AND CAREFUL MEASURING ARE NEEDED TO INSURE THAT THE MANTEL WILL JUST REACH THE FLOOR.

wood ledge that constitutes the mantel, project no more than the depth of a brick into the living room. The forms are simple and rectilinear, and the brick is often painted.

Repair

To replace a missing add-on mantel, scavenge salvage yards, and because mantels are becoming something of a collector's item, peruse antique shops. Painted or stripped mantels with beveled glass, cost about $150–$600 second-hand at Sunrise Salvage, Berkeley. As long as the design is architecturally sensitive, there is no need to duplicate the original precisely. The selection of the original add-on mantel was a matter of the first owner's taste, and so the replacement may be an expression of yours.

To reconstruct a damaged built-in mantel, consult a cabinetmaker, or do it yourself. Erect a simple wood box, with a ledge on top, and chamfered corners perhaps. For ornamentation, add standard molding, separately or in creative combinations, as explained in the section "Walls: Trim." To incorporate hearth tile in the mantel ornamentation, cement it in place with a product suitable for wall tiles, and frame it with moldings.

While a reproduction of the original mantel is not essential for a well-designed result, a reasonable facsimile entitles you to the rules of applicable code. (Consult Chapter 3.) In contrast, a redesigned rebuilt mantel must conform to modern standards established by the Uniform Building Code. Its requirements, however, do not preclude an architecturally sensitive replacement. For example:

- Clearance of at least 12″ between the fireplace opening and any combustible materials. (In other words, a facing 12″-wide of fire resistant brick or tile between the fireplace opening and the wood mantel.)
- Hearth dimension of no less than 20″ in front and no less than 12″ to either side of a fireplace opening that measures six square feet or more; hearth dimension of no less than 16″ in front and 8″ to either side of a fireplace opening less than six square feet.

Whether replacing or rebuilding a mantel, follow these design guidelines:
- The size of the mantel should be in proportion to the shape of the room and to the size of the fireplace opening.
- The woodwork, tiles and trim should be consistent with the other decorative motifs in the room and on the house.
- The size of the fireplace opening should never be changed for esthetic purposes only. (See below.)

If an existing fireplace was thoughtlessly painted, the paint can be removed from tile, marble, stone and wood by the stripping techniques described under "Walls: Wood." If clinker brick has been painted, the only effective solution is sandblasting, and regrettably so. The process engenders an incredible mess, threatens surrounding wood and plaster with pockmarks, and releases arsenic dust. Natural brick should never be painted as painting it, for all practical purposes, is an irreversible action.

To remove soot stains from brick, tile or stone facing, use detergent and water. For stubborn stains, a solution of water and muriatic acid, half-and-half, should do, but gloves and eye protection are a must.

Internal Workings

A fireplace in poor repair constitutes two very serious hazards. Insufficient draw permits smoke to fill the room and deoxygenate the breathing air. Poor draw may be the result of a blocked or sooty flue, a faulty damper or an ineffectual ratio of fireplace opening to flue size. It usually takes only a small newspaper fire to identify this problem. Make certain the damper is operative first, and open it.

A leaky flue may allow sparks or flames to contact the building's structural frame and ignite the wood. Leaks result from cracks in the flue liner, crumbling mortar, missing bricks, and the separation of the fireplace from the chimney as a result of settlement. Since accumulated soot is combustible, a dirty chimney sets the stage for a flue fire. Look for these symptoms of a situation susceptible to a flue or structural fire:

- separation of hearth from floor plane

PARTS OF A FIREPLACE

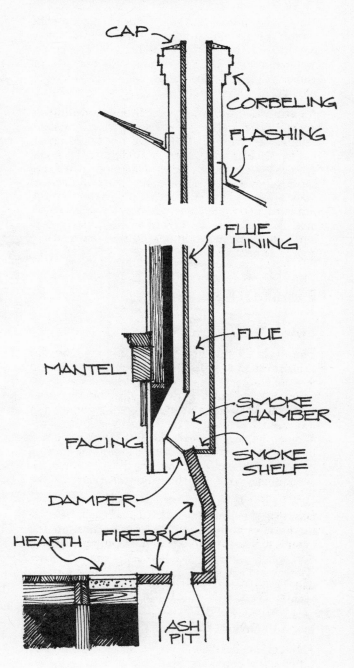

117

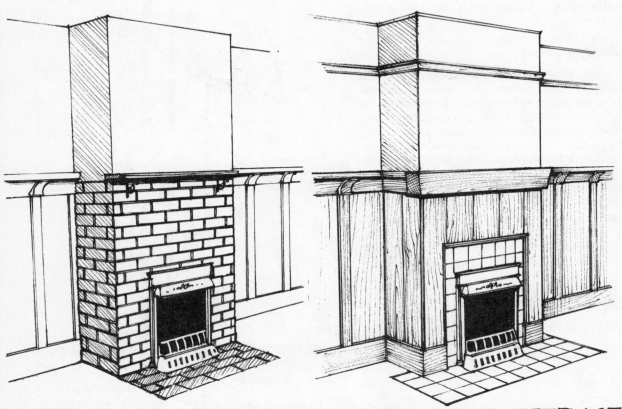

IN THIS MISGUIDED REMODEL-LING EFFORT, IMITATION BRICK HAS BEEN APPLIED, A SKIMPY MANTEL REPLACES THE ORIG-INAL AND THE REMAINING PANELLING HAS BEEN PAINTED AND THE CORNICE REMOVED. OTHER TECHNIQUES ARE USED TO ALTER FIREPLACES BUT LOSS OF CHARACTER OFTEN RESULTS.

RESCUING THE FIREPLACE FROM THIS SADLY COMMON DISGUISE ENTAILS REMOVING THE BOGUS MATERIALS AND ADDING MANTEL, BASEBOARD, AND CORNICE MOLDING WHICH MATCH THE SURVIVING CRAFTS-MAN PANELLING IN PROPORTION. (STRIP THE PANELLING FIRST). UNGLAZED TILE IS USED FOR HEARTH AND SURROUND.

- separation of mantel from the wall, even as little as 1/8″
- no daylight visible up through the chimney (use a mirror to reflect the rays)
- accumulated soot in the throat of the chimney (use a flashlight).

Unfortunately, most cities do not offer inspectional services to specifically evaluate fireplace safety. Professional consultation and service (listed in the *Yellow Pages* under "Chimneysweep" and "Fireplaces") are available and advisable for the more sophisticated operations associated with fireplace repair, like replacing a flue lining. Detecting hazardous problems and correcting insufficient draw requires deftness and equipment as well as expertise. Before hiring a fireplace firm, make sure they have damage and liability insurance. Chimney dust is extremely fine, and can permeate a house if mishandled. Also confirm a contractor's license if structural work is involved. (See Chapter 6.)

Repair of the internal working order of a fireplace can be accomplished without disturbing the original exterior appearance. Home repair manuals offer basic instruction in pertinent techniques, such as installing firebrick and repointing fireclay. The May 1977 and January 1985 issues of *The Old-House Journal* have a thorough discussion of other technical problems.

Never enlarge a small fireplace opening if the flue size is to remain the same. The proportion of the flue size to the fireplace opening is a critical factor for successful draw. The rule of thumb is that the fireplace opening should be not more than 10 to 12 times the area of the flue opening. (For example, a fireplace has an existing flue measuring 9″ × 12″, or 72 square inches. By the guideline, the fireplace opening should be 36″ by 24″, an opening of 864 square inches, or 12 times the flue.) Additional axioms for good draw are; width greater than height, and depth at least two feet.

Do not be frustrated by the limited size of a small Victorian fireplace. It can be used for burning wood as long as the logs are chopped to fit, burned in reasonably small quantities, and the rest of the fireplace mechanisms are in working order. Better yet, use coal, the fuel for which the fireplace was originally intended. A 100-pound sack costs $12.00 at Larm's Building Materials in Oakland. Add coal to an already glowing wood fire for a longer lasting, more intense heat.

It is possible to correct draw problems by reducing the size of a fireplace opening and improving its ratio to the flue. Experiment by lining the bottom, sides, or back of the firebox with firebrick, but without mortar. When you discover the configuration that works best, make the installation permanent with fireclay. For new fireplaces, the Uniform Building Code requires that the firebox be at least 20" deep, with top, bottom and side walls made of at least 4" of firebrick backed by at least 4" of common brick, and fireclay joints ¼" thick.

Never place a gas heater in the fireplace, nor direct its gas vent through the chimney. This is dangerous, illegal and architecturally inappropriate. (Consult "Utility Systems: Mechanical.") Call the City's Inspectional Services Department for information on mechanical permits necessary for the installation of a gas heater. If this condition exists, consider relocating or replacing the gas heater and restoring the fireplace.

The chimney itself may not be structurally sound, as evidenced by leaning, separation of the chimney from the house, cracks, crumbling mortar and loose bricks. Consult Chapter 4, under "Roof: Chimney," and a standard home repair book.

When preparing to buy a house, evaluate the condition of the fireplace and estimate the cost of repair prior to agreement on the sales price. The cost of making the fireplace operative can be a factor in negotiating the deal, much as the cost of termite repair is.

To clean the chimney, call a chimneysweep. Chimneys need cleaning every 15 to 20 years to optimize draw and minimize the danger of a flue fire. But according to an Oakland fireplace specialist, most chimneys have never been cleaned at all. The going rate is about $53.

STAIRCASE

Think of the amount of space a staircase takes up in a two-story house, and the quantity of materials.

Why, it's easily as important as an entire room, and probably more so because it can be seen from so many angles, and it is *sine qua non* of circulation. The staircase structure and ornamentation are unique within the house. When improvements are made, the original combination of function and decoration should be respected, and wherever possible, retained.

Style

In two-story Italianate and San Francisco Stick style Victorians, the staircase is straight and narrow, running the length of the entry hall. To maintain the tall, thin proportions of the architectural style, and to traverse the considerable vertical distance from first to second floor—remember the 12' ceilings—the risers are especially high and the treads short. In the large Queen Anne house, the entry hall merged with the living area and the stair sequence became a focal point. It assumed a square configuration, the direction of the steps doubling back at a landing midway up the flight. Victorian stairways are distinguished by turned balusters, one or two per tread, carved spandrels, and substantial newel posts. Often the partition wall concealing the stringers is surfaced with lincrusta-Walton.

During the Colonial Revival era, the landing at the kink in the staircase was elaborated upon, with built-in benches, hidden storage and stained glass windows. The balustrade, simpler than the Victorian and more classical in detail, was often, but not exclusively, painted. The staircase is faced with wainscotting, like the other walls within view.

On large Brown Shingle and Prairie School houses, the balustrade derives its decorative aspects from the structure itself. The wood is natural, the lines are simple, and the forms massive. There is typically one baluster per tread, and it is rectangular in profile. Craftsman wainscotting covers the open-stringer side.

Repair

The question of applicable code, introduced in Chapter 3, is especially pertinent to the repair or reconstruction of staircases. As interpreted by the City of Oakland, repair means to

NEWEL POST

NEWEL POSTS ARE THE OFTEN HEAVILY ORNAMENTED POSTS WHICH ANCHOR THE ENDS OF THE HANDRAIL. SPANDREL ORNAMENTS ADORN THE AREA UNDER THE TREAD END TRIM.

replace treads, risers or handrails. To rebuild means to replace the entire works, including the structural support, called stringers or horses. The Inspectional Services Department generally advises that for purposes of safety, rebuilt stairs be constructed to modern standards, since staircases are a common location for household falls. Fortunately for the architecture, however, reconstruction to modern code is not required.

Thanks to an amendment to the State of California Health and Safety Code (by Senate Bill 2348) owners of single-family and duplex dwellings are entitled to the replacement, retention and extension or original materials and the use of original methods. **If you want to rebuild the staircase exactly as it was**—even if the risers are too high, the treads too short, or the width too narrow, according to the Uniform Building Code—**you can.** No variance is necessary.

The law, however, does not permit any changes in the design unless those changes meet modern code standards. For example, a staircase that originally had 9″ risers could be completely rebuilt and still have 9″ risers, even though today's code establishes a maximum of 8″ risers for new construction. But, it would not be permitted to rebuild the same staircase with 8½″ risers as this is neither original, nor in conformance with the code.

Rebuilding a complete staircase is a sophisticated job for an amateur. If you are game, thorough guidance can be found in the *Stair Builders Handbook* by T.W. Love, available at the Oakland Public Library. If you hire a contractor or a carpenter, make certain your intentions to retain the original staircase design and ornamentation are quite clear before work begins.

When dismantling the remains of an expired staircase, keep the valuable component parts (the baluster, handrail, spandrel, wainscotting) for re-use as is, or as samples for replication. Once the support structure of the staircase is rebuilt, the more superficial parts should be replaced exactly as they were originally—this is easy if you were able to salvage them—or as sympathetically as possible. Always maintain the original proportions and materials, even if the design does not duplicate the original.

It is likely that part of the staircase may need repair, even if the whole structure need not be rebuilt. The balustrade is a likely spot for problems. It may be wobbly, damaged, or missing altogether. (Balustrades are a popular item with knowledgeable

vandals.) The newel post is the anchor of the balustrade at each story and at the landing, so it must be securely attached for the balustrade to be sturdy.

To tighten a loose baluster, drive wedges into the gap between it and the handrail. Begin with a strip of hardwood, slightly larger than the gap. Sand or plane it into a wedge shape, with the grain running the length of wedge. When the size is right for a snug fit, coat the wood strip with glue and tap it into position. Another technique is to drill a hole through the post at an upward angle toward the rail. Drive a screw, and countersink it.

A baluster can be removed in order to strip the paint, or for use as a pattern to make replacements. Typically, the bottom of the baluster fits into a slot in the tread, and the top into a hole on the underside of the railing. Pry off the end trim on the tread in order to slide the baluster out of its slot. Then pull down to free the top from the handrail.

To reproduce missing turned balusters, a lathe is essential. Equipment and instruction are available at the evening adult school in Piedmont. (See Chapter 7.) If most or all of the balusters are missing, you may select a different but compatible design that is easier to build in multiples. Craft a flat baluster that retains the silhouette of its more shapely ancestor, or construct a simple composition of standard geometric pieces and moldings that retains the proportion of the original posts. (Refer to Chapter 4, "Porch: Railings.") If the handrail needs replacement, it too can be rebuilt in character by combining standard pieces of lumber and molding. (Consult Chapter 4, "Stairs: Handrails.") New handrails can be ordered from the Bartley Milling Company, Oakland.

To replace missing balusters, scour salvage yards for a matched set. Or, arrange for a new group to be crafted by a local carpenter or mill yard. One source for new balusters is Haas Wood and Ivory Works, 64 Clementina, San Francisco. **Never substitute a prefabricated wrought iron unit for an original wood balustrade.**

If the balustrade is natural wood, leave the grain exposed. If it is already painted and needs a new coat, refer to "Walls: Paint" for advice on color and

PARTS OF A STAIRCASE

A. CLOSED STRINGER
FREQUENTLY, THERE ARE 2 CLOSED STRINGERS. THE GROOVES THAT HOLD THE TREADS AND RISERS ARE SHAPED TO ALLOW THE INSERTION OF SECURING WEDGES.

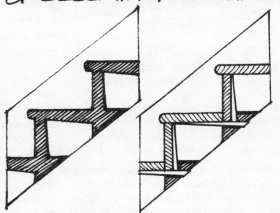

B. A WOODEN BEAM IS SOMETIMES USED AS A CENTER STRINGER, EMPLOYING SECTIONS OF 1 × 6 BOARDS TO BRACE THE TREADS.

C. OPEN STRINGER

D. TREAD
OFTEN TREADS AND RISERS ARE MORTISED FOR A CLOSE FIT (SEE STAIR CARPETING ILLUSTRATION).

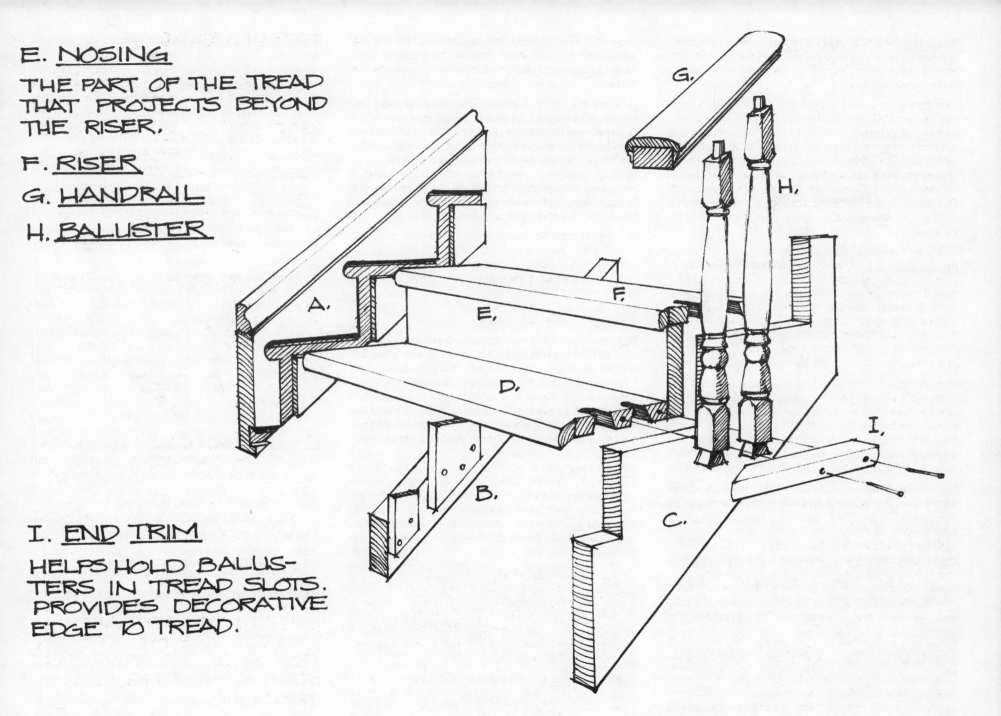

E. **NOSING**

THE PART OF THE TREAD
THAT PROJECTS BEYOND
THE RISER.

F. **RISER**

G. **HANDRAIL**

H. **BALUSTER**

I. **END TRIM**

HELPS HOLD BALUS-
TERS IN TREAD SLOTS.
PROVIDES DECORATIVE
EDGE TO TREAD.

121

STAIRCASE CARPETING: DOS AND DON'TS

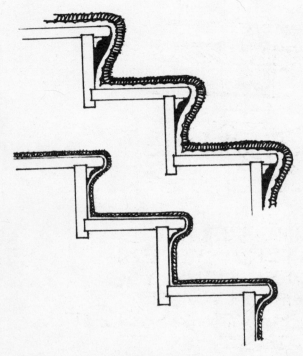

SHAG OR DEEP-PILE CAR-
PETING COUPLED WITH A
THICK PAD (TOP SKETCH)
CAUSES A LUMPY, OVER-
STUFFED LOOK OUT OF
CHARACTER WITH EARLY
STAIRCASES DESIGNED
FOR RUNNERS. THINNER
BUT DENSER CARPETING
WILL STILL WEAR WELL
(LOWER SKETCH) WHILE
RESTORING VISUAL DEF-
INITION TO THE NOSING.

product selection. Before re-painting, it may be necessary to scrape or strip at least the surface layers of accumulated paint in order to uncover the real form of the wood elements underneath.

When it comes to surfacing the staircase, **the intriguing sequence of right angles** that epitomizes the structure should be revealed. The obvious way is to leave the wood exposed, but even if the stairs are to be carpeted, the configuration of step and nosing need not be obliterated. By selecting a carpeting with a short, dense pile and a minimum of padding underneath, the carpeting can be contoured to the shape of the step and the architectural angles captured.

UTILITY SYSTEMS

Electricity, heating and plumbing are the central nervous system of the house. Subject to continual use, older systems are susceptible to breakdowns; victims of progress, they are likely to become outmoded by the conveniences which typify modern living. This section does not provide specific instructions for the repair or upgrading of a building's infrastructure. Rather, it is **an aid to evaluating systems that are there, and to improving them without disastrous effects on the architecture.**

Electrical

To begin to understand the way the electrical system in your house is put together and recognize its shortcomings, become conversant with some basic vocabulary. Electricity is moved through wires by pressure, much the way water is moved through pipes. The amount of pressure is called **voltage** and it is measured in units called **volts. Current** is the rate at which electricity is delivered—to the house from the power pole or to an individual appliance from the wall socket—and it is measured in amperes, commonly referred to as **amps.** The voltage forces the current along the electrical wires. The amount of current that can be transported is determined by the diameter of the wire.

The route of the wiring is called the **circuit.** Typically, several fixtures and sockets share a circuit, while

heavy duty appliances, like refrigerators or washing machines, have a circuit all their own. Each circuit is protected from overload by its own fuse or circuit breaker. The **fuse** contains a strip of soft metal which is melted by excessive current. The **circuit breaker** has a spring which is activated when excessive current passes through it, and the circuit is broken as if a switch had been turned off.

Service

Service relates to the total amount of voltage and amperage available to a house, and to the number of wires which carry that electrical power from the transmission pole to the meter box on the building.

In Oakland, most houses built before World War II originally had **two wire, 30 amp, 120 volt service.** Pacific Gas and Electric estimates that 15% to 20% of the single-family residences in Oakland (10,800 to 14,500 homes) still do. While this was perfectly adequate for electrical needs when first installed, and may still be for lifestyles with spartan energy demands, two-wire, 30 amp service is very limited for today's appliance-reliant family. Typically there are only two circuits. The amps on the fuses, combined, must not exceed 30 amps, resulting in combinations of one 10 amp circuit and one 20 amp circuit, or two 15 amp circuits. The amperage is sufficient to allow a refrigerator, television, stereo, hot water heater, and other "basic necessities," but it will not accommodate several small appliances turned on all at once or even one heavy duty appliance, like a washing machine.

Another 10% of the single-family housing stock in Oakland (some 7,200 homes) have **three-wire 120-240 volt, 30 amp service.** Three-wire service more than doubles the electricity available from a two-wire system. It permits at least twice the number of 120 volt circuits and an additional 240 volt circuit. The increased capacity accommodates the simultaneous use of more small appliances, like a kitchen busy at breakfast. However, the low amperage level precludes the use of major appliances like an electric dryer, which alone requires 40 amps, despite the increased voltage offered by the 240 volt circuit.

P.G.&E. surmises that another 25% of the single-family houses (about 18,000 homes) have **three-**

wire, **120-240 volt, 70 amp service.** There are enough circuits for all those electrical wedding presents. There is also enough voltage and amperage to support an electric dryer and an electric range.

Postwar houses are normally outfitted with **three-wire, 120-240 volt, 100 amp service.** This level of service is the minimum standard established by FHA and GI housing loans, for new and old houses alike.

Improving the electrical service is one of the most effective ways to modernize an old house without harm to the architecture. It is generally advisable to upgrade 30 amp service, whether two-wire or three-wire, to 100 amp service. It is generally unnecessary to upgrade a 70 amp system that is otherwise operating safely. The going rate charged by a licensed electrical contractor, with union labor, for increasing service from 30 amps to 100 amps is $650 to $850. This includes the permit, installation of a new circuit breaker panel, and all the wiring upstream (on the service side) of that point. The additional wiring downstream (on the house side) that makes the upgraded service utilitarian costs from $150 up. Downstream work is within the grasp of the electrically knowledgeable homeowner.

Two-wire service, and the original two-wire portion of an upgraded three-wire system, were typically installed by the knob-and-tube method. By this technique a conductor wire wends its way through the house, with a porcelain knob to support the wire where it crosses the wood. A porcelain tube encases the wire where it crosses other wire and in vertical runs through wood members.

In modern or modernized residential wiring systems, BX and Romex wire replaced the knob-and-tube method. BX wire encases two wires in an armor shield and Romex wire encases two wires in a non-metallic sheathing. Although BX and Romex are the more up-to-date methods, **knob-and-tube, properly installed, is a safe and efficient system that does not require replacement just because it is old-fashioned.** However, when extensive problems exist in a knob-and-tube system, it is practically impossible to repair it in-kind because the new, or "good as new" parts required by the electrical code are very difficult to come by.

IDENTIFYING YOUR ELECTRICAL SERVICE

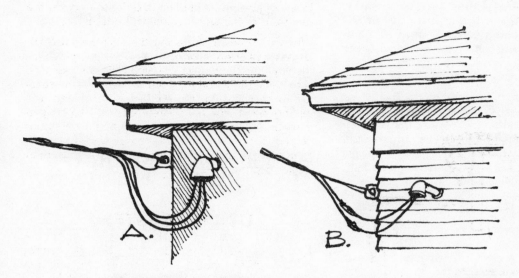

A.   B.

A BRIEF LOOK AT THE ELECTRIC POWER HOOKUP WHERE IT ENTERS THE HOUSE CAN TELL YOU THE VOLTAGE OF YOUR SERVICE BUT NOT THE AMPERAGE (AMOUNT OF CURRENT) AVAILABLE. A 3 WIRE HOOKUP (SKETCH A) INDICATES 110 - 220 VOLT SERVICE. THE AMPERAGE MAY VARY FROM 30 - 100 AMPS. 2 WIRES (B) MEANS 110 VOLT SERVICE THAT MAY BE 20 OR 30 AMPS. <u>WIRE SIZE</u> IS THE KEY TO AMPERAGE. FUSE SIZE AND FUSE PANEL LABELS CAN BE MISLEADING. ASK AN INSPECTOR OR QUALIFIED ELECTRICIAN

All new electrical installations must conform with the most recent electrical code. **Existing installations are acceptable if they have been safely maintained and the original integrity of the system has not been altered or abused.** Overfusing, for example, is one type of abuse which could very well have damaged the electrical system, whether or not alterations were involved.

If you feel competent enough to do the wiring downstream of the service box yourself, you can apply for an electrical permit. Before the permit is issued, the Inspectional Services Department visits the house to assess whether or not the homeowner can handle the job. Lack of expertise can be fatal. Electrical malfunctions were the number one cause of fires during 1975 in the United States, according to the national Fire Protection Association.

The proportion of electrical permits issued directly to homeowners has increased to 25% of the total residential work. The electrical inspector makes an average of nine house calls to the do-it-yourselfer, in comparison to three trips to review the professional electrician's work. If you have to be told to **turn off the main power switch before working on the electrical system,** you should probably hire an electrician.

When looking for an electric contractor:

- Always check for a State Electrical Contractor's License, C-10.
- Always get competitive bids in writing.
- Never pay more than 10% of the fee in advance. You are entitled to this limitation by the State Contractor's License Law.
- Never make the closing payment until the final inspection is made by the City and the work is approved.

If you sell the house within a year, you are required by Article 7004 of the Contractor's State License Law to use a licensed electrical contractor for all work. That way the buyer has recourse should anything go wrong. (Refer to Chapter 6.)

If you are uncertain about the condition of your electrical system, the City will conduct a complete survey and provide a written report for $26 an hour. It usually takes one hour to complete. The report enumerates applicable code violations, inadequacies

and recommended changes. Following the report, the Inspectional Services Department requires that any hazards be corrected, but they do not insist that all improper installations be redone according to code.

To do your own survey, make a map of each room in the house, noting the electrical fixtures and outlets. Then, by trial and error, determine which fuse or circuit breaker controls each one. Using a loud portable radio to test the outlets saves trips back and

ADDING A WALL SWITCH FOR AN OVERHEAD LIGHT

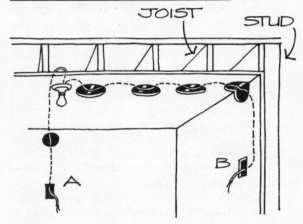

JOIST   STUD

A   B

SWITCH LOCATION A.
THIS IS THE EASIEST.
WIRING IS RUN IN THE CAVITY BETWEEN JOISTS. ONE HOLE IS MADE TO FISH THE WIRE THROUGH.

SWITCH LOCATION B.
AVOID IF POSSIBLE.
A HOLE MUST BE CUT IN THE CEILING AT EACH JOIST TO ALLOW NOTCHING FOR WIRING CLEARANCE.

NOTE: INSTALL PROPER SIZED ELECTRICAL BOXES AT SWITCH AND FIXTURE.

forth. Assign numbers to the fuses, if there are none on the service panel. Then mark the number of the circuit that controls it next to each fixture or outlet on the plan. Make a reverse list which enumerates all the fixtures controlled by each circuit.

Wiring

When the level of electrical service is upgraded, it's time to add new circuits. When the present service is adequate, but inconvenient and under-utilized, it's time to add a new circuit, or at least add a more convenient socket, switch or fixture to an available circuit. When a portion of an otherwise acceptable electrical system breaks down, it's time for repairs. Each one of these situations requires work behind the walls of an existing house, so **wiring becomes a matter of carpentry as well as of electrical know-how.**

The technique used to wire or rewire behind solid walls can have little effect on the architecture, or can totally devastate it. It's up to the homeowner to protect his or her house from the expedient electrician who pokes holes, slashes molding, or recommends ripping out an entire wall. **There is no need to destroy good lath and plaster in order to rewire,** nor to gut the innards of a house in order to modernize the electrical system.

Remember that the more walls that are ruined to make the electrician's job easier, the more difficult and more expensive it will be for you to replace or repair them. **To keep the cost of wall repairs from inflating the cost of wiring, and to safeguard the architecture of the house, follow these guidelines:**

- Lay out the route of the wiring yourself, before the electrician goes to work. Compare notes.
- If one or more walls are slated for repair, take advantage of the exposed frame to accomplish necessary electrical work in that area. Even if the rest of the system will not be completed for some time, install the wires while the wall is open, and cap the ends for future use.
- Whenever possible, route the wire through hidden passages (crawl space, pipe chase, abandoned vents, or the like) instead of through the wall itself.

SOCKET AND SWITCH: DOS AND DON'TS

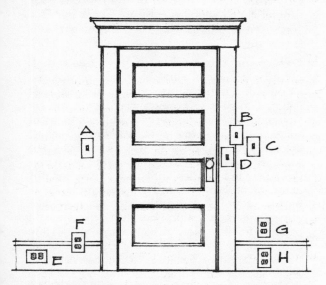

SOCKETS – E ⫛ H ARE PREFERRED (CORDS ARE UNOBTRUSIVE, FACE PLATES ARE CLEANED WITH BASEBOARD). G IS ACCEPTABLE, F DEFACES BASE MOLDING.

SWITCHES – C IS THE BEST LOCATION. B ⫛ D MAR THE DOOR TRIM, A IS ON THE WRONG SIDE OF THE DOOR SWING.

- For ceiling runs, like wiring an overhead light fixture with a pull chain into a wall switch, send the wire parallel to the joists in the void between them.
- For bottom-of-the-wall runs, like adding a series of convenience sockets, remove the baseboard and scrape a channel in the plaster behind it as a bed for the wire. If the wire is closer than 1" from the surface, code requires that it be covered with a metal plate to protect the wire from piercing nails. Replace the baseboard after the wire is

inspected. Elaborate cornice moldings can hide wiring in a like manner. (See "Walls: Trim" for the best method to remove molding.)

- For first floor sockets, use the open cellar ceiling for the wire, and come up into the room behind the baseboard.
- For vertical wall runs which require notches in obstacles like studs and firestops, use adjacent rooms or closets where patched surfaces are less noticable, less important or scheduled for wallpaper.
- Go fishing. Fishing is the electrician's art of sending a wire through a hole at one end of a wall or ceiling and mysteriously retrieving it out another. Fish wire is steel tape 3/16" wide and 1/16" thick. It is stiff enough to bend around corners. As with the sport, the essential skill in fishing is patience, and there's no need to pay an electrician's rates for that.
- Resort to surface wiring only where exposed circuits will not detract from the architecture, nor give the room a jury-rigged appearance. In a kitchen, for example, multiple outlet strips can prove a great convenience along countertops. They are so in keeping with the appliances they serve, that their obtrusive appearance can be acceptable. In most other rooms, however, surface wiring along wall or baseboard looks amateurish.
- Locate switchplates, sockets and other surface hardware so that it is entirely in the wall or baseboard, but not half-and-half. Never place a switch or socket in the door trim.

Light Fixtures

An electric light fixture is essentially a decorative shell for wires, socket and bulb. **Wherever possible, it is desirable to retain and utilize the light fixture original to the house.** If the illumination level is insufficient, try to supplement the original light with extra fixtures elsewhere in the room rather than substituting a new fixture for the old one in the same place.

Electricity came to Oakland on January 2, 1885, and in 1892 the Oakland Gas, Light and Heat Company built the first A.C. generator at 5th and Grove. Houses built prior to that time, the early Victorians, used gas and kerosene as a fuel for light.

The fixtures were massive in form, made of cast iron and white metal with ceramic ornaments and etched shades. Later Victorian and some Colonial Revival houses built or "modernized" subsequent to electrical service had fixtures with separate electric lights and gas jets, just in case. These fixtures were made of brass or bronze, and because the metal was shaped rather than cast, the form of the fixtures was more graceful. The shade was typically opalescent or vaseline glass. After the turn-of-the-century, electrical lighting became increasingly common, and by 1915 there were 45,279 consumers of electricity in Oakland. Initially, the electric fixtures looked a lot like the gas fixtures that preceded them. Often they were made of square brass stock, and the oxidized copper finish was introduced. For shades, artglass, such as the Tiffany dome, became popular, although the utilitarian bare bulb fixture persisted into the 1920s.

If there are original fixtures or remnants thereof, they can be made servicable. Often this is just a matter of installing new standard electrical parts, an inexpensive operation. If you don't know enough about electricity to do this yourself, an electric repair shop can do it for you and it usually costs less than $20 for labor.

If you choose to replace old fixtures in kind, seek an original or a legitimate reproduction at salvage yards and historic specialty stores. To satisfy the electrical code, replacement light fixtures must be UL labeled. Typically this disqualifies used fixtures. When selecting reproductions, make sure they are authentic and not just suggestive of "olden days." Pick a simple reproduction instead of the most elaborate one you can find. Make sure the materials are honest. If the copy is nothing more than a chintzy imitation, the house is better off with a straightforward modern fixture. Authentic reproductions of Victorian, Colonial Revival and Craftsman light fixtures are available at Ocean View Lighting in Berkeley and by mail from Rejuvenation House Parts in Portland, Oregon.

Modern electric light fixtures are usually necessary to replace and to supplement originals. Furniture stores often sell lamps along with other home furnishings, and lighting stores are so well stocked that

HOW TO "FISH"

FISHING PREVENTS UNDUE DAMAGE TO WALLS, CEILINGS AND ORNAMENTATION WHEN THERE IS NO EASY WIRING ACCESS. THE FOLLOWING SKETCHES SHOW THE BASIC TECHNIQUE. SOLID BLOCKING ABOVE THE WALL, FIRESTOPS BETWEEN STUDS AND LUMPS OF PLASTER ARE AMONG THE HIDDEN OBSTACLES THAT MAY COMPLICATE AN ALREADY DIFFICULT PROCESS. PARTICULAR PROBLEMS AND VARIANTS ON THE TECHNIQUE ARE COVERED IN BACK ISSUES OF "THE OLD HOUSE JOURNAL".

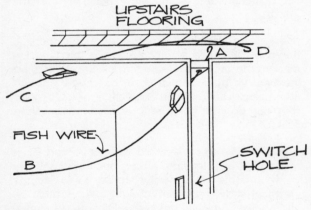

UPSTAIRS FLOORING

FISH WIRE

SWITCH HOLE

• OPEN A HOLE IN THE WALL 5" OR 6" FROM THE CEILING. WITH AN 18" DRILL BIT, MAKE AN ANGLED HOLE INTO THE CAVITY ABOVE THE CEILING. RUN FISH WIRE INTO THE CAVITY FROM THE CEILING FIXTURE HOLE AND THE WALL HOLE. "FISH" UNTIL HOOKED ENDS A AND D INTERLOCK (PERSISTENCE AND PATIENCE ARE NEEDED HERE). PULL ON END C UNTIL A EMERGES FROM CEILING HOLE. ATTACH ELECTRICAL CABLE TO HOOK A, MAKING SURE THE CONNECTION IS NOT TOO BULKY TO PASS THROUGH THE DRILLED HOLE.

PULL ON END B UNTIL THE CABLE APPEARS AT THE WALL HOLE. RUN FISH WIRE UP FROM SWITCH HOLE TO WALL HOLE. FASTEN CABLE TO FISH WIRE AND PULL DOWN TO SWITCH HOLE.

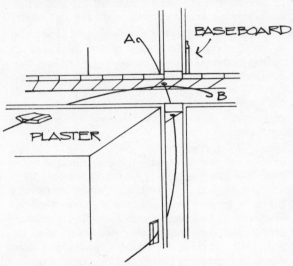

BASEBOARD

PLASTER

• WHEN THERE IS A WALL DIRECTLY ABOVE THE SWITCHPLATE WALL, THE EXTRA WALL HOLE IS UNNECESSARY. REMOVE THE UPSTAIRS BASEBOARD AND DRILL AN ANGLED HOLE INTO THE LOWER WALL CAVITY. FEED FISHWIRE INTO WALL AND OUT SWITCH HOLE. PULL END A BELOW UPSTAIRS FLOORING. HOOK ENDS A AND B AND PROCEED AS IN THE FIRST EXAMPLE, BUT DRAWING THE CABLE DIRECTLY OUT OF THE SWITCH HOLE.

they are overwhelming. To keep a clear head, use these guidelines:

• **Determine the function of the light.** Is it for general illumination? Is it light to work by? Is it concealed or indirect light? Is it a spotlight? Is it for security?

• **Determine the quality of light desired.** If only the quality of sunlight could be captured indoors! It is the easiest to read by and the most flattering to people's appearance. The choices are limited however, to fluorescent and incandescent lights. Basically, white light is a mixture of all colored lights together. In fluorescent light, the wave lengths at the blue end of the spectrum predominate; in incandescent light the wave lengths at the red and yellow end of the spectrum prevail. Incandescent light is warmer than fluorescent. It also seems more natural because while sunlight has a red-yellow glow in early morning and late afternoon, it never seems blue. Incandescent light throws a shadow because the light is directed, again like the sun. Fluorescent does not because the light is more evenly diffused, like on a foggy day. **Indoors, use incandescent light as a general rule.** Reserve fluorescent light for work areas, like a shop, and for indirect lighting, like behind a valance. Although normally used in the kitchen, fluorescent light makes food look unappetizing, so think twice before making this common decision. Wherever fluorescent is a must, buy the "warm white" type to minimize its inherent disadvantages.

• **Select as simple a fixture as possible.** Select geometric forms without ornamentation, plain surfaces without gaudy glamour and honest materials, not vinyl look-alikes.

• **Select a fixture in scale with the room and the wall.** If there is a high ceiling, use a pipe or pole fixture to bring the chandelier down to a practical level. If the room is small use a wall fixture that minimizes intrusion into the useable space. Do not use a gigantic or ostentatious lamp in a small room, or that is all you will see.

• **Install the fixture high enough** to cast light down on the people and objects in the room, Immobile wall fixtures should be above eye level, but below the cornice molding.

- **Do not feel obligated by convention to install a central ceiling light.** Although it provides the convenience of illuminating a dark room by a switch at a door, it is otherwise relatively useless in providing good light for specific activities. A combination of wall lights and floor or table lamps is much more effective in illuminating given areas for work or leisure, and far more flexible in accommodating the different uses of a room. If there is a ceiling socket in place and it's time for a new fixture there, consider track lighting. It provides several direct and adjustable light sources, and it is visually compatible with all the architectural styles discussed in REHAB RIGHT that have a plain ceiling (without a rosette). Also consider the use of dimmers, as the optional light levels let you create different atmospheres for different occasions.

Plumbing

The plumbing system is made up of two separate lines. The fresh water supply line brings water into the house under 50 to 80 pounds per square inch of pressure from the main in the street. The supply line is divided at the hot water heater, where part of the incoming flow is heated. From there, pipes with hot and cold fresh water run parallel to one another and serve plumbing fixtures throughout the house. The second line is the drain-waste-vent line (DWV). It carries used water out to the sewer by gravity, and noxious fumes up into the air at roof level.

In most Oakland houses built before World War II, the water supply line is constructed of galvanized steel and the DWV line of cast iron. Galvanized pipes may become fragile with age due to corrosion and frozen fittings, but **if the plumbing system is in good or reparable condition, there is no need to update it** to copper or plastic. Additions to the existing system can be made with copper or plastic, as long as a proper transition fitting is used.

The service from the water main to pre-war houses is typically a ½" pipe. In 1949, ¾" pipe became the standard. When the service pipe becomes encrusted, the inside diameter may be considerably smaller than its name implies. It is only necessary to consider upgrading plumbing service from ½" to

LIGHT FIXTURE: DOS AND DON'TS

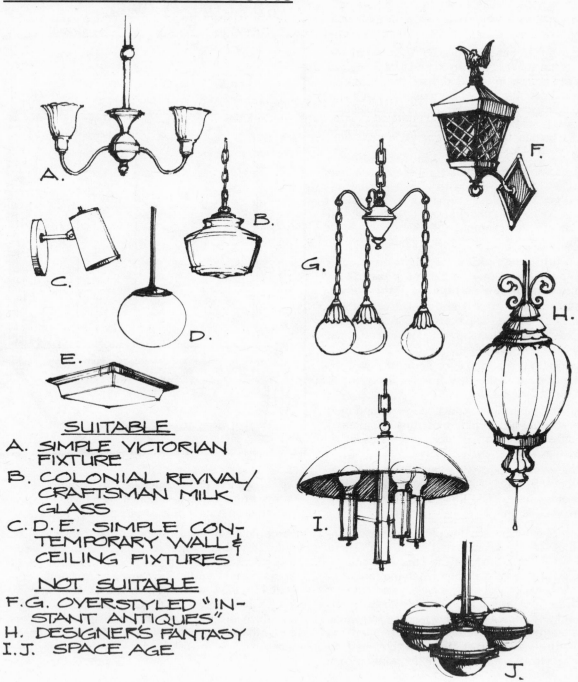

SUITABLE

A. SIMPLE VICTORIAN FIXTURE

B. COLONIAL REVIVAL/ CRAFTSMAN MILK GLASS

C. D. E. SIMPLE CONTEMPORARY WALL & CEILING FIXTURES

NOT SUITABLE

F. G. OVERSTYLED "INSTANT ANTIQUES"

H. DESIGNER'S FANTASY

I. J. SPACE AGE

¾" if you experience a disturbing reduction in the quantity of water available when two fixtures are used at once, or if you are building an additional bathroom.

The connection between the DWV line and the sewer on the street is broken in practically one out of four old houses in Oakland, according to a City inspector. Look for rodent burrows, broken curbs and a bright green tree in a brown lawn as evidence. If you suspect a broken sewer connection, call the Sewer Maintenance Department at (415) 273-3846.

Most of the plumbing system is hidden and has a limited bearing on the architectural character of the house. However, like electricity, installation and repair of pipes in an older house is a matter of carpentry as well as plumbing know-how. A drill with a hole saw bit, for example, is as handy as a pipe wrench.

When adding new pipes, or when improving the old, do as little damage as possible to the original materials and spaces of the house:

- Installation of a second story toilet or bathtub requires a P-shaped trap below the floor. Conceal this pipe between the joists; never lower the first story ceiling to hide it.
- Use existing holes in wall or floor for pipe connections, even if the new holes will be out of sight behind cabinets.
- Use hidden passages, crawl space, abandoned vents and the like to hide new runs of pipe and minimize destruction of valuable wainscot or plaster walls.
- On the exterior, locate pipes and vents as inconspicuously as possible, preferably on the back or sides of the house. Paint the pipe the same color as the wall behind it.

The most obvious parts of the plumbing system are the fixtures in the kitchen and bathroom. These two rooms, in that order, are the most commonly remodeled and redecorated rooms in the American house. As a result, valuable porcelain and vitreous china sinks, tubs and toilets, many with luxurious brass hardware, were removed in favor of something more modern, though undoubtedly less sturdy. **If the original plumbing fixtures are still in place, retain them.** There is nothing intrinsically

A CLAWFOOT TUB WITH ADDED SHOWER

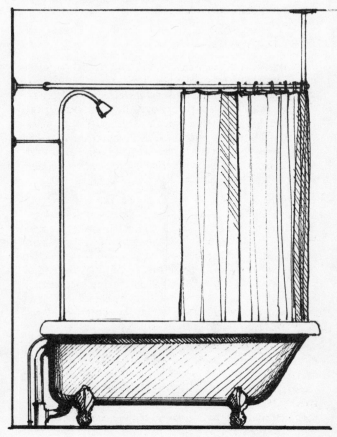

wrong with a pull-chain toilet, for example, if it works properly. A testimonial to its value is the price tag on a new one: approximately $600.

Porcelain often shows signs of age. Stains can be reduced with a Clorox solution. Use about ¼ cup to a gallon of water, and let it soak the stains for 24 hours. Cracks and chips can be permanently corrected by the Porcelain Patch and Glaze Company in Oakland. They have developed a special process by which the tub is re-surfaced with a high-gloss plastic that is "good as new," according to a company representative. You can see for yourself at their showroom at 966—86th Avenue. Clawfoot tubs can be

re-surfaced right in the home, and the cost is about $295. The price for resurfacing porcelain sinks begins at $125. Call them for precise information on a specific fixture, (415) 635-2188.

A temporary improvement to dings in porcelain is a special epoxy glue, but those who have tried it report mixed results. Success depends a great deal on the efficacy of cleaning the surface first. The easiest option is to learn to love the cracks as badges of antiquity. Care for porcelain with a non-abrasive cleanser.

An older sink, toilet or tub may have a cross-connection, and this demands correction. A cross-connection occurs when the supply line is placed in so low a position on the fixture that accumulated "used" water could enter the fresh water line and contaminate it. For a toilet with a cross-connection, install a new Fluidmaster type ball-cock. It costs about $6, certainly less than a brand new toilet. If the faucet of a clawfoot tub is below the rolled tub rim, the spigot can be replaced with a spout that arches above the waterline, although swan neck spigots are fragile. To meet the Oakland codes, the spout must be at least one inch above the overflow.

Clawfoot tubs can be converted into a combination shower and bath without modifying the pipes. A single piece of hardware, with faucets, extension pipe and showerhead, is available at several plumbing supply stores, like Meyer's and J & J, and costs from $72 and up, depending on the brand. Try hardware stores for the requisite circumferential shower curtain rods. The price depends on the exact brand and design, varying from $20 for the oval or d-shaped, wall flange and ceiling support type, to $35 for a u-shaped frame.

If the clawfeet are covered by so many layers of paint that they look as if they are wearing socks, use a chemical stripper to disclose the detail. Mask the area around the tub carefully. Use enamel spray paint suitable for metal to repaint the feet and the outside of the tub. If masking is not possible, use a brush-on enamel paint suitable for metal, like Rustoleum, and a good quality brush with fine bristles. A cheap brush will leave stroke marks.

While it is preferable to keep the tub unenclosed

and display it like a piece of sculpture, some people choose to box it in. If you do, be certain to leave a 12″ by 12″ hinged access panel to the above-floor pipes at the head of the tub, as these require occasional attention.

If the original bathroom accessories are gone, simplicity is the rule for selecting modern fixtures. Look for real materials. Marbleized plastic that is meant to look like stone is an obvious fake that drives up the price of lavatories and vanity tops.

To replace missing porcelain fixtures with the real thing, try salvage yards like Berkeley Architectural Salvage, and Urban Ore, also in Berkeley. A used tub, 5′ long, as is and without hardware, costs $15 to $150. To replace missing brass or brass-plated plumbing hardware, try salvage yards again or order by mail from DEA Bathroom Machineries, 495 Main Street, Murphys, CA 95247. Reproductions of original brass hardware are available from DEA, from Rejuvenation House Parts, 4543 N. Albina Avenue, Portland, OR 97217, and other sources. Many hardware and department stores now carry brass for the bathroom too.

In kitchen and laundry porch, a common problem is dry rot in the wood structure around sinks. If the original design did not include an effective splash area, the wall and floor can become deteriorated with continual exposure to water. Correct dry rot around sinks before replacing them, and make sure there is adequate drainage and waterproofing to prevent recurrence of the same situation.

A plumbing permit is required for all plumbing work other than minor repairs. Except for complicated mid-run re-piping, plumbing is within reach of the technically adept homeowner. Approximately one out of four plumbing permits is issued to a "do-it-yourselfer."

If the job is beyond your ability, or if you plan to sell the house within a year, hire a professional plumber. He or she should have a C-36 Plumbing License. While a general contractor is allowed by law to take out a plumbing permit and do the work if they are the prime contractor on a job involving three or more separate crafts, it is generally wise to stick with a specialist. One pro has observed that among plumbers, those that have been in the business for

10 to 15 years have the most reliable combination of experience and enthusiasm. Any contractor doing plumbing work in Oakland must register with the Plumbing Inspection Section.

Mechanical

The mechanical system is so named because it involves machines, unlike electricity and plumbing which are essentially delivery systems. In the home, the mechanical system manages the distribution of air: heating, ventilation and air conditioning. With a few exceptions, noted below, improvements to the mechanical system have limited bearing on the architectural character of the house, so the repair aspects are not addressed in detail here.

A variety of heating devices are represented in Oakland's older houses. The assortment includes: floor furnace, wall heater, single space or room heater, floor and wall combination heater, central steam heat with radiators, central warm air with ducts and registers, central forced air with ducts and registers, and, where modernization has occurred, electric heat. The individual units listed first are typical to smaller houses, while the central heating systems are more common to larger houses.

The floor furnace is associated with the Craftsman and California Bungalows, but in fact, it was installed in new houses well into the 1950s. **If you can arrange to child-proof it, there is nothing intrinsically wrong with a floor furnace,** despite the fact that FHA frowns on them. Check underneath the house to make sure that the pipe which vents the floor furnace is still connected and in good repair. It is prone to rusting, and unless its condition is intentionally examined, a malfunction can go unnoticed.

At the insistence of FHA, floor furnaces are often replaced with vertical wall heaters. This is a very poor trade-off. The floor furnace is safer, more efficient, and much better suited to the architectural style of the house than a wall heater. The drawback of the floor furnace is the hot grill cover, but this can be remedied by constructing a cover made of dowels mounted on a simple frame. For a free construction diagram, contact Bananas Childcare Information and Referral Service, 6501 Telegraph Avenue, Oakland, CA 94609.

Steam radiators in older houses can be a symphony of noises. Replacement of the central furnace will do nothing to stifle the hisses, gurgles and thuds because they are generated by the steam distribution mechanisms—the pipes, radiators and air valves. *The Old-House Journal* offers technical guidance for tracking down the cause of the noise and silencing it.

The Oakland Housing Code requires that in all new residential construction the heating facilities be adequate to maintain a temperature of 65 degrees three feet off the floor in all habitable rooms. A habitable room is defined as any space used for living, sleeping, eating or cooking. Bathrooms, closets, halls, storage and utility areas are not regarded as habitable areas. While this can be used as a guideline for older houses, the legal requirement for houses built prior to 1958 is entirely different. In those dwellings, there is no requirement for heating, other than retaining the level that the original heating facility provides. If, for example, a floor furnace is the only heater in the house, there is no City requirement that additional heaters be provided in unserved rooms. Or if, in a single-family dwelling, there is no heater at all and there never was, the Oakland Housing Code does not require that a heater be installed. However, FHA and other lending institutions have more stringent standards, and they may demand installation of additional heaters in a house as part of the financial agreement.

Additions to an inadequate heating system invariably have a visual impact, so try to minimize the intrusion. Consider upgrading the system you already have—with the installation of supplementary registers, for example—rather than switching to a brand new set-up that engenders exposed duct work or bulky room units. If you must introduce a new permanent heating device to an unserved room, baseboard heaters are usually the least obtrusive. The Intertherm type is considered especially good by some, due to its safety, control and humidity features. Remember, a mechanical permit is required by the City for all mechanical work done except minor repairs.

Before expanding the heating system in the house, make sure that the building is properly insulated to prevent heat loss. You may find that new insulation is a better solution than a new heater. The best reference is *Retrofit Right: How To Make Your Old House Energy Efficient*, available from the Oakland City Planning Department. (See last page for order form.) Also, examine your heat consumption habits to determine if heat and energy are being unnecessarily wasted.

For safety purposes, make sure that all gas appliances are vented to approved flues which terminate above the roof with a cap. As evidence of an appliance malfunction, look for sooting atop the vent. The City will make a survey of the mechanical system of the house for $26.50, minimum, and pinpoint its hazards and shortcomings. Contact the Inspectional Services Department.

If you install a window-type air-conditioner, it is advisable for aesthetic reasons to place it in a side window rather than a front window. This keeps the façade of the house uninterrupted, and the street scene more orderly.

Chapter 6

FOR YOUR INFORMATION

WHEN SHOULD YOU HIRE A PROFESSIONAL?

And When to Do-It-Yourself

A common way to keep the rehab budget in line with the housing budget is to do the work yourself. While this saves money, it may cost more in time, quality and general aggravation. One prediction has it that "remodeling your house can bust up your marriage, force you into bankruptcy, drive you to a nervous breakdown—or all three."

There is a time for professional help in any rehab job. The professionals who could become involved are: *civil engineers* to evaluate structural conditions; *architects* to design structural changes; and *contractors* to perform the construction work. A general contractor, usually a carpenter by trade, oversees the entire job, coordinating the work of various specialists, while a subcontractor is the specialist himself, like a plumber or electrician. The subcontractor can be hired directly, as well as via the general contractor.

It is wise to **hire a professional when:**

- the job requires technical skills you do not have, or are not readily learned
- the job requires tools and equipment that are unfamiliar to you or infeasible to rent
- you want the job completed in a short or specified period of time
- your time is worth more than your money
- codes completely baffle you, to the detriment of the final product

- the quality of your workmanship is so poor that it may cause additional damage, or signal additional costs of doing it over to a prospective buyer, in other words
- when you don't know what you're doing.

The law requires that you **hire a licensed contractor if:**

- the applicable code so states
- the loan contract so stipulates
- you plan to sell the house within one year of completing the improvements.

Despite these precautions, there are many opportunities to participate in the rehab process and save money doing so. Most people will be able to identify certain portions of the rehab project which they can comfortably handle. Once you have consulted Chapters 4 and 5 for the particular repair problems you face, you will probably discover that you can do much more than you had suspected. In fact, **rehab work that is sensitive to existing architectural features is often a lot easier to do than a contractor's solution of modernization.** Many general contractors are amenable to letting the owner play a part, but this must be agreed upon in advance.

Handy men and women experienced in construction may choose to be their own general contractors. This is a very complicated undertaking, requiring full-time attention to detail. It can, however, save 15%–20% of the total construction cost, the equivalent of the contractor's profit and overhead.

Whether you face a major construction project, or an individual case of disrepair, **identify tasks to do yourself which:**

- require a sensitivity to architectural features, as described in Chapters 2, 4 and 5—these are the very chores the contractor is likely to avoid in pursuing the route of modernization
- utilize your skills and equipment, or skills you would like to learn and equipment you can conveniently rent or acquire
- are time intensive but require limited skill (like stripping woodwork or scraping out stucco cracks) —here, rehab work can really become a family affair

- will give you a sense of pride and satisfaction in your accomplishment.

With all this in mind, outline those portions of the rehab job which you can realistically handle yourself, and which assignments require professional skills.

Selecting a Contractor

Selection of the right contractor or architect is a skill in itself. Effectively sifting through the candidates is the key to a successful outcome, and critical to your long-term state-of-mind. Here are some guidelines:

1. **Get recommendations** from friends, relatives, neighbors, owners of similar style houses, building suppliers, hardware merchants, subcontractors and bankers. It's important to get first-hand information about the quality of the contractor's work. How understanding is he or she, and how easy to understand? Be certain that you can talk to the contractor, or your plan to REHAB RIGHT may be stymied. Most contractors have their own way of doing things, which is often contrary to the architectural sensitivity advocated in this manual. Find out if they are willing to read this book. Maybe they already have.

2. **Reliability is critical.** Be certain the contractor has an established business. The home improvement racket constitutes the largest number of consumer frauds in the United States, according to *The Complete Book of Home Remodeling, Improvement and Repair.* Fly-by-night characters abound. A business office, no matter how small, and at least one staff member, are some assurance that your contractor is not just operating out of a glove compartment. Check the Better Business Bureau for registered complaints. Reliability also includes being on time, abiding by estimates, and general honesty. Ask the people who recommend him or her about these traits.

3. **Check for a contractor's license.** Any person contracting for a building job worth $200 or more must be licensed by the State of California Department of Consumer Affairs. The license is granted only when the applicant has passed required tests, and has had four years of experience. You can verify license status by calling the

State Contractor's Licensing Board, or by asking to see the contractor's license. The latter assures you that he or she is not an imposter. The license, however, does not guarantee that the contractor is perfect, or that he or she is the right person for your job. *Caveat emptor*—buyer beware.

Unlicensed contracting is a category which lumps together all sorts of folks, from the crooked shyster, to the ambitious handyman, to the talented craftsman. While the unlicensed contractor may be performing in violation of the Contractor's License Law, he or she will probably charge less money and therefore seem more attractive to you. Even if a maverick shows more sensitivity to architecture, be careful. Hiring an unlicensed contractor entails considerable risk on the property owner's part.

- A licensed contractor is responsible for installations that meet code requirements. If the contractor is not licensed, the burden is on the owner. If any construction is found to be in violation of code, then the owner must pay to have the job done over correctly. The second time he or she usually hires a licensed contractor.

- A licensed contractor is required by law to carry worker's compensation insurance. If you hire an unlicensed contractor, you too must carry worker's compensation. While most homeowner's insurance policies have a worker's compensation clause, it is usually limited to an employee who works no more than 20 hours a week. This can be amended to cover a full-time worker for additional premiums. Be certain to check with your insurance agent first.

- A licensed contractor can also carry property damage insurance and public liability insurance, although this is not required by law. He or she will pay several thousand dollars a year in premiums for the privilege of this kind of commercial insurance—not available to the homeowner who is hiring unlicensed workers.

- A licensed contractor carries bonds to guarantee that there is monetary recourse if he or she walks out on the job before it is completed. An unlicensed contractor is rarely eligible to offer such assurance.

4. Find out in advance **what kind of insurance and bonds** the licensed contractor you are interviewing carries and if the amounts are sufficient for your particular job. The state requires a minimum bond of $$5000, but if you have a job worth $8000, the bonding is inadequate.

5. Evaluate the **contractor's experience** on problems and houses similar to your own. **Pay special attention to his or her sensitivity to architectural features,** like those described in Chapter 2 for the style of your house. Compare examples of his or her work to the "Don't" sketches in Chapters 4 and 5, as listed in the Table of Illustrations. If the contractor has been the culprit of such architectural crimes, look elsewhere, or see how cooperative he or she would be about treating your house differently.

6. See if the contractor has a thorough **understanding of the building codes** affecting your project. Find out some basic information from the City, and then quiz him or her on it in a naive way. See if he or she knows the answer, and whether he or she talks down to you, or explains it comfortably. Find out if the services include acquiring necessary permits for you.

7. Once you have narrowed the list down, **get competitive bids in writing from different contractors on the same set of written specifications.** Tell each one exactly what you want, the quality of materials you expect, the time frame, and the fact that they are in competition. Write it down. If a contractor suggests adding something, have him or her bid that separately. Each contractor should also indicate their hourly charge for work beyond the contract, as unanticipated items are inevitable. The lowest bid may not be the best bid. Throw out any excessively high or low bids, and decide among the mid-range by using the factors listed above.

Similar rules apply in the selection of an architect, if your project warrants one. Get recommendations, make sure the two of you can communicate, and evaluate his or her experience on similar projects. Typically, an architect's work is in two parts: the preliminary design drawings to arrive at mutual agreement and show to the banker, and the working drawings for the actual construction. The architect's

fee for rehab jobs is usually 15%, or more, of the final construction cost.

Drafting a Contract

Once you have selected a contractor or an architect, **define your mutual obligations in a legal contract.** Although consultation with a lawyer is general preferable, most contractors have a standard form, or you can get one for $1.15 from the American Institute of Architects. The contract should safeguard your interests and include:

1. The **work** the contractor agrees to do, including dimensions, specifications, type and quality of materials. Instead of drawings, you can use photographs of the part of the house where work will occur. Make photocopies of the picture, then add notes which define the scope of work.

2. The date the work is to begin, and a **time schedule** of how the project is to proceed, until its completion.

3. A schedule of **payments** in pace with the work, with 10–20% to be paid after you have inspected the final product.

4. A precise description of the **appliances** or fixtures to be bought if any.

5. Responsibility for **cleanup** and removal of debris, like a requirement that the contractor leave the premises "broom clean" daily or at stated intervals.

6. Release for you from **liability** should the contractor go bankrupt before he or she has completed your work. Otherwise, under the mechanic's lien law, an owner can be held accountable for any money owed by the contractor for labor or materials used on the owner's project.

If you are using a standard form and these, or any other items you are concerned about, are not listed, write them in. As long as the additions are neither illegal acts, nor prohibited by laws governing public funds used for the loan, the amended contract is valid when both the owner and contractor sign. It is also advisable to double-check your homeowners insurance policy and your mortgage before signing the contract, as these documents may have clauses pertinent to remodeling or improvement of the property.

Never sign a Certificate of Completion until after the final City inspection and until the job is finished to your satisfaction. Otherwise the certificate entitles the contractor to final payment, and it will be difficult to get him or her to return and correct errors.

Finally, be understanding of the professional's problems too. Contracting is a nerve-wracking business, and a little sympathy on your part will probably go a lot further than perpetual nagging or accusation.

HOUSE HISTORY

Discovering the history of your old house is not essential to good rehab. However, if you plan a restoration for tax purposes, local landmark review or personal satisfaction, your building's biography may provide clues for accurate design decisions. For example, an old family photograph might reveal in the background what the original mantle looked like before it disappeared. Letters or reminiscences might allude to color, ornament or floor plan.

Historical data or anecdotes can enhance your enjoyment of the house, and provide a setting and characters to visualize as you scrape, scrub and hammer.

Consult building departments, libraries, preservation and historical groups, and SHPO-funded architectural surveys for original building permits, tax records, photographs and architectural ratings.

In Oakland, start with a phone call to the Oakland Cultural Heritage Survey, (415) 273-3941. The OCHS, under the auspices of the City Planning Department, is conducting an inventory of all buildings in Oakland to determine architectural and historical significance. If your house is in one of two intensively studied areas—the Central Business District or Adams Point—or in one of 15 target neighborhood centers, there will be a file on the house which includes the date of construction, the builder or architect, other pertinent data and a definitive evaluation of its significance.

If the house is outside a focal area, it will nevertheless have a rating in the Citywide Preliminary Historical and Architectural Survey. An estimated construction date, and a general evaluation of importance and extent of remodeling, will enable Survey staff to determine if the building might be eligible for landmark designation or National Register status. You are urged to call OCHS as a first step in pursuing historic designation of any type.

Building permit records can be the most useful tool because they provide a history of building alterations. In Oakland, visit the Inspectional Services Department, City Hall, second floor, and expect to stand in line with applicants for new building permits. The permit material is recorded by address and retrieved on microfiche. For two-story woodframe buildings, do not expect to find the original plans or permit.

You can, however, examine the actual handwritten ledgers which record building permits from 1905 to 1947. Your second step in City Hall is the Cultural Heritage Survey office on the sixth floor.

To find yet more, go to the Oakland History Room, Oakland Main Library, second floor. Use the Sanborn maps dating back to 1882 to determine the general period of construction. The Sanborns will show the footprint of the house on the lot. For even earlier houses, study the "Bird's Eye View of Oakland, circa 1870," and pinpoint the house in its original form on this remarkably detailed illustration.

Next, refer to the tax assessor's roles, also in the Oakland History Room. They are organized by block and lot, year by year. Find the first year a value was given to a house on the lot, and you have a construction date. But be careful of mistaking a previous building on the site for the one that still stands.

The block books will also inform you, in exquisite and flowing penmanship, of the original owner's name. To find out more about that person, use the library's colleciton of City Directories, which goes back to 1869. Alphabetical listings will tell you whether the owner presided at the house in question, and the owner's occupation. Another source of information on individuals is the voting registers.

If you suspect from your findings that the owner was important—and this can be a factor in National Register status, although not directly bearing on archi-

tectural form—there are several Oakland History Room indices for more biographical background.

Pictures of houses are likely of more interest to the restorer than narratives about occupants. The Oakland History Room has pictorial sourcebooks and files to find houses similar to your own. Shelter magazines from earlier eras, like *Architect & Engineer*, *Sunset*, and *Craftsman* are replete with prototypes. Find these on open shelves in the library at the College of Environmental Design, University of California, Berkeley.

ACCESS

The special needs of a disabled person can be met, and met well, by the older residential styles. In fact, in many of its features **an old house is better suited to wheelchair access than a modern tract house.** The public rooms—whether formal parlors or living and dining areas—flow together in most old houses, freeing up circulation otherwise constrained by doorways and corridors. Many doorways are wide enough for adequate clearance, and the hardwood floors are an ideal surface for wheelchairs. Wall-to-wall carpets, especially high pile and those with pads underneath as featured in newer homes, are difficult to traverse.

The old kitchens are room-like, with adaptable appliance layout, unlike the modern galley kitchen with built-in appliances, which is narrow and inflexible. The old kitchen has few of the base cabinets which obstruct chair movement, especially under the sink. The absence of counter space is not a disadvantage: a table of appropriate height makes an accessible work surface.

Double-hung windows in good working order can operate so smoothly that, depending on a person's disability, they may be easier to use than aluminum windows with stubborn hardware.

Other components of the old house do require modification for wheelchair users and people with other disabilities. These alterations can and should be accomplished in a manner sympathetic to the architecture.

Ramps

Just scan the cover of this book and it is obvious that the main floor is raised well above ground level on most old houses in Oakland. Admittedly, this is the biggest drawback to old houses in terms of accessibility. Typically, the vertical distance between front path and front door is between 2½' and 4'. This dimension, and the size of the front and side yards, are the critical factors in determining the feasibility of graceful ramp installation.

For every foot of vertical height that separates door level from ground level, a run of 12' of horizontal space is needed for the ramp. And, for every 30' of ramp and every change in direction, a landing is required as well. Thus, for an entry just 3½' above the ground, some 50 linear feet are needed to accommodate a straight ramp, an intermediate landing and a landing in front of the door. The ramp would be over 6' tall at its highest point, which includes a 34"-high handrail.

Clearly, the ramp structure becomes a major landscape feature, a part of the neighborhood scene. Here are some **guidelines for blending the ramp in with the house and its setting.**

Choose a house with an **entry and main floor as close to grade as possible.** A quick way to estimate the dimension is to count the number of stair risers and multiply by six inches. (If the stairs are steep, the actual vertical distance may be up to a foot more than the estimate.) Don't forget the step between sidewalk and front path. Look for deep front yards and fairly wide side yards.

The choice between front and side or rear entry to the house from the ramp should be made depending on the grace of the design solution, rather than by predisposition.

A **sideyard ramp** does not interrupt, or bisect, the front façade of the house, nor does it alter or eliminate the front stairs which may be characteristic of the architectural style. Leading to a side or rear entry, the side yard location allows a long, straight run, perhaps down a driveway. It reduces the apparent length of the ramp by concealing all or a portion of the structure between houses. In one very successful example in the Rockridge section of Oakland, the side yard ramp is hidden behind a fence and gate built at the front corner of the house. A gentle grade change at ground level in front of the gate forms a subtle approach.

Another effective solution is to direct the side yard ramp to a generous back yard deck. The deck serves double-duty as a landing for the back entry and as useable outdoor living space.

There may be zoning limitations for the side yard ramp. A minimum side yard is required by the zoning code, and in Oakland, any structure over 6' high within this setback is in conflict with the regulations. To determine the required side yard in your zone, and if need be, apply for an administrative variance, contact the Planning Department, Zoning Division. (See Chapter 7, "City Offices.")

When positioning a **front yard ramp**, be careful not to give the appearance of cutting the house down the middle. An asymmetrical placement is natural for houses with entries to one side of façade.

Where possible, try to incorporate the original porch design as part of the landing. Or, incorporate the ramp itself into the original porch, as at the Victorian house in DeFremery Park in West Oakland. There, the balustrade and frontal appearance of the porch are maintained, but on one side there is a ramp instead of a porch floor.

For the horizontal line of bungalow-style homes, a ramp parallel to the building and joining the porch at one end can be compatible in appearance. Cover the sides and base of the ramp with shingles or stucco, in the same manner as the base of the house and the porch railing itself.

The front yard ramp can be absorbed into a spacious front deck which serves as an outdoor room, as well as a front door landing. There is an elegant example on Russell Street, above College Avenue, in Berkeley, which takes good advantage of a southern exposure. This should not be done, however, at the expense of an original front porch in decent condition, or other architectural assets of the entryway.

When choosing a **railing design**, remember that a railing with vertical members is more pleasing to the eye than one with horizontal members. The vertical lines are parallel to the many vertical lines of the house and tie in with windows, doors, etc. Angled lines are distracting in the composition, and vertical railing members de-emphasize the angle of the ramp and the handrail. Horizontal railing members tend to repeat the angle of the ramp and handrail, contradicting the lines of the house.

Another approach is to use minimal or non-directional material for the side of the guardrail, such as wire grid painted black or the color of the base of the house, so that it disappears into the background.

In general, repeat the railing features of the porch itself if possible.

Use **landscaping** to screen the support structure, as open and exposed underpinnings are usually unattractive. The contour of the plant material softens the geometric outline of the ramp, and blends it into the setting. Otherwise, the transition from wood ramp to front lawn is quite abrupt.

Plant shrubs of differing heights along the base of the ramp, and consider training vines along the rail. Use color and scent to create a more pleasant passage.

A **ground-level unit** may be discovered inserted underneath what was once a single-story house. These flats are often directly accessible from the outside without ramping. Perhaps a previously unfinished space had been converted to a second unit. (Ceilings must be 7½' to meet code.) Or, when the building was raised for foundation work, additional height—from a few feet to a full story—was garnered at the same time for the sake of more floor space or rental quarters. In fact, **if a single-story house must be raised** anyway, **consider adding an accessible unit at the same time.** The Tenant Access Program or the Rental Rehab Program, described in Chapter 7, may provide a grant or low-interest loan toward the cost.

Other Design Considerations

Transforming an old house into accessible home is mostly a matter of choice. The extent of work is up to the owner, and following recommended standards makes practical sense. However, **if the old house is being adapted for non-residential use, accessibility is mandated** by California State law. Consult Title 24 of the California Administrative Code or Access California, (415) 273-3723, for complete requirements. Exceptions can be made for designated historic buildings, per the SHBC, as described in Chapter 3.

Some additional design considerations for an accessible old house are outlined below. Use the list in conjunction with the more general discussion of rehabilitation techniques and design concerns in Chapters 4 and 5 under the same headings. Consult an access reference for a thorough treatment of accessibility standards. Look for a book by the Center for Independent Living, Berkeley, entitled *Making Home Accessible*, available in late 1986.

For funding, refer to Chapter 7 under "Rehabilitation Assistance Programs." Of special interest is Oakland's Tenant Access Program (TAP) which provides grants of up to $6000 per unit for access modifications to rental units, and the HMIP Loan Program for homeowners.

Front Stairs

For the visually impaired, cane users and others, the stairs can be left in place—but with certain changes which respect a person's disability.

Put a non-skid surface on stair treads. For wood steps, use a sand or walnut shell additive in the deck paint. If the original wood stairs have been replaced with concrete, it should have a medium broom finish.

Use solid risers, and paint the risers and treads a different color from the tread nosing. The contrasting color allows someone with a visual impairment to discern the stepping surface. Similarly, a perceptible 2"-wide line should be painted at the leading edge of the top- and bottom-most tread. Select colors which contrast without clashing. Use colors in the same hue, but of different values: for example, light gray-blue for the risers and treads and dark gray-blue for the nosing.

If the porch light does not illuminate the steps, or puts them in shadow, relocate it, or add an outdoor lamp at the base of the stairs.

The handrails should extend at least one foot beyond the first step. If the railing, and possibly stairs, are being reconstructed, use the original design motif but carry it the extra distance. The hand-rail itself must be "grippable," that is, not too large in diameter to grasp firmly. You may also need a rail for the step up between sidewalk and path. Choose something plain and unobtrusive.

Front Door

The threshold should be no higher than ½", beveled to ¼" on each side. Minimum clearance of 32" should be available on the front door of most old houses.

The door knob may be inoperable for the resident. One solution used in a Berkeley cottage is the equivalent of an automatic garage door opener. The device is not visible, and the original door knob and faceplate remain a pleasure for the eye. Alternately, replace the doorknob with a lever. Select a lever design which is approved for use by disabled persons. These generally have a return at the end of the handle.

For a kickplate select a heavy-duty plastic, so that the panel is still visible, though protected. The kickplate should span from stile to stile.

Floors, Walls and Windows

Inside the front door, place a wheelchair doormat to clear the wheels before they proceed onto the hardwood floors. Finish hardwood floors with a product recommended for an extra-durable surface. Do not use rugs; they can interfere with circulation.

Protect wall plaster from chips and nicks with guard-strips. Use plexiglass, prefabbed at right angles or in strips, delicately tacked in. Or, use flat wood trim or corner boards, as advertised in *The Old-House Journal.*

Install window latches where they can be reached, and repair sash cords to good working order.

Doors

Ideally, door clearance is 36" wide, but 32" can be adequate. Much depends on hall configuration just outside the door. Removing the door itself, if privacy is not a factor, can be the simplest solution. If a door is needed, install offset, or swing-clear hinges.

Altering the door opening is a carpentry project. However, you can gain up to 1½" of extra clearance simply by removing the door stops. If the opening must be widened further, try not to disrupt design elements. If necessary, widen both sides of the door to avoid a lopsided appearance. Maintain the original door height, installing a new header as needed. Replace and match original trim.

In certain cases, removing an entire wall may be the best solution. In a bungalow, for example, removing the wall between kitchen and the living room/dining room space may provide a continuous living area, with a counter defining the kitchen area but allowing passage.

Pocket doors are appropriate when the door swinging into a hall takes up what little circulation space there is, yet some type of separation is needed for privacy or temperature control.

As with the front door, use appropriate knobs or levers and kickplates on interior doors. If needed, protect the door jamb with plexiglass. If there is no change in floor level or floor surface between rooms, a threshold is not necessary.

Bathrooms and Kitchens

Spacial layout is the main consideration in getting into the bathroom and having access to all the fixtures. Original wall-hung sinks offer more room for circulation than vanities. Grab bars and other devices should be tailored to the resident's disability.

For kitchen access, spacial layout, clearance under the sink and a convenient work area are the main considerations. Use roll-out shelving in pantry units and in general, easy-to-reach, good quality hardware.

ASBESTOS

In recent years, there has been considerable press coverage of the asbestos problem in public buildings, particularly schools. Only now are federal officials beginning to examine the potential danger of asbestos in home construction. This discussion, therefore, cannot provide conclusive findings or recommendations. Rather, it is intended to alert you to a potential hazard and inform you about options for addressing it. You would be well-advised to keep abreast of the topic as more data becomes available.

Asbestos is present in many forms in both old and new houses. It was not until 1978 that the Environmental Protection Agency banned the use of asbestos in all building products but two. Six years later the exceptions, vinyl asbestos tile (VAT) and sheet vinyl with asbestos backing, were also taken off the market.

Asbestos-containing materials (ACMs) in the old house may date from original construction, or from the advent of a remodeling effort. In addition to flooring, ACMs in the old house often include: duct, furnace and pipe insulation, roofing felt and roofing shingles, cementitious shingle-type siding, caulking putties, sealants, mastics and many others.

Asbestos fibers are incorporated in various binders or sizings, depending on the building product. For example, in roofing felt the asbestos is held by asphalt, in caulk by linseed oil, and in VAT by DVC. The hazard comes about when the binder begins to disintegrate from age, wear or abrasion, and the mineral fibers are released into the air.

Some asbestos fibers are large enough to be screened by the body's own air filter, the nose. However, microscopic mineral fibers, much smaller and more buoyant than dust, pass unobstructed to the lungs. The breathing of airborne asbestos has been found to be carcinogenic among those who regularly work with the material.

In the home, old or new, the presence or extent of danger from airborne asbestos particles is as yet undetermined. What is clear is that **ACMs which are intact pose negligible exposure, while those that have been cut, eroded or otherwise disturbed do indeed release asbestos.** Since the process of removing an asbestos-containing product can unleash more villainous particles than leaving it alone, some authorities recommend just that: If you have asbestos, leave it alone.

For flooring, this means covering VAT and sheet vinyl with a new surface without removing the old. You'll recognize VAT immediately: it is pastel and white and comes in 9" or one-foot squares. The sheet vinyl is practically any sheet flooring installed before 1984. According to the Consumer Products

Safety Commission in Washington, D.C., sealing in an ACM floor is preferable to taking it out. Breaking up the tile or sheets, disengaging the mastic or, worse, sanding the mastic residue, sets the offending fibers aloft. This is disappointing for those who would otherwise choose to reveal and refinish a hidden softwood floor. Also, layering floors creates an uneven threshold between rooms. Nevertheless, non-friable ACMs like flooring, siding, roofing and others, can become hazardous if cut, drilled, sanded or broken during repairs or renovation.

For duct and furnace insulation, and other friable ACMs, the "do not touch" warning is meant quite literally: Hands off! The aging binder may crumble so readily that hand pressure could free the fibers. Cutting or sawing the insulation in the course of adjusting ducts or pipes for rehabilitation can release even larger quantities of hazardous particles. Look for white cementitious coating, or material resembling corrugated cardboard with a white, chalky surface, around heating ducts, furnaces, plumbing pipes (especially out of the Oakland area), and boilers (in old mansions converted to multi-family use). In the basement, examine exposed duct insulation for brown spots. These rust stains suggest that the underlying sheetmetal may have rusted through, providing asbestos fibers entree to the forced air heating system.

Alternatives to leaving the ACM alone are: encapsulation, enclosure, repair and removal. A deteriorated binder may warrant intervention, or you may side with those researchers who favor a once-and-for-all removal, particularly of friable material. They reason that disintegration of the sizing can only increase over time, and that as long as asbestos is present, there is a chance of it being handled naively by an uninformed adult or a child—with dire consequences.

- **Encapsulation** refers to the spraying of the ACM with penetrating sealant. It should only be used, according to the EPA, on accoustical plaster, rarely found in old houses.
- **Enclosure** involves construction of an airtight compartment, usually sheetrock, around an ACM.
- **Repair** is an abatement approach when damage to the insulation is limited. Non-asbestos plaster

can restore open joints; duct tape is not suitable for exposure to high temperatures.

- **Removal** of short lengths of asbestos pipe insulation can be addressed fairly simply with a glovebag. However, a basement full of duct insulation requires airtight containment of the work space: protective gear including masks, respirators and disposable clothing; and, wetting down, bagging and disposal of the contaminant at a hazardous dump site. Experts urge follow-up testing for airborne particles.

Homeowners and conventional contractors should never remove, repair or enclose friable asbestos themselves. Hire an OSHA-licensed contractor to handle or excise it in an approved manner. Careless removal can disseminate fibers throughout the house, much exacerbating the problem. To obtain a list of OSHA-licensed contractors and independent testing laboratories in California, call CAL-OSHA, (800) 652-1476. Elsewhere, contact your state OSHA, or EPA Regional Asbestos Coordinator.

One recent estimate to remove duct and furnace insulation from an Oakland basement was $3500, not including post-operative testing. This may cost an additional $300-$500 per sample because expensive electronic microscopy is required.

Clearly there is no simple solution. The best strategy may be to keep informed. Contact the EPA for publications on asbestos and its abatement. One local architect who follows asbestos research is Anthony Bernheim, AIA. His assistance in providing material for this section is gratefully acknowledged.

Also note that the California Association of Realtors' standard Disclosure Form (described in Chapter 3) does not itemize asbestos insulation or other ACMs.

EARTHQUAKE SAFETY

The major damage to structures and the most readily apparent sensation felt by people during an earthquake is caused by ground shaking. Consult Chapter 4 for information on quake-safe foundations. In addition, simple precautions which can reduce the hazard should be incorporated in your rehab plans:

1. Know where the **turn-off valves** are for the building's water and gas supply. Keep a wrench handy in case the valve is sticky.

2. Strap the **water heater** to the wall with a metal strap, or bolt it to the floor. Otherwise it is likely to fall over in an earthquake, rupturing gas lines and/or water lines.

3. Tall, free-standing **bookcases or cabinets** should be anchored to wall studs with metal tie straps or steel angles. Keep the heaviest and most valuable items on the lower shelves. Consider adding a guard rail to the shelf edge to prevent items from sliding off. Make sure cabinet doors close tightly.

4. Hang **pictures** on hooks screwed into studs, not just into plaster. Never hang pictures or other objects over the head of the bed. Ceiling mirrors are extremely dangerous.

5. **Keep the exit area clear** of large bookcases, breakable items, or anything else that might block the path and make an emergency exit more difficult, especially in the dark.

6. Be extremely cautious of **chimneys**. During or shortly after an earthquake, the mortar of older chimneys may disintegrate, and the bricks topple over. The top of the chimney above the house may come crashing through the roof. Keep beds away from that area, and determine an exit route which will not take you near the chimney.

7. Be mentally prepared for an earthquake and learn basic first aid procedures. Keep an **earthquake emergency kit** in what should remain an accessible location even after groundshaking. The kit should include:

- flashlight with extra batteries
- transistor radio with extra batteries
- first aid kit
- several days food supply
- plastic-bottled water
- portable fire extinguisher.

Chapter 7

SOURCES AND RESOURCES

CITY OFFICES

Civil servants are available to help you, but sometimes it's hard to track down the right person on the telephone. Use this list as a shortcut to the City of Oakland offices which handle matters related to rehab. In other cities, expect the names of departments and their responsibilities to be similar to these. For general information about Oakland call *Cityline,* a joint project of the Oakland Public Library and Volunteers for Oakland, at (415) 444-CITY.

CITY PLANNING DEPARTMENT
Plans and Programs Divisions
City Hall, 6th Floor
273-3941
8:30–5:00

Service:	Advanced Planning for specific neighborhoods and the City as a whole
Ask for:	Public Information Officer
When to call:	If you desire information, publications and referrals regarding the City's land use plans for all districts in Oakland, or census data
Ask for:	Secretary to the Landmarks Preservation Advisory Board
When to call:	If you are interested in landmark designation, development in a preservation zone, or design review of a landmark building
Ask for:	Oakland Cultural Heritage Survey Coordinator
When to call:	If you are seeking National Register status; if you are researching house or neighborhood history; if you would like to volunteer time to work on the survey

Development Controls Division
City Hall, 2nd Floor
273-3911
8:00–4:00

Ask for:	Zoning Technician
Service:	Explanation of the *Zoning Regulations,* the legal document which governs the use and amount of building allowed on a parcel Processing requests for variances and use permits that may be required to make improvements or meet applicable code Upon request, a member of the Development Controls Division will explain the *Zoning Regulations* to assembled groups, such as neighborhood associations.
When to call:	Before buying a house Before creating more dwelling units, whether by building an addition or dividing up the interior Before planning new construction
Fees:	No charge for zoning information Minor Variance and Minor Conditional Use Permit: $190 Major Variance and Major Conditional Use Permit: $380

OFFICE OF COMMUNITY DEVELOPMENT
Housing Department
1417 Clay Street
273-3531
8:30–5:00

Ask for:	Mortgage Advisor
Service:	Administration of rehabilitation assistance programs (Refer to list of programs in this chapter.)
When to call:	If you are investigating the best way to finance a rehab project
Fee:	No charge for information

Housing Conservation
1417 Clay Street, Room 305
273-3881
8:00–4:30

Ask for:	Housing Representative
Service:	Building inspection for violation of applicable codes
When to call:	If you are planning to rehabilitate a house for resale through

an FHA, GI, or other loan program
If you need a Certificate of Occupancy
If you want to register a complaint against a probable housing code violation
If a hazard clearance is required

Fees: $110 per building for a full inspection to determine compliance with applicable housing, building, electrical, plumbing and mechanical codes.
$17 for each additional unit.
The fee includes the certificate of occupancy if corrections are completed, or substantial progress made, within six months.
The Housing Representative is obliged to report any observed violations of applicable code, and to follow up on the report. The correction of safety hazards is required.

Housing Counseling Agency
1417 Clay Street
273-3056
8:30–5:00

Ask for: Housing Counselor

Service: Counseling services on home purchase and maintenance, budget management, default and delinquency, discrimination

When to call: For general information or specific counseling on the purchase or rehabilitation of a house in one of the Community Development Districts

Fee: No charge

Program Planning and Coordination
1417 Clay Street
273-3716
8:30–5:00

Ask for: District Coordinator for your Community Development District

Service: Information on community development plans for neighborhoods in Community Development Districts
Schedules of public meetings and hearings related to such neighborhood improvements

When to call: If you are interested in a specific neighborhood in a Community Development District

Fee: No charge

OFFICE OF PARKS AND RECREATION
Parks Services
7101 Edgewater Drive
273-3151
7:00–3:30

Ask for Park Services Manager or Greenstreets

Service: Development and maintenance of City parks and street trees

When to call: To find out if any new parks are planned for your neighborhood or if improvements are slated for existing parks
To participate in planning for new parks
To find out how to have street trees planted

Fee: No charge for information

OFFICE OF PUBLIC WORKS
Engineering Services
City Hall, 8th Floor
273-3871
8:00–4:30

Ask for: Engineering Information Counter

Service: Provision of engineering records
Issuance of grading and encroachment permits
Information on flood hazards and seismic study zones
Review of building plans, parcel maps, and subdivision maps

When to call: Before buying a house or property
When contemplating improvements that may affect public property

Fee: No charge for information

Inspectional Services
City Hall, 2nd Floor
Building Section: 273-3441
Electrical Section: 273-3341
Plumbing Section: 273-3291
8:00–4:00

Ask for: Building Inspector, Electrical Inspector, Plumbing or Mechanical Inspector, between 8:00 and 9:00 a.m.

Service: Issuance of permits
Review of permit applications and plans
Inspection of buildings and construction for compliance

with the *Oakland Building Code*, *Oakland Electrical Code*, *Oakland Plumbing Code*, *Oakland Mechanical Code* and other related laws

Administration of regulations pertinent to residential rehabilitation

When to call: When the extent of proposed work is determined, but the work has not yet begun

Fee: The fee for permits is derived from the cost of construction and the number of hours required for inspection.

REHABILITATION ASSISTANCE PROGRAMS

The City of Oakland administers or supports programs that help finance residential rehabilitation. The programs are subject to change, and should be confirmed with the representative indicated.

In other cities, you are also likely to find HMIP, 312, NHS, Rental Rehab, single-family bond and self-help paint and weatherization programs. Call your city or county Community Development Department.

312 Loan Program

Summary: The 312 program offers rehabilitation low interest loans to encourage rehabilitation in declining neighborhoods.
The maximum loan amount is $27,000 per dwelling unit.

Eligibility: The house must be located in a Community Development District. Preference is given to lower income families.

For more information: Office of Community Development
Mortgage Servicing
273-3531

Home Maintenance Improvement Program (HMIP)

Summary: HMIP offers below-market interest rate loans to owner-occupants for rehabilitation, particularly the correction of code violations. Loan amounts are up to $30,000 for a single-family house and $5,000 for each additional dwelling unit up to four units.

Eligibility: Owner-occupied one- to four-unit house in a Community Development District. Owner is within HUD's moderate income limits.

For more information: Office of Community Development
Mortgage Servicing
273-3532

Single-Family Bond Program

Summary: To provide low cost mortgage and rehab loans to owner-occupant. The loan terms are set at the time of bond issue.

Eligibility: There are income limits and purchase price limits, and these differ depending on whether the property is located in a target area. A minimum down payment of 5%, earthquake insurance and 100% private mortgage insurance are required.

For more information: Office of Community Development
Housing Development Service
273-3052

Weatherization Program

Summary: Free insulation, caulking, weatherstripping, replacement of broken windows, etc. are available under these programs to help lower fuel consumption.

Eligibility: Owner-occupied house in a Community Development District. Low income status.

For more information: Social Services
Weatherization
273-3310

Self-Help Paint Program

Summary: The City provides free paint and equipment (brushes, pans, rollers) for people who are painting their own houses. Attendance at a one-session training course is required.

Eligibility: Owner-occupied house in a Community Development District. Moderate-income status.

For more information: Office of Community Development
Housing Counselor
273-3056

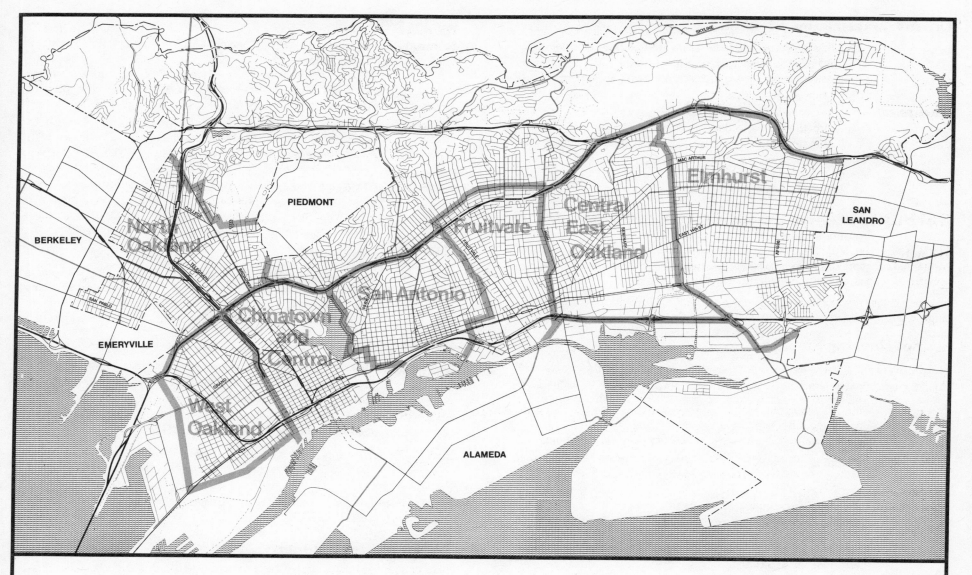

Oakland, California
Community Development
District Boundaries

4000 ft.

**OAKLAND
CITY PLANNING
DEPARTMENT**

Urban Homesteading Program

Summary: The City acquires property in designated areas of the City. The selected homesteaders receive the property for a low down payment plus their agreement to rehabilitate the property and to occupy it for five years.

Eligiblity: Family owns no other real property
Family has the ability to pay rehab costs
Head of household is 18 years or older and U.S. citizen or resident alien
Moderate-income family
Preference given to applicants who are: Oakland residents (for a year prior to applying), families with children, handicapped, over 62 years of age, supporters of elderly parents who live in household, veterans.

For more information: Office of Community Development
Housing Counselor
273-3056

Vacant Housing Program

Summary: To address the increasing need for housing and the problem of vacant housing, the City identifies vacant houses for acquisition and rehab. Financing may be available under other programs.

For more information: Office of Community Development
Housing Counselor
273-3502

HMIP Deferred Payment Loan

Summary: To provide rehab resources to homeowners unable to qualify for interest bearing loans. Can be used for repairs required by code and access features for the disabled homeowner. Maximum loan of $15,000.

Eligibility: One- to four-unit property located in a Community Development District. Family income within HUD's definition of very low income.

For more information: Office of Community Development
Mortgage Services
273-3531

Rental Rehab

Summary: To assure an adequate supply of affordable housing to low-income tenants. The loan provides 50% of rehab costs, up to $5,000 per unit to correct substandard conditions and repair major systems in danger of failure. Can be used to provide disability-related access features.

Eligibility: Privately-owned, residential rental properties. Preference to target areas within CD Districts. Preference to buildings with four or more two-bedroom units.

For more information: Office of Community Development
Mortgage Services
273-3531

Housing Counseling

Summary: Provides counseling in default and delinquency, low- and moderate-income home ownership, landlord-tenant relations and rehabilitation programs. Offers classes and workshops in simple home maintenance, home purchase and housing-related issues.

For more information: Office of Community Development
Housing Counseling
273-3056

Neighborhood Housing Services (NHS)

Summary: This non-profit corporation supports rehabilitation and neighborhood conservation in the Elmhurst District.

For more information: Neighborhood Housing Services
632-8892

Tenant Access Program (TAP)

Summary: Grants to landlords owning rental property to make alterations which accommodate the special needs of the physically disabled, including ramps, handrails, wider doorways and kitchen and bathroom modifications. Up to $6,000 per unit, or $24,000 per building. Landlords and tenants are invited to inquire.

For more information: Access California,
Social Services Department
273-3723 (Voice or TTY)
They can also provide information on other possible funding sources for access modifications.

CLASSES, CONFERENCES AND WORKSHOPS

Classes

There are many opportunities in the East Bay to learn more about architectural history and home repair. Outside Oakland, check with your community college, school district adult education program and local preservation groups.

Merritt College
12500 Campus Drive
Oakland, CA 94619
531-4911
- Real Estate, Home Improvement, Surveying, Carpentry
- Daytimes, Evenings
- $5 per unit, maximum $50

Laney College
900 Fallon Street
Oakland, CA 94607
834-5740
- Carpentry, Architectural and Engineering Technology
- Daytimes, Evenings
- $5 per unit, maximum $50

Owner-Builder Center
1516 Fifth Street
Berkeley, CA 94710
526-9222
- Remodeling, House Building, General Contracting, Home Inspection
- Evenings, weekends
- $50–$325; can volunteer time in lieu of tuition

Piedmont Adult School
800 Magnolia Avenue
Piedmont, CA 94611
653-9454
- Architectural Heritage of the East Bay, Architectural History of California, Cabinet Making, Interior Decorating, Home Inspection
- Evenings and weekends
- $30 Registration fee (for one or more classes)

Camron-Stanford House
1418 Lakeside Drive
Oakland, CA 94612
836-1976
- In-depth programs on Oakland history and domestic lifestyles for guide trainees
- Daytimes, evenings, weekends
- $70

Conferences and Workshops

Many statewide preservation groups sponsor an annual preservation conference, and these can be extremely educational. Check the program for topics of interest to rehabbers. The annual conference is an excellent way to tap your state's preservation resources, to meet professionals and enthusiasts and to see important preservation projects first-hand. In California, the highly respected annual conference is organized by the California Preservation Foundation. Call (415) 527-7808.

Some State Historic Preservation Offices (SHPOs) fund lay-oriented workshops on preservation subjects. The state of Oregon, for example, funds a workshop series which includes a video presentation. Contact your SHPO for locations and registration. You will find a national SHPO directory later in this chapter.

Some cities hold preservation-related events. In Oakland, the Camron-Stanford House Preservation Association sponsors an annual Preservation Fair on their grounds during September. Call (415) 836-1976.

Your local preservation group probably has speakers at regular meetings, conducts house tours for fund-raising, and perhaps arranges tours of manufacturing facilities that specialize in a preservation product. Contact the group and let them know you are interested in topics relating to rehab right.

Other conferences are conducted by national groups, such as the National Trust for Historic Preservation and the Association for Preservation Technology. Program topics may not be specific to the rehab of old houses. Find their addresses in this chapter under "Preservation Organizations."

BOOKS, PERIODICALS AND A FILM

While this is a selected bibliography only, the list provides further reading on specific subjects addressed in preceding chapters. Additional books and periodicals of special interest are alluded to in the text.

Architectural History

These publications figure prominently among the reference material used in the preparation of REHAB RIGHT architectural profiles.

Bean, Walton E. *California: An Interpretive History.* New York: McGraw-Hill Book Co., 1968.

Dykstra, John Beatty. *A History of Physical Development of the City of Oakland: The Formative Years, 1850–1930.* Thesis for a Masters Degree in City Planning. University of California, Berkeley.

Fleming, John, Hugh Honour, and Nikolaus Pevsner. *The Penguin Dictionary of Architecture.* Hammondsworth, England: Penguin Books, Ltd., 1966.

Freudenheim, Leslie Mandelson, and Elisabeth Sacks Sussman. *Building with Nature: Roots of the San Francisco Bay Region Tradition.* Santa Barbara: Peregrine Smith, Inc., 1974.

Gebhard, David, et al. *A Guide to Architecture in San Francisco and Northern California.* Santa Barbara: Peregrine Smith, Inc., 1973.

Kirker, Harold, *California's Architectural Frontier.* Santa Barbara: Peregrine Smith, Inc., 1974.

Oakland City Planning Department. *Oakland's Form and Appearance: An Evaluation Based on the 701 Urban Design Study.* Oakland, 1968.

Olwell, Carol, and Judith Lynch Waldhorn. *A Gift to the Street.* San Francisco: Antelope Island Press, 1976.

Richey, Elinor. *The Ultimate Victorians of the Continental Side of the San Francisco Bay.* Berkeley: Howell-North Books, 1970.

Whiffen, Marcus. *American Architecture Since 1780: A Guide to the Styles.* Cambridge: The M.I.T. Press, 1969.

Woodbridge, Sally, et al. *Bay Area Houses.* New York: Oxford University Press, 1976.

Yoho and Merritt. *Craftsman Bungalows.* Seattle: 1910.

Rehabilitation and Repair

Basic Home Repairs Illustrated. The Editors of Sunset Books and *Sunset Magazine.* Menlo Park: Lane Books, 1974.

Diane Maddex. *The Brown Book: A Directory of Preservation Information.* Washington, D.C.: The Preservation Press, 1983.

Handyman Book. The Staff of *The Family Handyman.* New York: Charles Scribner's Sons, 1970.

New Life for Old Dwellings: Appraisal and Rehabilitation. U.S. Department of Agriculture, Agriculture Handbook 481, Washington, D.C., 1975.

Preservation Briefs. U.S. Department of the Interior, National Park Service, Technical Preservation Services, Washington, D.C. 20240 or regional NPS office.

Reader's Digest Complete Do-It-Yourself Manual, Pleasantville, New York: The Reader's Digest Association, 1973.

Remodeling Old Houses Without Destroying Their Character. New York: Alfred A. Knopf, 1976.

Respectful Rehabilitation: Answers to Your Questions about Old Buildings. Technical Preservation Services, U.S. Department of Interior. National Trust for Historic Preservation. 1982.

Retrofit Right: How To Make Your Old House Energy Efficient. Sedway Cooke Associates, City of Oakland Planning Department, Oakland, CA 1983.

The Old-House Journal Yearbooks: 1976–1986 and *The Old-House Journal Cumulative Index, 1973–1985. The Old House Journal,* Brooklyn, New York.

Buyer's Guides

Bay Area Consumer's Checkbook. Center for the Study of Services, 222 Agriculture Building, 101 Embarcadero, San Francisco, CA 94105. Quarterly.

Heritage Directory. The Foundation for San Francisco's Architectural Heritage. The 1977 directory of services and products is currently being revised.

The Old-House Journal Buyers' Guide Catalog. The Old-House Journal, 69A–7th Avenue, Brooklyn, NY 11217. 1986.

The Owner/Builder Directory. The Owner/Builder Center. 1516 Fifth Street, Berkeley, CA 94710. 1985.

Pamela McGuire. *Recreating Authentic Interiors: A California Directory of Products and Services.* State of California Office of Historic Preservation. Sacramento: 1979.

Rejuvenation House Parts Company Catalog. 901-B N. Skidmore, Portland, OR 97217. 1986.

Lawrence Grow. *The Third Old-House Catalog.* New York: Collier Books, MacMillan, 1982.

Also, scan advertisment in preservation periodicals (listed below).

Periodicals

Bulletin and *Communique.* Association of Preservation Technology. P.O. Box 2487, Station D, Ottawa, Ontario, K1P 5W6, Canada.

Common Sense Pest Control Quarterly. Bio-Integral Resource Center. P.O. Box 7014, Berkeley, CA 94707.

Conserve Neighborhoods. National Trust for Historic Preservation. 1785 Massachusetts Avenue, NW, Washington, D.C. 20036.

Design Book Review. 2508 Ridge Road, Berkeley, CA 94709.
Fine Homebuilding. 52 Church Hill Road, Newton, CT 06470.
Historic Preservation. National Trust for Historic Preservation. 1785 Massachusetts Avenue, NW, Washington, D.C. 20036.
Nineteenth Century and *The Victorian.* The Victorian Society in America, 219 E. 6th Street, Philadelphia, PA 19106.
The Old-House Journal. 69A—7th Avenue, Brooklyn, NY 11217
Small Town. Small Towns Institute. Box 517, Ellensburg, WA 98926.
Urban Conservation Report. 1016—16th Street, NW, Suite 275, Washington, D.C. 20036.

Local and statewide preservation groups generally publish newsletters of extreme interest and value.

Booklists

American Life Foundation
Box 349
Watkins Glen, NY 14891

Builders Booksource Catalog
1801–4th Street
Berkeley, CA 94710

The Old-House Journal Bookshop
69A–7th Avenue
Brooklyn, NY 11217

The Preservation Press
National Trust for Historic Preservation
1785 Massachusetts Avenue, NW
Washington, D.C. 20036

Technical and Preservation Services
Publications and Price List
U.S. Department of the Interior
National Parks Service
Preservation Assistance Division
Washington, D.C. 20013-7127

Film

Houses Have History. Directed by Paul Fillinger for Churchill Films
662 North Robertson Boulevard
Los Angeles, CA 90069

This upbeat and award-winning 20 minute film is based in part on REHAB RIGHT. While intended for elementary and junior high school classrooms, it can be used equally well as a preservation primer for adult audiences. In Oakland, the film can be borrowed from the City Planning Department, 273-3941. For curriculum suggestions to accompany the film, contact the Planning Department or Churchill Films.

PRESERVATION ORGANIZATIONS

Preservation and historic organizations provide an opportunity to meet people who share an interest in old houses. The groups schedule lectures, slide shows, and house tours for their membership. Often, the general public is invited too. To varying degrees, preservation organizations are also involved in the political process, lobbying for landmarks legislation and governmental action to save valuable buildings from demolition and insensitive remodeling.

National Preservation Organizations

Preservation Action
1700 Connecticut Avenue, N.W.
Suite 400
Washington, D.C. 20036
(202) 659-0915

Association for Preservation Technology
P.O. Box 2487, Station D
Ottawa, Ontario K1P 5W6, Canada
(613) 238-1972

National Trust for Historic Preservation
1785 Massachusetts Avenue, N.W.
Washington, D.C. 20036
(202) 673-4000

National Trust for Historic Preservation Regional Offices:

Mid-Atlantic Regional Office
6401 Germantown Avenue
Philadelphia, PA 19144
(215) 438-2886

Delaware, District of Columbia, Maryland, New Jersey, Pennsylvania, Puerto Rico, Virginia, Virgin Islands, West Virginia

Midwest Regional Office
53 West Jackson Boulevard, Suite 1135
Chicago, IL 60604
(312) 353-3419, 353-3424

407 South Dearborn Street, Suite 710
Chicago, IL 60604
(312) 353-3419

Illinois, Indiana, Iowa, Michigan, Minnesota, Missouri, Ohio, Wisconsin

Mountain/Plains Regional Office
511–16th Street, Suite 700
Denver, CO 80202
(303) 844-2245

1407 Larimer Street, Suite 200
Denver, CO 80202
(303) 844-2245

Colorado, Kansas, Montana, Nebraska, North Dakota, Oklahoma, South Dakota, Wyoming

Texas/New Mexico Field Office
500 Main Street, Suite 606
Fort Worth, TX 76102
(817) 334-2061

New Mexico, Texas

Northeast Regional Office
45 School Street, Second Floor
Boston, MA 02108
(617) 223-7754

Connecticut, Maine, Massachusetts, New Hampshire, New York, Rhode Island, Vermont

Southern Regional Office
456 King Street
Charleston, S.C. 29403
(803) 724-4711

Alabama, Arkansas, Florida, Georgia, Kentucky, Louisiana, Mississippi, North Carolina, South Carolina, Tennessee

Western Regional Office
One Sutter Street
San Francisco, CA 94104
(415) 974-8420

Alaska, Arizona, California, Guam, Hawaii, Idaho, Micronesia, Nevada, Oregon, Utah, Washington

Statewide Preservation Organizations

ALABAMA

Live-in-a-Landmark Council
c/o Alabama Historical Commission
725 Monroe Street
Montgomery, AL 36130
(205) 832-6621

ALASKA

Alaska Association for Historic Preservation
524 West Fourth Avenue, Suite 203
Anchorage, AK 99501
(907) 272-8018

ARIZONA

Heritage Foundation of Arizona
P.O. Box 25616
Tempe, AZ 85282
(602) 438-9443

ARKANSAS

Historic Preservation Alliance of Arkansas
P.O. Box 305
Little Rock, AR 72203
(501) 372-4757

CALIFORNIA

California Preservation Foundation
55 Sutter Street, Suite 593
San Francisco, CA 94104
(415) 527-7808

COLORADO

Colorado Preservation, Inc.
1501 West Cucharras
Colorado Springs, CO 80904
(303) 635-2065

CONNECTICUT

Connecticut Trust for Historic Preservation
152 Temple Street
New Haven, CT 06510
(203) 562-6312

DELAWARE

Historical Society of Delaware
505 Market Street Mall
Wilmington, DE 19801
(302) 655-7161

DISTRICT OF COLUMBIA

D.C. Preservation League
930–F Street, N.W., Suite 612
Washington, D.C. 20004
(202) 737-1519

FLORIDA

Florida Trust for Historic Preservation
P.O. Box 11206
Tallahassee, FL 32302
(904) 224-8128

GEORGIA

Georgia Trust for Historic Preservation
1516 Peachtree Street, N.W.
Atlanta, GA 30309
(404) 881-9980

HAWAII

Historic Hawaii Foundation
P.O. Box 1658
Honolulu, HI 96806
(808) 537-9564

IDAHO

Idaho Historic Preservation Council
P.O. Box 1495
Boise, ID 83701
(208) 334-4685

ILLINOIS

Landmarks Preservation Council of Illinois
407 South Dearborn, Suite 970
Chicago, IL 60605
(312) 922-1742

INDIANA

Historic Landmarks Foundation of Indiana
3402 Boulevard Place
Indianapolis, IN 46208
(317) 926-2301

KANSAS

Kansas Preservation Alliance
c/o The Wichita-Sedgwick County
    Historical Museum Association
204 South Main
Wichita, KS 67202
(316) 265-9314

KENTUCKY

**Commonwealth Preservation Council of
    Kentucky**
c/o Landmarks Association
P.O. Box 1812
Bowling Green, KY 42101
(502) 781-8106

LOUISIANA

Louisiana Preservation Alliance
P.O. Box 1587
Baton Rouge, LA 70821
(504) 342-7393

MAINE

Citizens for Historic Preservation
597 Main Street
South Portland, ME 04106
(207) 775-3652

MARYLAND

Preservation Maryland
2335 Marriottsville Road
Marriottsville, MD 21104
(301) 442-1772

MASSACHUSETTS

**Architectural Conservation Trust
    for Massachusetts**
45 School Street
Boston, MA 02108
(617) 523-8678

MINNESOTA

Preservation Alliance of Minnesota
c/o Kensington Properties
730 Hennepin, Suite 200
Minneapolis, MN 55403
(612) 338-4885

MISSOURI

Missouri Heritage Trust
P.O. Box 895
Jefferson City, MO 65102
(314) 635-6877

NEBRASKA

Nebraska Historical Network
Route 3
Seward, NE 68434

NEW HAMPSHIRE

Inherit New Hampshire
4 Bicentennial Square
Concord, NH 03301
(603) 224-6714

NEW JERSEY

Heritage Studies, Inc.
20 Seminary Avenue
Hopewell, NJ 08525
(609) 466-9606

NEW YORK

Preservation League of New York State
307 Hamilton Street
Albany, NY 12210
(518) 462-5658

NORTH CAROLINA

**Historic Preservation Foundation of North
    Carolina**
P.O. Box 27644
Raleigh, NC 27611
(919) 832-3652

OHIO

Ohio Preservation Alliance
22 North Front Street
Columbus, OH 43215
(216) 861-7688

OREGON

Historic Preservation League of Oregon
P.O. Box 40053
Portland, OR 97240
(503) 243-1923

PENNSYLVANIA

Pennsylvania Trust for Historic Preservation
P.O. Box 297
Lancaster, PA 17603
(717) 431-6917

Preservation Fund of Pennsylvania
2470 Kissell Hill Road
Lancaster, PA 17601
(717) 569-2243

RHODE ISLAND

Heritage Foundation of Rhode Island
1 Hospital Trust Plaza
Providence, RI 02903
(401) 751-2110

SOUTH CAROLINA

**Confederation of South Carolina Local
Historical Societies**
Box 11669
Columbia, SC 29211
(803) 758-5816

SOUTH DAKOTA

Historic South Dakota Foundation
P.O. Box 2998
Rapid City, SD 57709
(605) 341-5820

TENNESSEE

**Association for the Preservation of Tennessee
Antiquities**
110 Leake Avenue
Nashville, TN 37205
(615) 352-8247

Tennessee Heritage Alliance
c/o Historic Nashville
100 Second Avenue North
Nashville, TN 37201
(615) 898-2544

TEXAS

Texas Historical Foundation
P.O. Box 12243
Austin, TX 78711
(512) 472-6784

UTAH

Utah Heritage Foundation
355 Quince Street
Salt Lake City, UT 84103
(801) 533-0858

VIRGIN ISLANDS

St. Thomas Historical Trust
9-33 Estate Nazareth
St. Thomas, USVI 00801

VIRGINIA

Preservation Alliance of Virginia
P.O. Box 142
Waterford, VA 22190
(703) 882-3018

WASHINGTON

Washington Trust for Historic Preservation
111 West 21st Avenue
Olympia, WA 98501
(206) 573-0099

WEST VIRGINIA

Preservation Alliance of West Virginia
P.O. Box 1135
Clarksburg, WV 26302
(304) 624-9298

WISCONSIN

Wisconsin Heritages, Inc.
2000 West Wisconsin Avenue
Milwaukee, WI 53233
(414) 931-0808

WYOMING

Wyoming Historic Preservation Association
P.O. Box 1041
Cheyenne, WY 82003
(307) 635-5044

Some Special Interest Groups
in Northern California

Art Deco Society of California
109 Minna Street, Suite 399
San Francisco, CA 94105
(415) 552-DECO

East Bay Negro Historical Society
4519 Martin Luther King, Jr. Way
Oakland, CA 94609
(415) 658-3158

Friends of Terra Cotta, San Francisco Chapter
P.O. Box 421393
Main Post Office
San Francisco, CA 94142

Victorian Alliance
4143 23rd Street
San Francisco, CA
(415) 824-2666

Prominent Citywide Preservation
Organizations in California

Alameda Victorian Preservation Society
P.O. Box 1677
Alameda, CA 94501

**Berkeley Architectural Heritage Association
(BAHA)**
P.O. Box 1137
Berkeley, CA 94701
(415) 841-BAHA

Chico Heritage Association
P.O. Box 2078
Chico, CA 95927

Los Angeles Conservancy
849 South Broadway, Suite 1722
Los Angeles, CA 90014
(213) 623-CITY

Oakland Heritage Alliance
5569 Lawton Avenue
Oakland, CA 94618
(415) 658-4915

Pasadena Heritage
80 West Dayton
Pasadena, CA 91105
(818) 793-0617

Sacramento Old City Association (SACA)
P.O. Box 1022
Sacramento, CA 95806
(916) 448-1688

Save Our Heritage (SOHO)
P.O. Box 3571
San Diego, CA 94103
(619) 297-9327

**The Foundation for San Francisco's
Architectural Heritage**
2007 Franklin Street
San Francisco, CA 94109
(415) 441-3000

There are also citywide preservation groups in
Claremont, Orange County, Riverside, Santa
Barbara, Glendale, Long Beach, Healdsburg, Vallejo
and elsewhere.

Oakland Groups with a Preservation, Design or Housing Focus

Adams Point Preservation Association
Naomi Schiff
238 Oakland Avenue
Oakland, CA 94611
835-4800

Brooklyn Neighborhood Preservation Association
Xandra Malandra
P.O. Box 29905
Oakland, CA 94604
532-3010

Camron-Stanford House Preservation Association
1418 Lakeside Drive
Oakland, CA 94612
836-1976

East Bay Asian Local Development Council (EBALDC)
310–8th Street
Oakland, CA 94612
763-2970

Jubilee West
1448–10th Street
Oakland, CA 94607
839-6776

Oakland Community Organization
3914 East 14th Street
Oakland, CA 94601
261-8440

Oakland Design Advocates
Chris Pattillo
337–17th Street, Suite 214
Oakland, CA 94612
465-1284

Oakland Heritage Alliance
Leslie Flint
5569 Lawton Avenue
Oakland, CA 94618
(658-4915)

Oakland Museum Association
1000 Oak Street
Oakland, CA 94607
Council on Architecture 273-3055
History Guild 273-3842

Oakland Neighborhood Housing Services
1641–98th Avenue
Oakland, CA 94603
632-8892

Oakmore Preservation Society
Mrs. Charles H. King, III
1727 Clemens Road
Oakland, CA 94602
531-7490

Old Oakland Association
Robin Wolf
5446 Carlton Street
Oakland, CA 94618
658-1333

Oak Center Neighborhood Association
1324 Adeline Street
Oakland, CA 94607
272-0902

OCCUR
1419 Broadway
Oakland, CA 94612
839-2440

Piedmont Avenue Neighborhood Improvement League (PANIL)
c/o H.E. Christian Peoples
4037 Howe Street
Oakland, CA 94611
655-4438

Rockridge Community Planning Council
Warren W. Chupp
6243 Rockwell Street
Oakland, CA 94618

Rose Garden Neighborhood Association
JoAnn Hawsler
687 Vernon Street
Oakland, CA 94610
568-1083

PRESERVATION ADMINISTRATIONS

National Park Service Regional Offices

These regional offices provide tax incentive and preservation services.

Alaska Region
National Park Service
2525 Gambell Street, Room 107
Anchorage, AK 99503
(907) 271-4230

Mid-Atlantic Region
National Park Service
600 Arch Street
Philadelphia, PA 19106
(215) 597-2283

Connecticut, Delaware, District of Columbia, Indiana, Maine, Maryland, Massachusetts, Michigan, New Hampshire, New Jersey, New York, Ohio, Pennsylvania, Rhode Island, Vermont, Virginia, West Virginia

Western Region
National Park Service
450 Golden Gate Avenue
P.O. Box 36063
San Francisco, CA 94102
(415) 556-7741

Arizona, California, Hawaii, Idaho, Nevada, Oregon, Washington

Rocky Mountain Region
National Park Service
655 Parfet Street
P.O. Box 25287
Denver, CO 80225
(303) 234-2560

Colorado, Illinois, Iowa, Kansas, Minnesota, Missouri, Montana, Nebraska, New Mexico, North Dakota, Oklahoma, South Dakota, Texas, Utah, Wisconsin, Wyoming

Southeast Region
National Park Service
75 Spring Street, SW
Atlanta, GA 30303
(404) 221-2633

Alabama, Arkansas, Florida, Georgia, Kentucky, Louisiana, Mississippi, North Carolina, Puerto Rico, South Carolina, Tennessee, Virgin Islands

State Historic Preservation Offices

ALABAMA
SHPO, Executive Director
Alabama Historical Commission
725 Monroe Street
Montgomery, AL 36130
(205) 261-3184

ALASKA
SHPO
Division of Parks
Office of History & Archaeology
Pouch 7001
Anchorage, AK 99510
(907) 762-4108

AMERICAN SAMOA
HPO, Director
Department of Parks & Recreation
Government of American Samoa
Pago Pago, American Samoa 96799

ARIZONA
SHPO
Arizona State Parks
1688 West Adams
Phoenix, AZ 85007
(602) 255-4174

ARKANSAS
SHPO
Arkansas Historic Preservation Program
The Heritage Center
225 E. Markham, Suite 200
Little Rock, AR 72201
(501) 371-2763

CALIFORNIA
SHPO
Office of Historic Preservation
Department of Parks & Recreation
P.O. Box 2390
Sacramento, CA 95811
(916) 445-8006

COLORADO
SHPO, President
Colorado Historical Society
1300 Broadway
Denver, CO 80203
(303) 866-2136

CONNECTICUT
SHPO, Director
Connecticut Historical Commission
59 So. Prospect Street
Hartford, CT 06106
(203) 566-3005

DELAWARE
SHPO
Bureau of Archaeology and Historic Preservation
Hall of Records
Dover, DE 19903
(302) 736-1903

DISTRICT OF COLUMBIA
SHPO, Director
Department of Consumer & Regulatory Affairs
614 H Street, N.W.
Washington, D.C. 20001
(202) 727-7170

FLORIDA
SHPO
Bureau of Historic Preservation
Division of Archives, History, & Records
   Management
Department of State
The Capitol
Tallahassee, FL 32301-8020
(904) 487-2333

GEORGIA
SHPO, Commissioner
Department of Natural Resources
270 Washington Street, S.W.
Atlanta, GA 30334
(404) 656-2840

GUAM
SHPO, Director
Department of Parks & Recreation
490 Naval Hospital Road
Agana Heights, Guam 96910
(477) 9620, ext. 4 Overseas Operator

HAWAII
SHPO
Department of Land & Natural Resources
P.O. Box 621
Honolulu, HI 96809
(808) 548-6550

IDAHO
SHPO, State Historian
Idaho Historical Society
610 North Julia Davis Drive
Boise, ID 83702
(208) 334-3356

ILLINOIS
SHPO, Director
Department of Conservation
524 S. 2nd Street
Springfield, IL 62706
(217) 782-6302

INDIANA
SHPO, Director
Department of Natural Resources
608 State Office Building
Indianapolis, IN 46204
(317) 232-4020

IOWA
SHPO, Executive Director
State Historical Department
East 12th and Grand Avenue
Des Moines, IA 50319
(515) 281-5113

KANSAS

SHPO, Executive Director
State Historical Society
120 West Tenth Street
Topeka, KS 66612
(913) 296-3251

KENTUCKY

SHPO
Kentucky Heritage Council
Capitol Plaza Tower, 12th Floor
Frankfort, KY 40601
(502) 564-7005

LOUISIANA

SHPO
Office of Cultural Development
P.O. Box 44247
Baton Rouge, LA 70804
(504) 922-0358

MAINE

SHPO, Director
Maine Historic Preservation Commission
55 Capital Street, Station 65
Augusta, ME 04333
(207) 289-2132

MARYLAND

SHPO, Director
Maryland Historical Trust
21 State Circle
Annapolis, MD 21401
(301) 269-2851

MASSACHUSETTS

SHPO, Executive Director
Massachusetts Historical Commission
80 Boylston Street
Boston, MA 02116
(617) 727-8470

MICHIGAN

SHPO, Director
Bureau of History
Department of State
208 North Capitol
Lansing, MI 48918
(517) 373-6362

MINNESOTA

SHPO, Director
Minnesota Historical Society
Fort Snelling History Center
St. Paul, MN 55111
(612) 726-1171

MISSISSIPPI

SHPO, Director
Department of Archives & History
P.O. Box 571
Jackson, MS 39205
(314) 359-1424

MISSOURI

SHPO, Director
State Department of Natural Resources
1915 Southridge Drive
P.O. Box 176
Jefferson City, MO 65102
(314) 751-4422

MONTANA

SHPO, Program Manager
Historic Preservation Office
Montana Historical Society
225 No. Roberts
Helena, MT 59620
(406) 444-7715

NEBRASKA

SHPO, Director
Nebraska State Historical Society
P.O. Box 82554
Lincoln, NE 68501
(402) 471-3270

NEVADA

SHPO, Director
Department of Conservation & Natural Resources
Nye Building, Room 213
201 South Fall Street
Carson City, NV 89710
(702) 885-4360

NEW HAMPSHIRE

SHPO
Department of Resources
Office of the Commissioner
P.O. Box 856
Concord, NH 03301
(603) 271-3255

NEW JERSEY

SHPO
Department of Environmental Protection
CN 402
Trenton, NJ 08625
(609) 292-2885

NEW MEXICO

SHPO
Historic Preservation Division
Office of Cultural Affairs
Villa Rivera, Room 101
208 E. Palace Avenue
Santa Fe, NM 87503
(505) 827-8320

NEW YORK

SHPO
Parks, Recreation & Historic Preservation
Agency Building #1
Empire State Plaza
Albany, NY 12238
(518) 474-0443

NORTH CAROLINA
SHPO, Director
Divison of Archives & History
Department of Cultural Resources
109 East Jones Street
Raleigh, NC 27611
(919) 733-7305

NORTH DAKOTA
SHPO
State Historical Society of North Dakota
Heritage Center
Bismarck, ND 58505
(701) 224-2667

NORTHERN MARIANA ISLANDS
HPO
Department of Community & Cultural Affairs
Commonwealth of the Northern Mariana Islands
Saipan, Mariana Islands 96950
Saipan 9722 or 9411 Overseas Operator

OHIO
SHPO
The Ohio Historical Society
1985 Velma Avenue
Columbus, OH 43211
(614) 466-1500

OKLAHOMA
SHPO, Executive Director
Oklahoma Historical Society
Wiley Post Historical Building
Oklahoma City, OK 73105
(405) 521-2491

OREGON
SHPO
State Parks & Recreation
525 Trade Street, S.E.
Salem, OR 97310
(503) 378-5019

PENNSYLVANIA
SHPO, Executive Director
Pennsylvania Historical & Museum Commission
P.O. Box 1026
Harrisburg, PA 17108
(717) 787-2891

COMMONWEALTH OF PUERTO RICO
SHPO
Office of Cultural Affairs
Office of the Governor
Box 82
La Fortaleza
San Juan, Puerto Rico 00901
(809) 721-3012

RHODE ISLAND
SHPO
R.I. Historical Preservation Commission
Old State House
150 Benefit Street
Providence, RI 02903
(401) 277-2678

SOUTH CAROLINA
SHPO, Director
S.C. Archives & History Department
1430 Senate Street
Columbia, SC 29211
(803) 758-5816

SOUTH DAKOTA
SHPO, Director
Office of Cultural Preservation
State Library Building
800 N. Illinois
Pierre, SD 57501
(605) 773-3458

TENNESSEE
SHPO
Department of Conservation
701 Broadway
Nashville, TN 37216
(615) 741-2301

TEXAS
SHPO
Texas Historical Commission
P.O. Box 12276
Capitol Station
Austin, TX 78711
(512) 475-3092

TRUST TERRITORY OF THE PACIFIC ISLANDS
HPO
Office of Historic Preservation
Trust Territory of the Pacific Islands
Saipan, CM 96950

UTAH
SHPO
Utah State Historical Society
300 Rio Grande
Salt Lake City, UT 84101
(801) 533-6017

VERMONT
SHPO
Agency of Development & Community Affairs
Pavilion Building
Montpelier, VT 05602
(802) 828-3211

VIRGINIA
SHPO
Virginia Historic Landmarks Commission
221 Governor Street
Richmond, VA 23219
(804) 786-3143

VIRGIN ISLANDS
SHPO
Virgin Islands Planning Office
Division for Archeology & Historic Preservation
P.O. Box 3099
Christiansted, St. Croix, USVI 00820
(809) 773-1082

WASHINGTON
SHPO
Office of Archeology & Historic Preservation
111 West 21 Street KL-11
Olympia, WA 98504
(206) 753-4011

WEST VIRGINIA
SHPO
Department of Culture & History
Capitol Complex
Charleston, WV 25305
(304) 348-0220

WISCONSIN
SHPO
Historic Preservation Division
State Historical Society of Wisconsin
816 State Street
Madison, WI 53706
(608) 262-0746

WYOMING
SHPO
Wyoming Recreation Commission
Herschler Building
122 W. 25th Street
Cheyenne, WY 82002
(307) 777-7695

City of Oakland
Landmarks Preservation
Advisory Board

Landmarks Preservation Advisory Board (LPAB)
City Planning Department
City Hall, 6th Floor
One City Hall Plaza
Oakland, CA 94612
(415) 273-3941

Local preservation laws are generally the province of a city planning department within the municipal government. The regulations may include landmark designation, preservation zones, design review, facade easement and other provisions. In Oakland, the LPAB is a mayor-appointed body acting in an advisory capacity to the City Planning Commission.

Technical support is provided by City Planning Department staff, specifically the LPAB Secretary and the Oakland Cultural Heritage Survey Coordinator. Board meetings are open to the public.

HOW TO ORDER THE SEQUEL TO THIS BOOK

If you are pursuing a rehab project, this is the best time to think about weatherizing your house to reduce fuel consumption—and your utility bill. RETROFIT RIGHT: HOW TO MAKE YOUR OLD HOUSE ENERGY EFFICIENT, provides all the information you will need to combine rehab and retrofit efforts.,

RETROFIT RIGHT is a ground-breaking publication in two respects. First, it addresses energy problems unique to the old house and offers solutions which are sensitive to its architectural style.

Second, RETROFIT RIGHT provides precise retrofit strategies. These were developed through careful consideration of individual house styles, occupant profiles, and whether the work would be done by the owner or a contractor. The architectural styles correspond exactly to those pictured in REHAB RIGHT.

RETROFIT RIGHT earned the top professional award from the American Planning Association, California Chapter, 1984, and was featured in *Sunset* magazine.

To order RETROFIT RIGHT, send your name, address and pre-payment to the City of Oakland Planning Department, One City Hall Plaza, Oakland, CA. The price is $7.95, plus 86¢ postage. California residents add $.52 sales tax. Inquiries on favorable bulk rates for retailers and community groups are welcome.

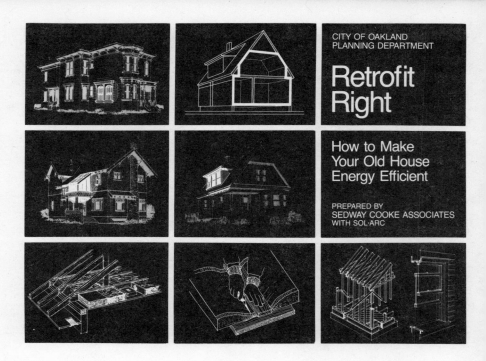

CITY OF OAKLAND
PLANNING DEPARTMENT

Retrofit Right

How to Make
Your Old House
Energy Efficient

PREPARED BY
SEDWAY COOKE ASSOCIATES
WITH SOL-ARC

TO: City of Oakland
Planning Department
One City Hall Plaza
Oakland, CA 94612

Please send RETROFIT RIGHT. I have enclosed a check for:

☐ $8.31

☐ $9.33 (California residents)

Name_____

Address_____

City_____ State_____ Zip_____

Make checks payable to the CITY OF OAKLAND. Thank you.

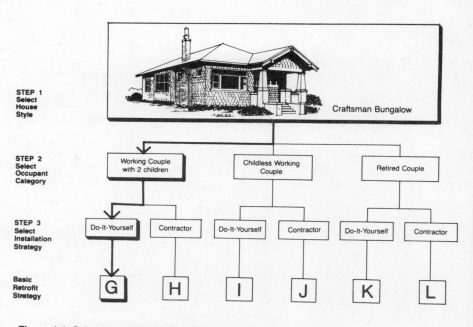

Figure 1-1 Selecting a Basic Retrofit Strategy